LEGENDARY LOCALS

OF

NEW HAMPSHIRE'S LAKES REGION

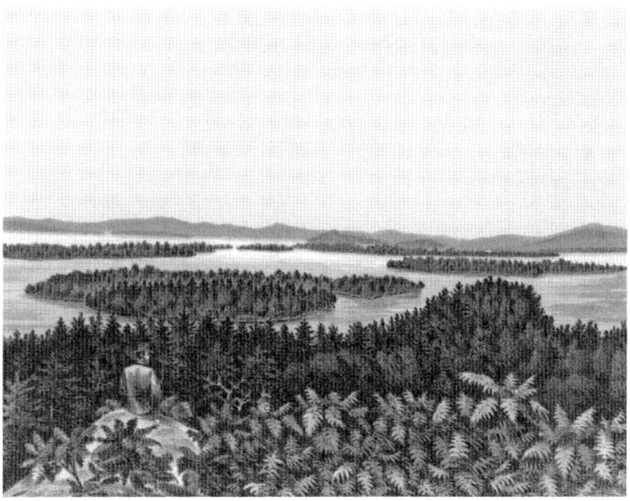

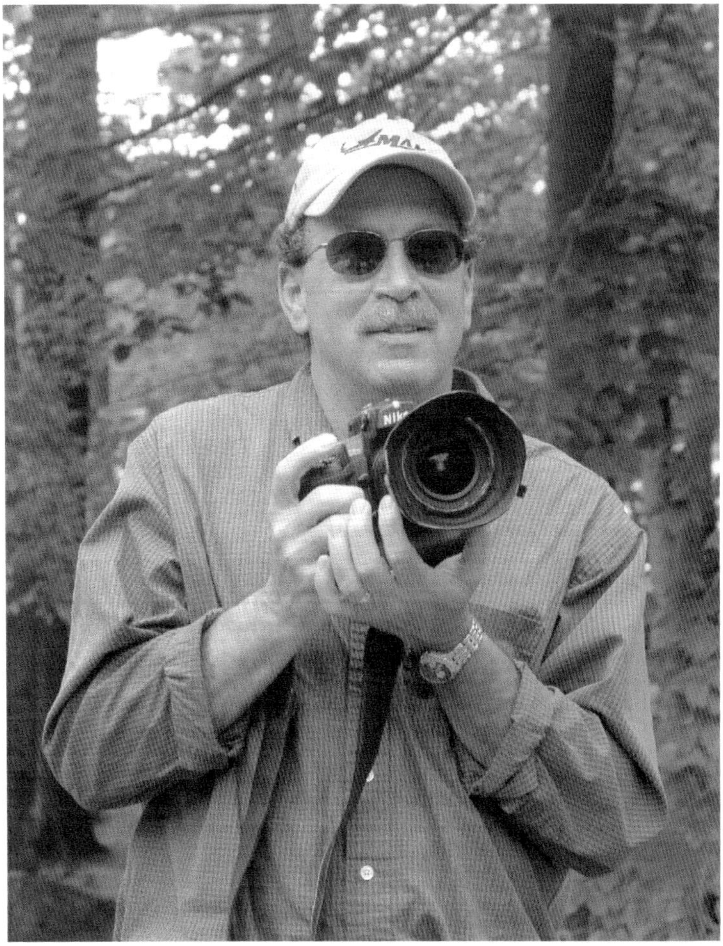

The Lakes Region Photographer

Daryl Carlson likes to say that he has taken photographs of everything in the Lakes Region—at least twice.

During his 12 years as photographic editor for the daily *Citizen* newspaper, Carlson filled his time shooting presidential primaries, town meetings, school plays, press conferences, arrests, and accident and fire scenes, and still found time to produce hundreds of outstanding nature photographs.

A lifelong resident of the area, Carlson has won more than two dozen Associated Press Photo of the Month awards and two New England Press Association awards, and has been featured on MSNBC's Picture of the Week. Carlson's work has appeared in various magazines and newspapers throughout the country and in galleries around New England.

Carlson has made significant contributions to three books: *The Lakes Region of New Hampshire: Four Seasons Countless Memories*, Images of America: *Laconia Motorcycle Week*, and this volume. He also teaches photography to both high school and college students. Recently, he taught digital imaging at the Laconia Adult Education program as well as the Elder Hostel Road Scholar Program at Geneva Point in Moultonborough. (Courtesy of Daryl Carlson/Kamara Image Photography.)

Page 1: **Idyllic Lakes Region**

This classic pencil illustration shows some of the more popular islands of Lake Winnipesaukee from a vantage point on the south side of Mark Island in Gilford. (Courtesy of the Lake Winnipesaukee Historical Society.)

LEGENDARY LOCALS

OF

NEW HAMPSHIRE'S LAKES REGION

RAY CARBONE

LEGENDARY LOCALS

ISBN 978-1-4671-0199-8

Legendary Locals is an imprint of Arcadia Publishing
Charleston, South Carolina

Printed in the United States of America

Published in cooperation with Carbone Productions LLC of Warner, New Hampshire

Library of Congress Control Number: 2014951749

For all general information, please contact Arcadia Publishing:
Telephone 843-853-2070
Fax 843-853-0044
E-mail sales@arcadiapublishing.com
For customer service and orders:
Toll-Free 1-888-313-2665

Visit us on the Internet at www.arcadiapublishing.com

Dedication
To my wonderful Lord Jesus, and with unending thanks to my wife, Jane, for her constant loving support.

On the Front Cover: Clockwise from top left: Ruth Doan MacDougall, writer (courtesy of Ruth Doan MacDougall; see page 63), a Laconia Motorcycle Week parade down Main Street (courtesy of Charlie St. Clair; see page 86), Barnard "Bun" McBride, longtime employee at Black's Paper Store in Wolfeboro (courtesy of *Granite State News*; see page 54), Annie Forts of Meredith, activist, with Pres. Bill Clinton and the late John F. Kennedy Jr. (courtesy of Jim McMillian; see page 46), Charles and Harry Smart, brothers who owned a mill together in Ossipee (courtesy of the Smart family; see page 21), Rueben Wentworth, owner of Alton Home and Lumber (author's collection; see page 27)

On the Back Cover: From left to right: Seth Stearns, standing in Center Harbor bandstand he helped build (author's collection; see page 38), Wallace Rhodes, Belmont historian (courtesy of Linda Frawley; see page 48)

CONTENTS

Acknowledgments	6
Introduction	7
CHAPTER ONE Early Days	9
CHAPTER TWO Growth	19
CHAPTER THREE Community Glimpses	37
CHAPTER FOUR Artists and Craftsmen	55
CHAPTER FIVE Tourism Then and Now	77
CHAPTER SIX In Service	89
CHAPTER SEVEN Here and There	105
Index	126

ACKNOWLEDGMENTS

The author gratefully acknowledges the valuable assistance of Daryl Carlson, award-winning professional freelance photographer and educator, and Warren Huse, local historian of Laconia, New Hampshire. Without the accomplished and skilled help of these two colleagues, this book would have been impossible to assemble.

Thanks also to photographers John Hession, Jim MacMillan, and Christine Randall.

Gratitude is also extended to the Lake Winnipesaukee Historical Society, the Laconia Historical and Museum Society, and the historical societies of Alton, Ashland, Center Harbor, Franklin, Gilford (Thompson-Ames Historical Society), New Hampton, Sanbornton, Tuftonboro, and Wolfeboro. Additional thanks to the New Hampshire Veterans Home, the Ashland Town Library, the *Granite State News*, the Wright Museum, the New Hampshire Boat Museum, LRGHealthcare, and the National Baseball Hall of Fame Library, Cooperstown, New York.

Finally, a debt of personal gratitude is due to historians, history buffs, artists, community activists, church leaders, business owners, and numerous other residents, former residents, and friends who have provided photographs, information, contacts, and precious memories about some of the most memorable people who have lived and worked in the Lakes Region.

It has been a privilege to work with you all.

Unless otherwise noted, all images are from the author's personal collection.

INTRODUCTION

Talking about legendary locals in the Lakes Region is bittersweet.

To begin, there is the thrill of discovering—or sometimes rediscovering—the rich character and characters of the area.

Rueben Whitten of Ashland kept his neighbors and friends fed in 1816, the infamous "Year Without a Summer." Thomas Cogswell was the Revolutionary War veteran who served as part of George Washington's inner circle and retired to Gilmanton. Tom Clairmont, a self-proclaimed Belmont pig farmer, changed medical care throughout the region during his tenure at LRGHealthcare. Franklin Fire Department chief Edgar Wheeler helped institute building safety codes in New Hampshire. Dudley Leavitt was a Meredith teacher obsessed with creating almanacs. And Jim Irwin was a Boston musician who created the popular Winnipesaukee Gardens, a Weirs Beach waterfront dance hall where some of the most popular musicians of the 20th century played.

Then there is Franz Nicolay, the Center Sandwich musician and writer now considered one of the "best punk accordionists in the world." Ernest Dane, a Massachusetts banker, helped save Center Harbor from the worst ravages of the Great Depression. Alton Civil War hero Gen. George Savage wanted his horse Old Tom buried alongside him—and eventually got his wish. Charles and Sophia Lane were former schoolteachers who retired to New Hampton and became internationally known as artistic arbiters. Brig. Gen. Harrison Thyng, a Barnstead pilot, was an ace in World War II and the Korean War. Penny Pitou went on from being a Center Harbor kid to winning two Olympic skiing medals. Ralph Morris was a Laconia theater manager who invented Christmas lights. And Thomas Plant, a Maine shoe tycoon, built a "castle in the clouds."

Still, for everyone included, there are so many others who should be but are not. Sometimes the reason is simple—it was impossible to get any kind of photographic image or illustration, or an image was available but the owner did not wish to share it. And these legends demand some kind of visual representation. Sometimes people were passed over because other subjects who were included were too similar, lived in the same area or town, or had a slightly more interesting background story. And sometimes the names and the legends were not sufficiently known, and time just ran out.

The bitterest part of the process is knowing some should be included but are not. In fact, the day this manuscript is off to the publisher, more and more of those names will begin rising to the top.

So, you will not find anything here about the Marsh family that lived in Laconia in the early 20th century and had a hand in inventing motorcycles—ironic, given that the city now hosts the oldest motorcycle rally in America. You will not read about Mel Hale, the Wolfeboro veterinarian who allegedly developed an allergy to penicillin, so he retired to Center Harbor and purchased a large farm that he later turned into the still-operating Waukewan Golf Club. Or Bolder Landry, a Laconia youth who taught himself cowboy rope tricks that led to touring around the country in Wild West shows and later to leading expeditions to countries like Costa Rica. Based on his experiences, Landry was eventually named a professor of anthropology at the University of California. And there is Moses Senter, the founder of Center Harbor and the source of an ongoing argument among locals about whether their town is named for him or for its geographic location.

You will miss out on Red Dunn of Laconia, who ran for governor, performed on local radio daily, and promoted his paving business by declaring, "When it's done by Dunn, it's done right." And Alton Wilkes is also missing, the man who renovated a Gilford barn into the Lakes Region Playhouse, where some of America's most notable theatrical stars of the 1950s, 1960s, and 1970s performed. Soong Mei-ling, better known as Madame Chiang Kai-Shek and the wife of the last leader of China before the communist takeover in 1949, was a beautiful, intelligent woman oftentimes called "the most powerful woman of the 20th century;" she also happened to have a home in Wolfeboro for years. Bruce Heald of Meredith is a well-known local author and historian, but he also directs a choir at the Immaculate Conception School in Center Harbor that sings intricate polyphonic Catholic Latin hymns, motets, and liturgical music. And there is the Tilton junk dealer who was as much a pastor and a philosopher as a business owner.

But, the cast in this collection does reflect some of the imaginative and fascinating range of people of the Lakes Region, and the captions will provide a quick glimpse into the rich nature of the area.

So, read and enjoy. And let these brief outlines lead you to a more thorough investigation through reading, meeting, and talking to people.

You are likely to find your own legendary local at the corner convenience store or the neighborhood diner.

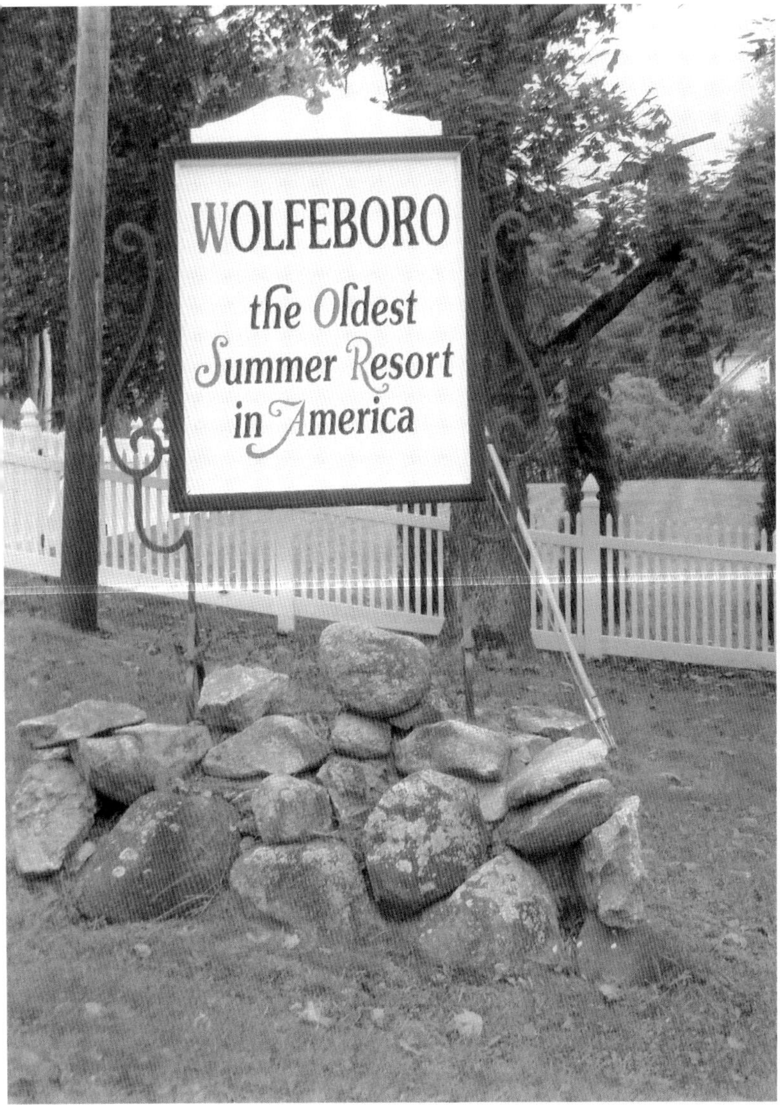

Welcome to the Lakes Region
Wolfeboro's iconic sign identifies the town as America's first resort, as Colonial governor John Wentworth set up a seasonal home here in 1769 (see page 12). Current seasonal residents include former Republican presidential candidate Mitt Romney, *Tonight Show* host Jimmy Fallon (his daughter Winnie is named after Lake Winnipesaukee), and Spencer Johnson, author of the popular business book *Who Moved My Cheese?*. Since Wentworth's arrival, the Lakes Region has continued to draw—and grow—a rich variety of people who have contributed to the region, the nation, and the world.

CHAPTER ONE

Early Days

As noted in the introduction, one of the charms of the Lakes Region is that there are easily more than the 100 legendary locals included in this modest volume. On almost any street corner one can find a business owner, church leader, environmental activist, or someone who is a hero to a family or similar group of people and who has had (or is currently having) an impact on the community, the region, or the nation that is in some ways incalculable.

Maybe it is the connection here between the lakes, mountains, farm stands, and factories; cool August evenings and cold February mornings; blue summer skies and whitened winter ski trails; green springs and burnt orange autumns; congenial summer people and industrious year-round residents. But, it seems to be in the nature of the Lakes Region to develop a keen sense of interconnection between people.

This chapter is devoted to that handful of people who distinguished themselves in a unique way and did so in what is vaguely referred to as the good old days.

The days past were probably not much better or worse than the present. And that is what makes the deeds of these people particularly striking. When the area was still largely a sometimes-dangerous wilderness, John Sherman and Harvard College student Jonathan Ince traveled to the place now called Weirs Beach to mark the outskirts of English authority. At a time when only about one-third of Americans favored the Revolutionary War, Thomas Cogswell served at the right hand of Gen. George Washington. And when the region's population was still sparse, Charles Tilton demonstrated indomitable faith in the development of his community by investing in its infrastructure and its artistic development.

Marks on a Rock

In the mid-17th century, property owners in coastal New Hampshire wanted to establish the northernmost point of the Merrimack River, where their land grant of the Massachusetts Bay Colony ended. John Sherman of Watertown, Massachusetts, and a Harvard College student named Jonathan Ince were hired to pinpoint the spot. The pair noted its latitude and longitude and marked their initials on a rock there.

However, the boulder was lost to history until more than 150 years later, when it was discovered by workers involved in a project to deepen the Weirs Channel. The New Hampshire legislature set aside funds to raise the rock up a few feet and construct a granite canopy around it.

On top was a life-size depiction of an Indian brave nicknamed "Captain Jack." The figure was executed in zinc by William Demuth and Company of New York, a purveyor of 19th-century cigar store items, such as the Indian figures that sat outside many tobacco shops of that era.

In 1983, lightning damaged the Indian figure. After it was repaired, the State of New Hampshire loaned it to the Laconia Historical Society; it is currently on display in the second-floor reading room of Laconia's Gale Memorial Library.

Five years later, the original Captain Jack above Endicott Rock was replaced by a white-metal likeness. Then, in the early 2000s, sculptor Robert Morton created a more historically accurate statue of what a Native American would have looked like if the explorers had met one in 1652. That figure now sits on top of the Endicott Rock granite canopy.

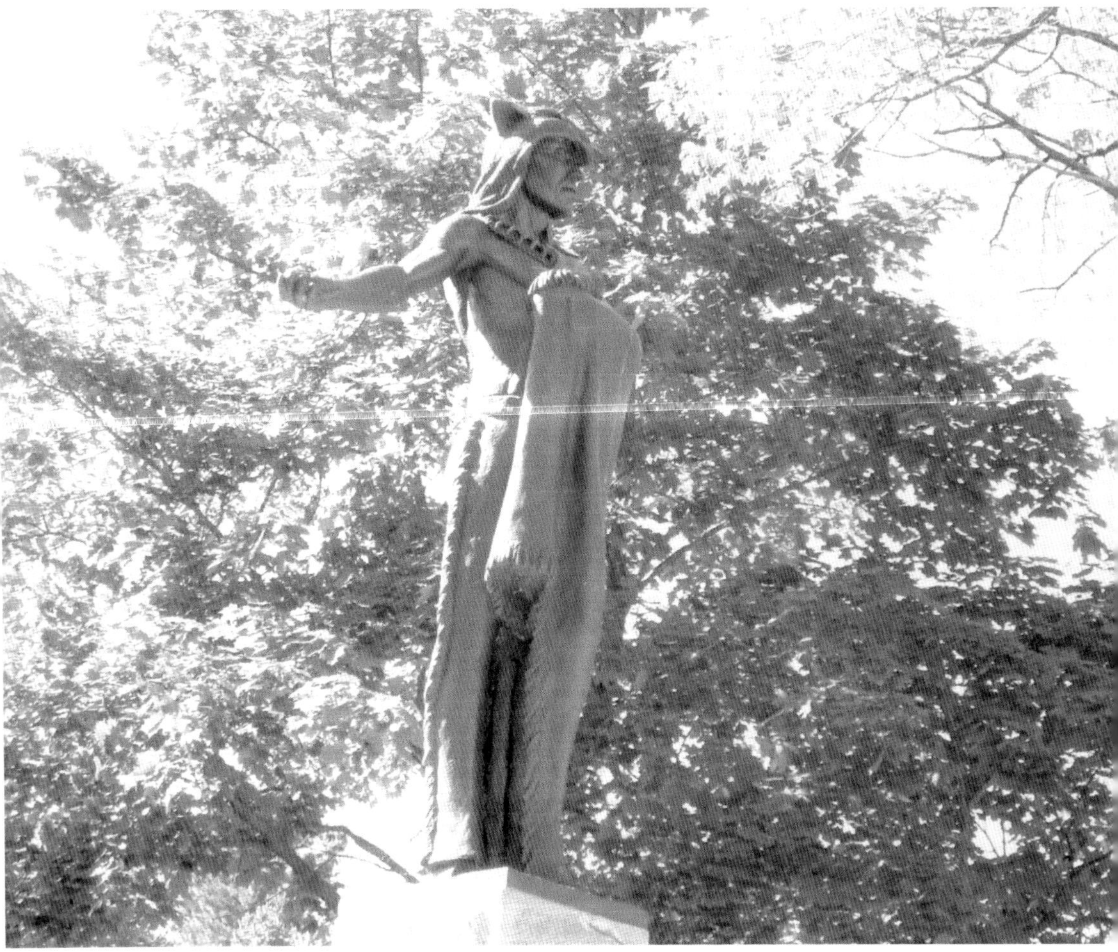

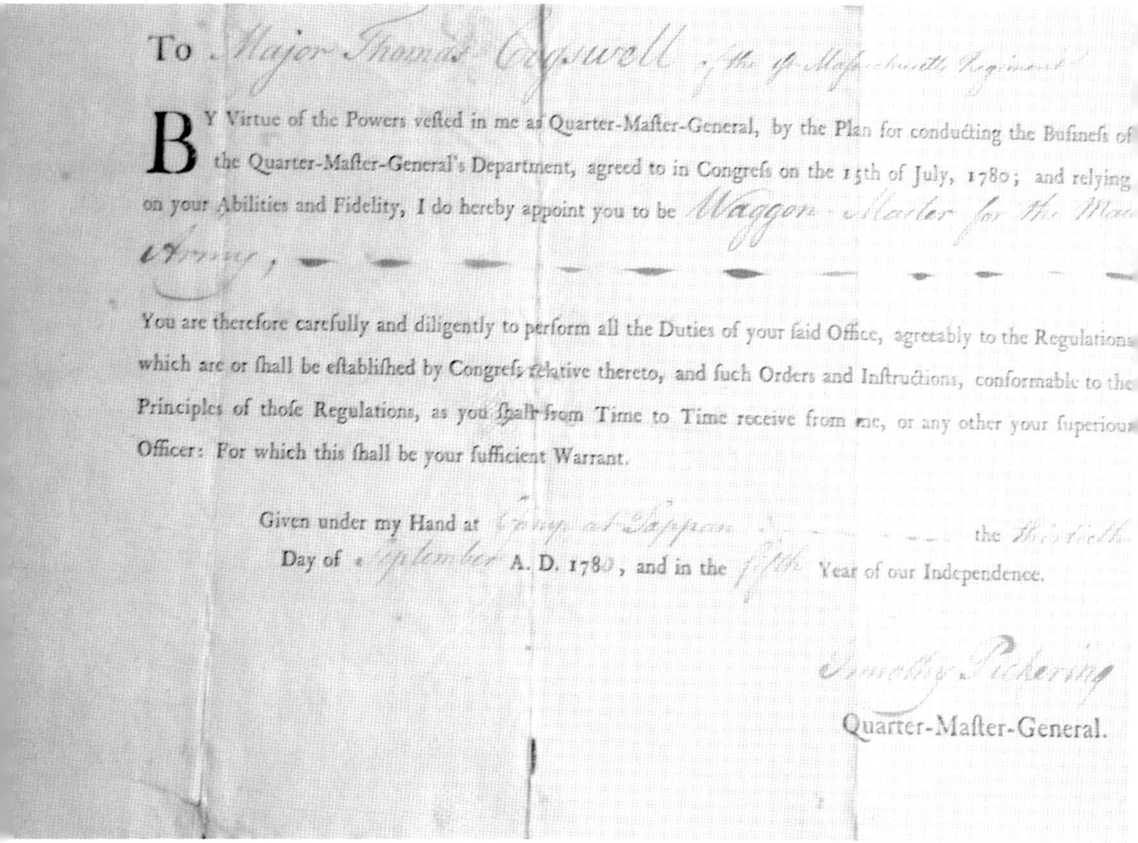

To Major Thomas Cogswell, of the Massachusetts Regiment

BY Virtue of the Powers veſted in me as Quarter-Maſter-General, by the Plan for conducting the Buſineſs of the Quarter-Maſter-General's Department, agreed to in Congreſs on the 15th of July, 1780; and relying on your Abilities and Fidelity, I do hereby appoint you to be Waggon Master for the Main Army,

You are therefore carefully and diligently to perform all the Duties of your ſaid Office, agreeably to the Regulations which are or ſhall be eſtabliſhed by Congreſs relative thereto, and ſuch Orders and Inſtructions, conformable to the Principles of thoſe Regulations, as you ſhall from Time to Time receive from me, or any other your ſuperiour Officer: For which this ſhall be your ſufficient Warrant.

Given under my Hand at Camp at Tappan the thirtieth Day of September A. D. 1780, and in the fifth Year of our Independence.

Timothy Pickering
Quarter-Maſter-General.

Washington's Inner Circle

Thomas Cogswell did not come from Gilmanton but his wife, Ruth, did. She was a descendant of one of the town's settlers, Joseph Badger, who later became a governor of New Hampshire.

Cogswell, who came from Haverhill, Massachusetts, was a patriot. He captained a troop of Minutemen who fought at the Battles of Lexington and Concord and was in charge of the defenses at the Battle of Bunker Hill.

When the Revolutionary War officially broke out, Cogswell enlisted and was sent to serve with Gen. George Washington's army. Cogswell served as Washington's wagon master, the person responsible for transportation of goods. (His official orders to serve with the nation's main army, approved by Congress, are seen here.) It was an important job, crucial to the Americans' success.

In 1781, when Washington moved his troops from New York to Virginia for the Battle of Yorktown, Cogswell oversaw the transport of hundreds of tons of equipment—cannonballs, gunpowder, and other materiel—over 400 miles in four weeks. It was a herculean feat and a decisive factor in the defeat of the British; the move allowed the Continental army to constantly bombard British general Lord Charles Cornwallis's troops until they surrendered on October 17, 1881. It was, in effect, the end of the war.

Cogswell retired to Gilmanton and lived in the house on Crystal Lake once owned by his father-in-law, Governor Badger. (When the house was built in 1784, it was called "the finest wood frame house in New Hampshire.") Cogswell served as chief justice for the town as well as stints as a selectman and the town moderator. (Courtesy of Ned Downing.)

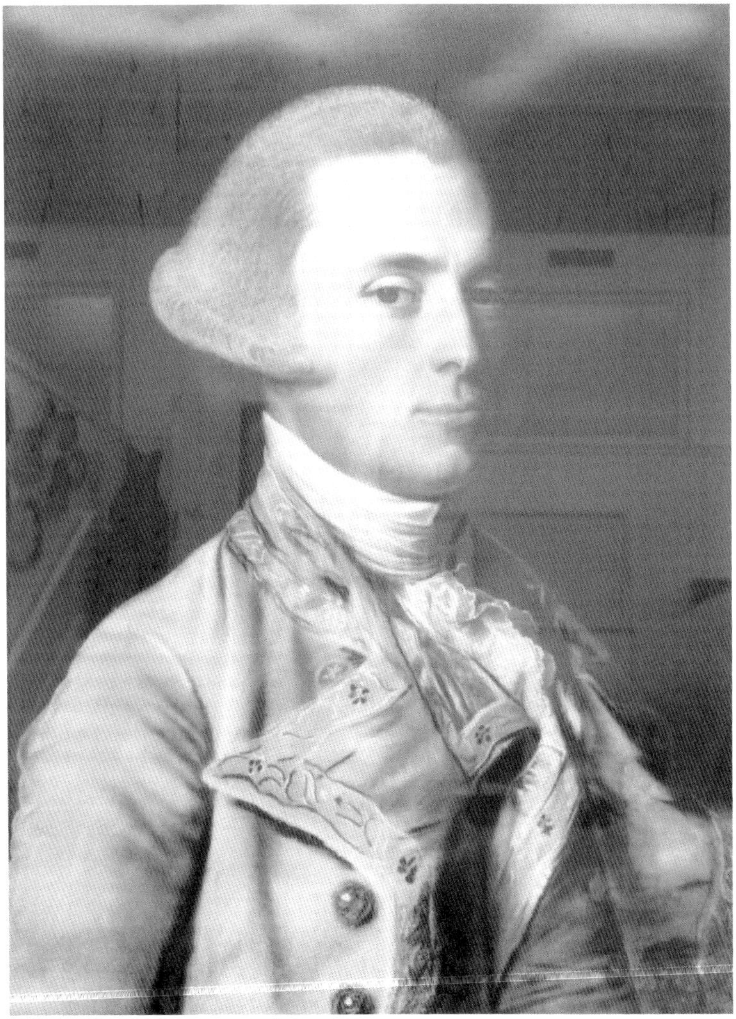

First Vacationer

The history of tourists coming to the Lakes Region from cities like Boston and New York dates back to the 1800s.

But even before that, Gov. John Wentworth saw the advantages of staying by Lake Winnipesaukee as a refreshing retreat.

Wentworth was born and raised in Portsmouth, New Hampshire, and although he was the last royal governor, appointed by King George III, he also had great affection for the New World. After he took office in 1767, he worked to strengthen the region, frequently criticizing English leaders who looked down on the colonists.

For most of his term, he was popular with New Hampshire residents. He helped establish Dartmouth College. He worked to improve roads. And, in 1769, he built one of the first vacation homes here on 4,000 acres in Wolfeboro. (It is the reason the town is known as "America's First Resort.") A road, which is still in use, linked the town with the Hanover area, where Dartmouth College is located. Wentworth hoped it would indicate the importance of both communities in the development of New Hampshire.

But, history caught up with Wentworth, and when the Revolutionary War began, he lost his popularity as he struggled to maintain British rule. He eventually fled New Hampshire and moved back to England. (Courtesy of Wolfeboro Historical Society.)

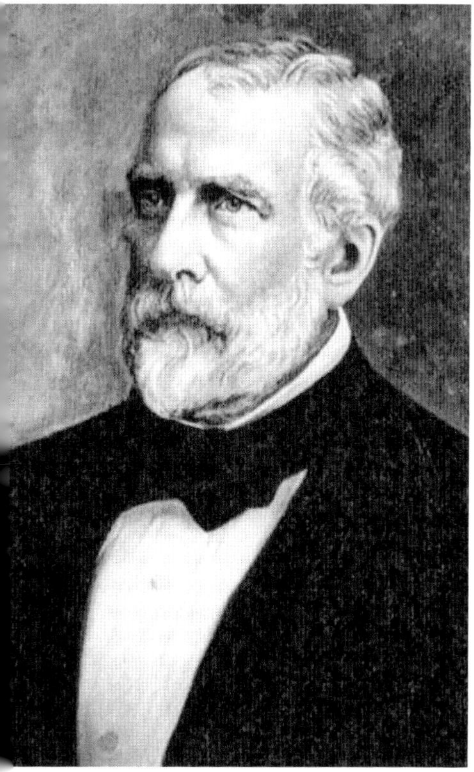

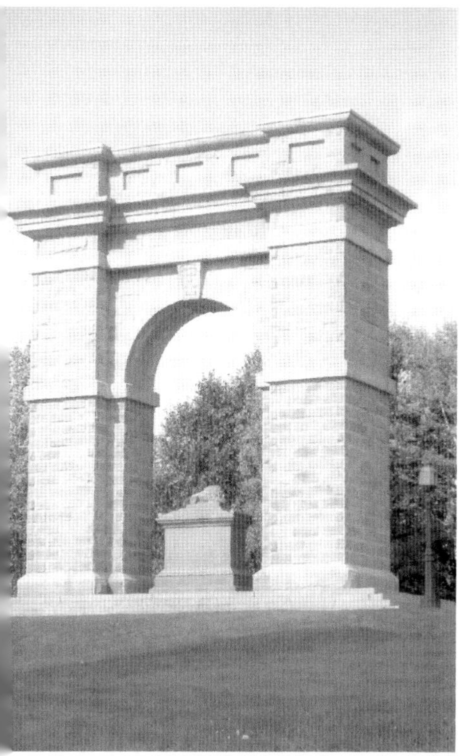

The Tilton Plan

No other single person impacted the development of a Lakes Region community as much as Charles E. Tilton. Originally part of Sanbornton, his town was incorporated as Tilton in 1869. Residents chose the name at his suggestion; Tilton said he wanted to honor his family, not himself. He was a member of the fourth generation in the area, and his ancestors were among its original settlers.

After making his fortune in the California Gold Rush, Tilton returned home determined to make his community one of the most beautiful places in America. He funded the construction of the town hall and two bridges, as well as the erection of several prominent public objets d'art, including the Tilton Memorial Arch, which sits near the town on a hill overlooking the Winnipesaukee River, in Northfield.

It is a dramatic edifice, and Tilton hoped his gift to Northfield would convince the residents to join Tilton and become a single town; he even had a mausoleum built underneath the arch for himself.

But, Northfield folks proved stubborn, and the two towns remain separate to this day. Tilton was buried in his town's Park Cemetery in 1901. (Top, courtesy of New Hampshire Veterans Home; bottom, author's collection.)

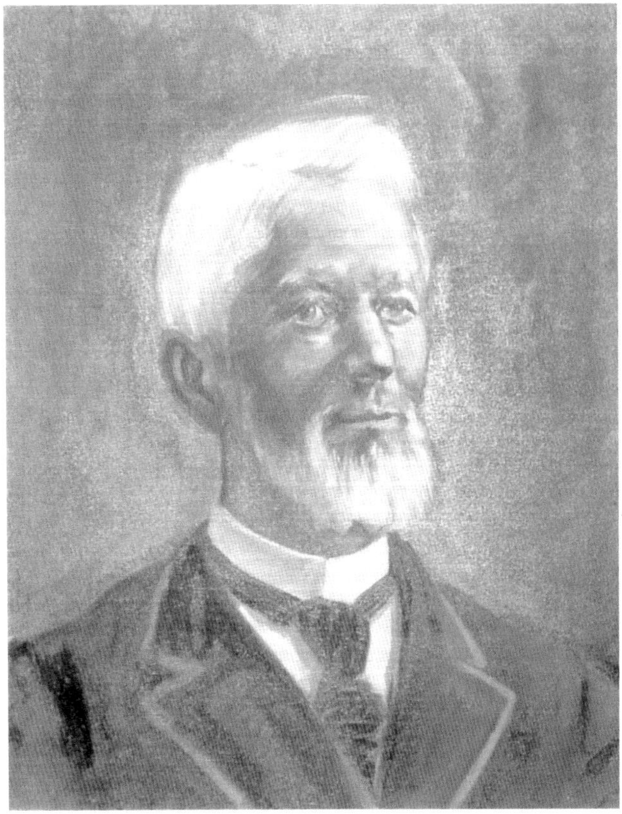

The Writing Preacher

In the late 18th and early 19th centuries, Moses Thurston Runnels was the pastor of the first church in Sanbornton. He treasured the community that was his parish, and folks there generally loved him.

But, his greatest impact came from writing their story for posterity. His two-volume *History of Sanbornton*, published in 1882, is still prized for its strong writing and thoroughly researched and accurate content. "One of the very best town histories to come out of the 19th century," wrote R. Stuart Wallace, former editor of *Historical New Hampshire*.

Runnels came to Sanbornton in 1865 and, with his wife and family, moved into the Sunshine Cottage, across the road from the still-standing Lane Tavern on Route 132. It was his job to get to know the community, and he enjoyed the task. Before long, his innate writing skills rose up, and he found himself writing down things he learned.

Runnels was not being paid for the work, but he loved it. "Not an hour of drudgery—not a cheerless hour—has ever been employed upon it!" he exclaimed, after his history was published.

Still, Runnels ran into difficulties. After the books were completed, he found himself heavily in debt and began working hard to pay off his obligations. He may have overdone it, as the church put him on a four-month sabbatical. He traveled to the southern United States, and when he returned, he learned that the congregation had resolved his debts.

Despite their generosity, Runnels was not satisfied. Although he loved writing, he saw his primary job as a preacher of the gospel, and was disappointed that Sanbornton did not experience the kind of spiritual revival seen in other parts of New England.

But, he treasured his time in the small town and offered some sage advice when speaking at his last Old Home Week celebration in 1901. "Take the hint, my younger hearers," he told his audience. "Be more free to converse with those aged parents of yours . . . Try to draw out those treasures of knowledge and experience of the past." (Courtesy of Sanbornton Historical Society.)

Making Almanacs in Heaven

Dudley Leavitt of Meredith was a farmer, but he was also a man with an insatiable quest for knowledge. He studied Latin, Greek, Hebrew, modern languages, and astronomy before he started publishing his own almanac. The first Leavitt's Farmers Almanac appeared in 1797, and the publication became a staple of farmers throughout the region until his death in 1851. In fact, before Leavitt passed away, he prepared six more years of almanacs. Leavitt reportedly said he hoped to make almanacs in the afterlife. This historical marker is on Whittier Highway in Center Harbor.

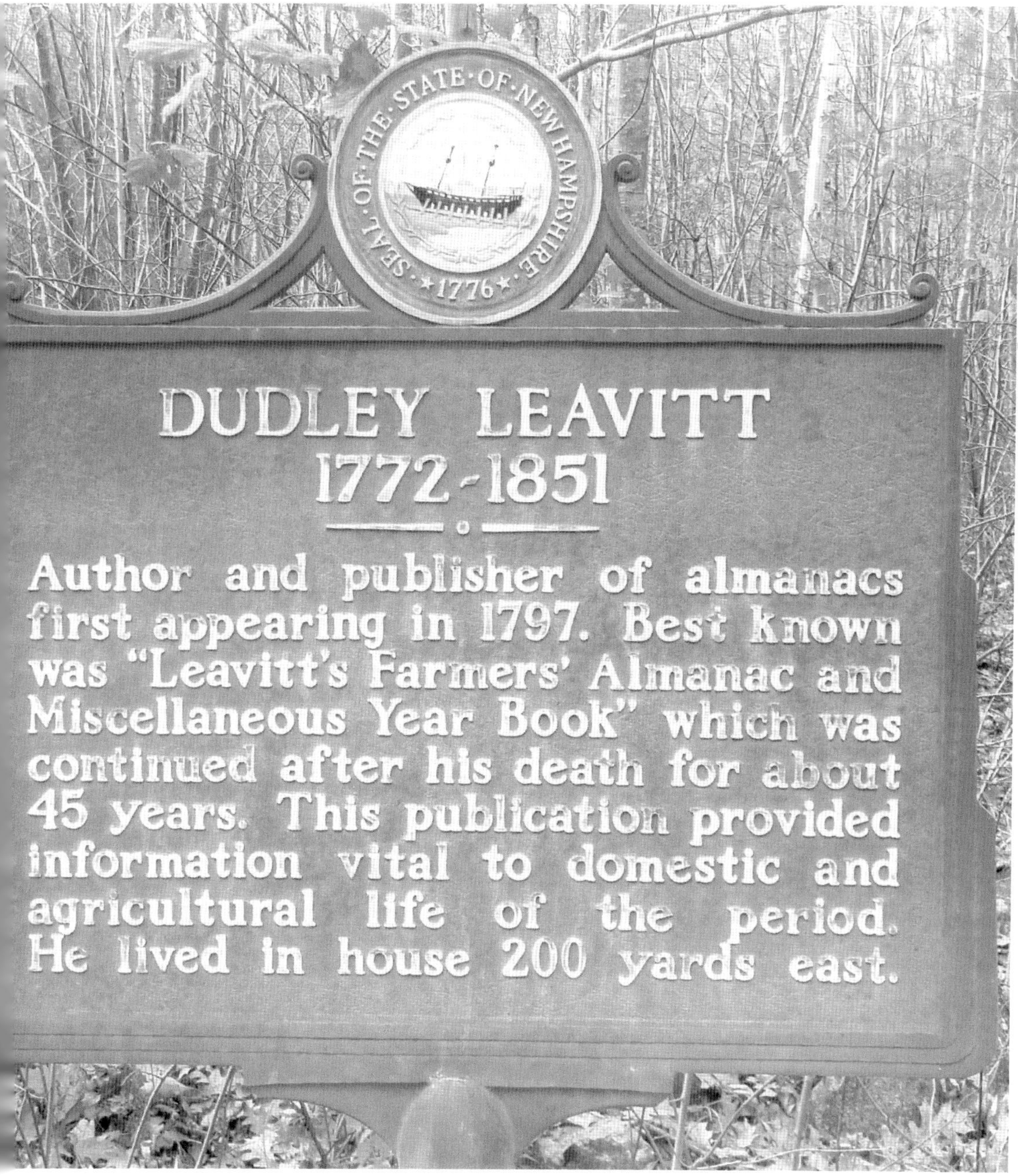

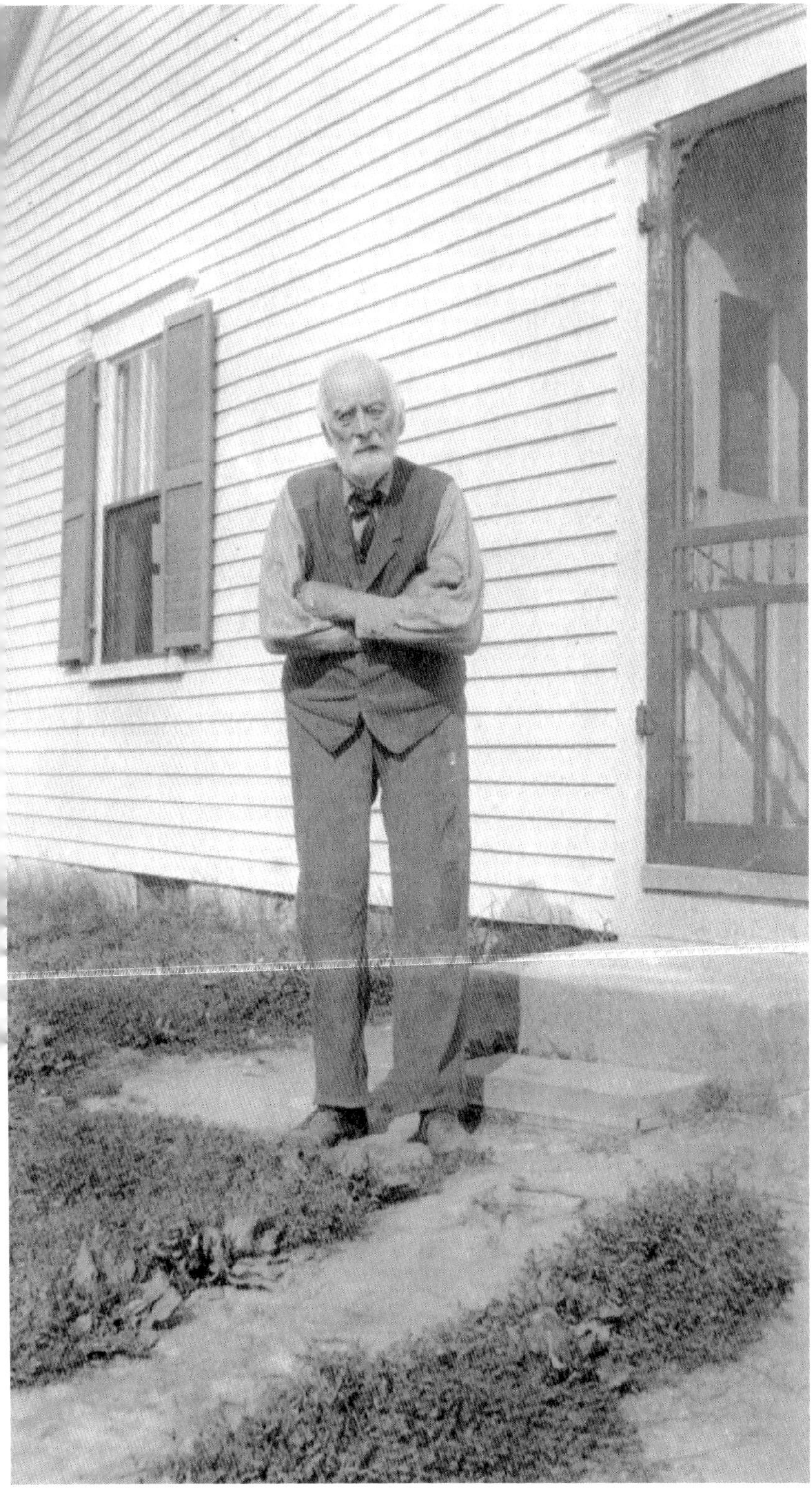

One of Alton's First Families

The Downings moved from New Hampshire's seacoast to the Lakes Region in the 1830s and have made a significant impact on the area for generations. Over the years, Downings owned the Bay Boat Company, Downing's Landing, Downing's Garage, the Alton Corner Store, the Winnipesaukee Hotel, and even the landmark Bay View Pavilion for a while.

Among the few families that were here before the Downings were the Bennetts, and inevitably, the families intermarried. Morrison Bennett, shown here at the age of 97, was named after his wife's father, Lyndia Morrison, who fought in the Revolutionary War. The original Bennett family homestead, built on New Durham Road around 1774, is likely the oldest home standing in town. (Courtesy of the Downing family.)

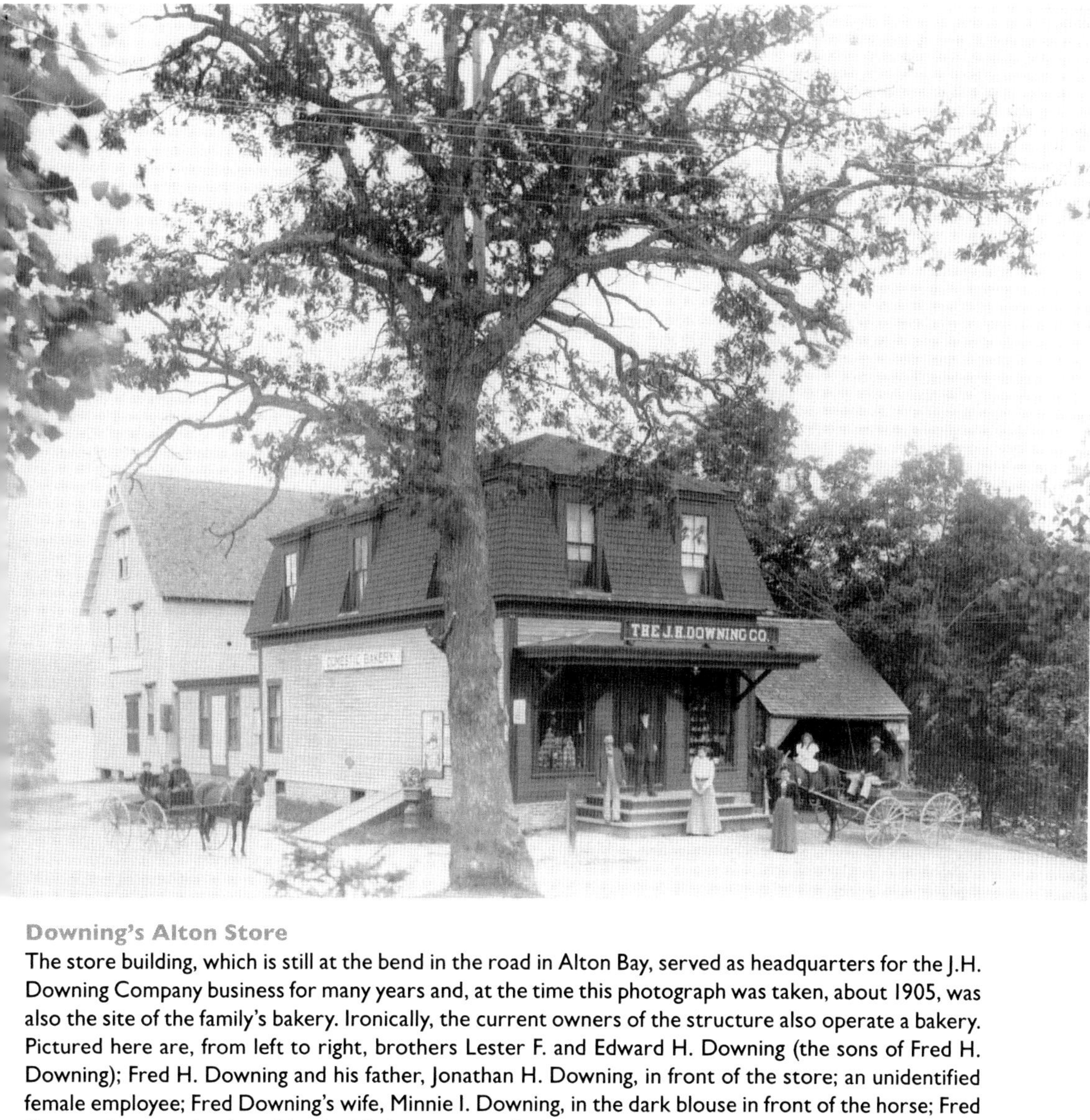

Downing's Alton Store

The store building, which is still at the bend in the road in Alton Bay, served as headquarters for the J.H. Downing Company business for many years and, at the time this photograph was taken, about 1905, was also the site of the family's bakery. Ironically, the current owners of the structure also operate a bakery. Pictured here are, from left to right, brothers Lester F. and Edward H. Downing (the sons of Fred H. Downing); Fred H. Downing and his father, Jonathan H. Downing, in front of the store; an unidentified female employee; Fred Downing's wife, Minnie I. Downing, in the dark blouse in front of the horse; Fred Downing's young daughter Blanche M. Downing, on the horse; and an unidentified male employee in the carriage. (Courtesy of the Downing family.)

The Biggest Man in the Country

More than 150 years after his death, Daniel Webster of Franklin remains New Hampshire's most illustrious son. He was born in a simple farmhouse on family property he called "the most beautiful place in all this earth."

Steven Vincent Benét writes, "For a while, he was the biggest man in the country. He never got to be President, but he was the biggest man . . . They said when he stood up to speak, stars and stripes came right out in the sky . . . They said when he walked the woods with his fishing rod, the trout would jump out of the streams right into his pockets, for they knew it was no use putting up a fight against him; and, when he argued a case, he could turn on the harps of the blessed and the shaking of the earth underground."

It is nearly impossible to gauge Webster's effect on 19th-century America. He was, first of all, the most important lawyer of his time, known for his impeccable logic and dramatic oratory skills. His arguments were sometimes used by Chief Justice John Marshall as reasoning behind important Supreme Court decisions.

Webster also served as a New Hampshire congressman and, after that, as a senator and congressman from Massachusetts. His strong support of the federal government fostered protective tariffs and a national bank. Some say he may have even delayed the start of the Civil War for several years; while the battle over slavery focused on the states' rights of Southerners, he argued for "Liberty and Union, now and forever, one and inseparable!"

Webster twice served brief terms as secretary of state and is now considered one of America's best. He negotiated the Webster-Ashburton Treaty, which settled a long-simmering dispute about the Maine–New Brunswick border. The agreement ended a threat of war with Great Britain.

Webster was so revered that in the 1930s, Steven Vincent Benét wrote a short story describing a fictional case in which Webster argued with the devil for the soul of a man and won. "The Devil and Daniel Webster" is still read in many American schools. His statue stands outside the statehouse in Concord.

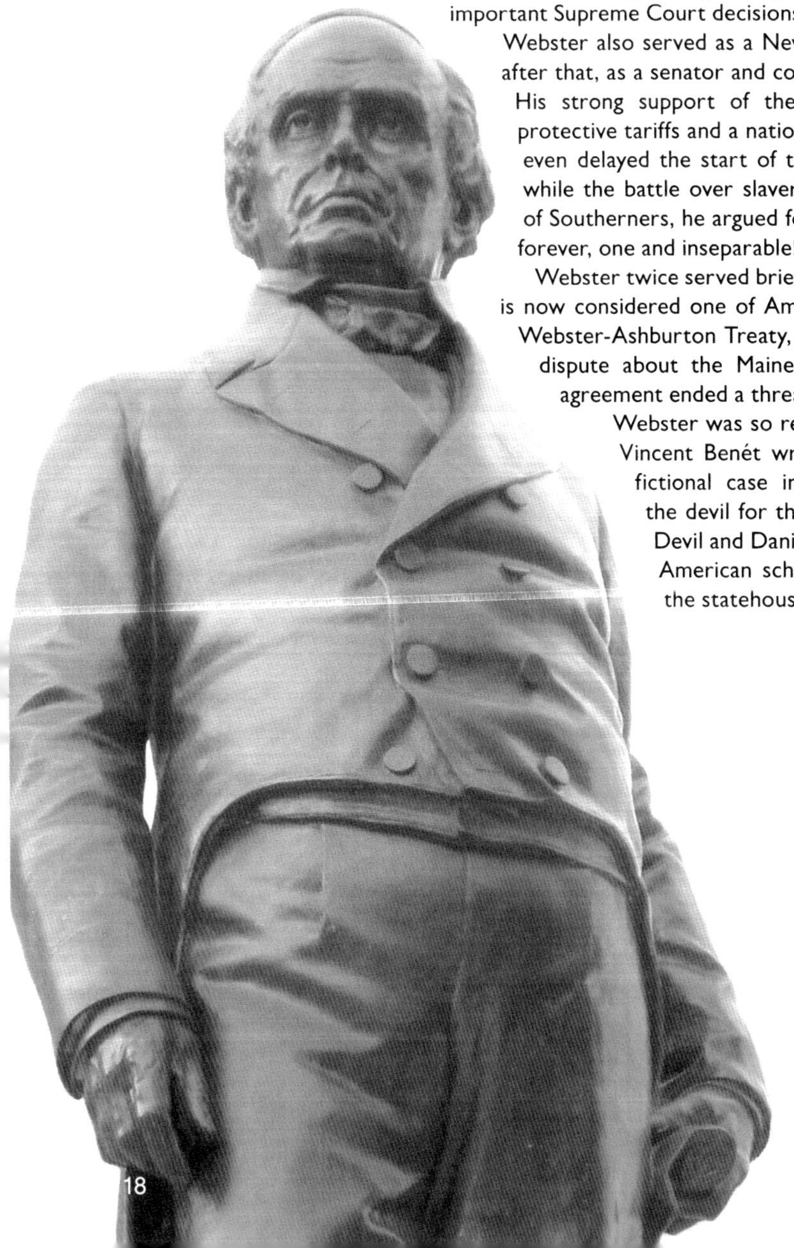

CHAPTER TWO

Growth

There are many reasons a community grows and thrives, but there is one sure sign. When commerce is robust, resources are plentiful, and people generally prosper.

That is why looking at those who are prominent in the local business community is always revealing. Poets can dream, preachers can inspire, and philosophers can theorize, but it is all so much air unless entrepreneurs stand side-by-side with inventors, investors, and marketers to create an environment of promise, expansion, and possibilities.

The Lakes Region has been blessed with some amazing businesspeople who have found opportunities around them that others missed.

Russell Clough of Alton kept trying his hand at anything—from poetry to machinery—until he developed a new way to remove a cork from the top of a medicine bottle. The results were a factory and jobs in his hometown and franchises all over Europe.

Henry Page of Gilmanton was interested in restoring old furniture until he learned how to become an expert in restoring old Colonial homes. He is still doing it almost 50 years later.

The Lawton brothers saw the fun people had when they came to Weirs Beach and turned that into the enormous year-round Funspot.

Sisters Shelli Shumway and Stephanie McKim took note of the gourmet inclinations of their neighbors and created an award-winning Tilton cupcake bakery.

Lin Bi was a college student who saw how local people love the food of his homeland and opened a restaurant that is still thriving.

Joseph Morin was a French Canadian immigrant who developed one of the most successful textile mills in the area, providing work for many of his fellow countrymen and helping to establish Laconia as an industrial hub of New England.

Anyone can imagine, but these are the people who make dreams into the real stuff of life, who gave form to the best intentions of artists, dreamers, and children.

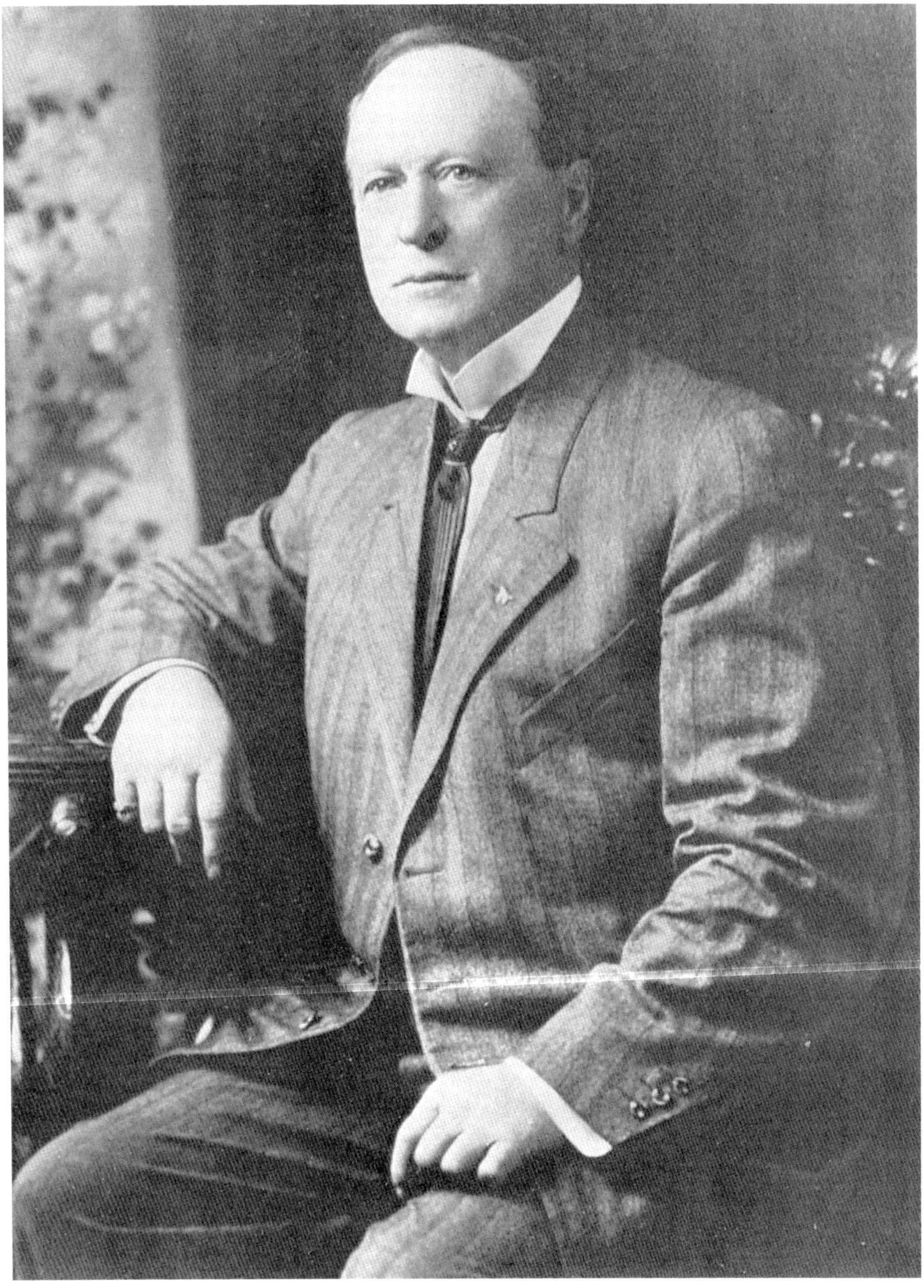

Twisting His Way into History

Rockwell Clough was one of the Lakes Region's most inventive sons. As a young man in the Union army during the Civil War, he wrote patriotic verses. When the war ended, he became an inventor—designing an improved hairpin, a diaper safety pin, a hook wall hanger, a buckle, and a reclining chair. His greatest success was inventing a corkscrew to open the cork tops that were used on top of medicine bottles in those days, or, more accurately, a machine that produced the corkscrew quickly and inexpensively. His machine won awards at exhibitions in Paris, Chicago, and Atlanta, and he established franchises throughout Europe. (Courtesy of the Alton Historical Society.)

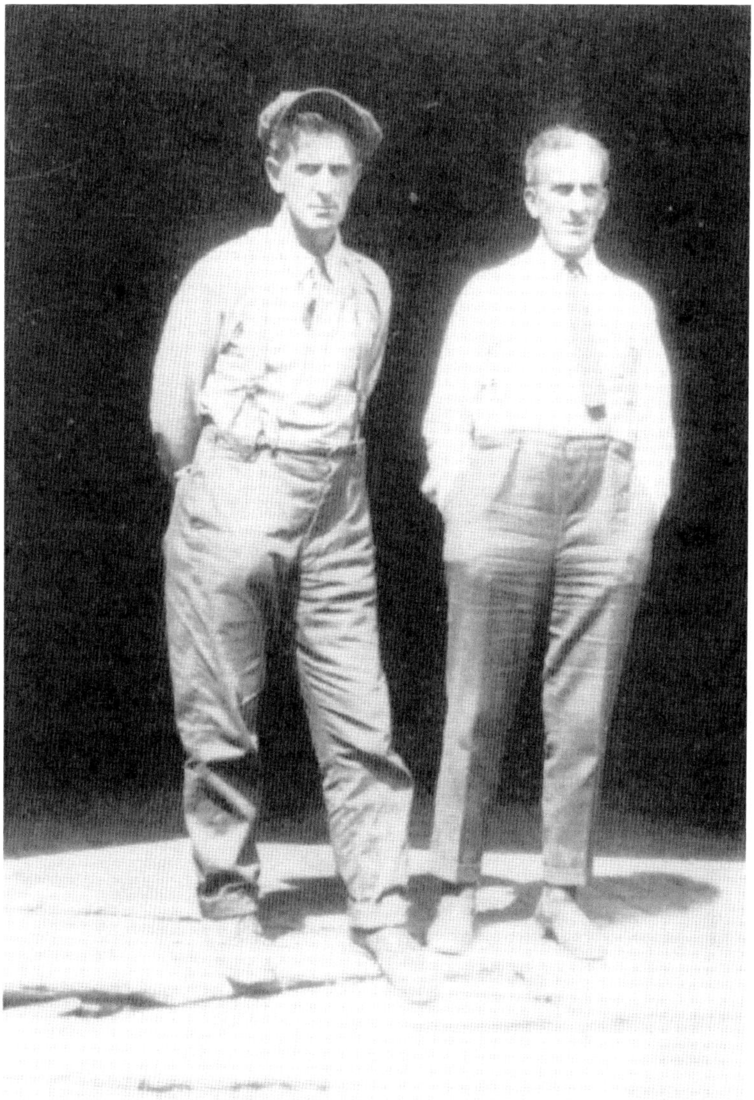

The More Things Stay the Same

Charles and Harry Smart of Ossipee made a good living operating the Smart Brothers Mill on Beech River in Ossipee. Their company, which was founded in 1851, primarily sold pine blinds and shutters—for $2 each, according to a mid-20th century price list—but it also ran logging operations, drawing lumber from the nearby Ossipee Mountains.

But things changed in the 1950s, when Japanese imports undercut the Smarts' prices. They hung on for as long as they could but issued their last checks to employees in 1967.

Harry Smart (left) served in the New Hampshire legislature with Sherman Adams, who later became President Eisenhower's chief of staff. In 1945, he introduced legislation to make the Old Man of the Mountain the official emblem of New Hampshire.

Meanwhile, the old Smart mill was purchased in 1982 by Greg Dale of Ontario, who revived the facility; his work was featured on an episode of PBS's *This Old House*. In 1989, the Oullette family bought the building and returned the Beech River Mill to making louvered and paneled products like doors, shutters, and blinds. (Courtesy of the Smart family.)

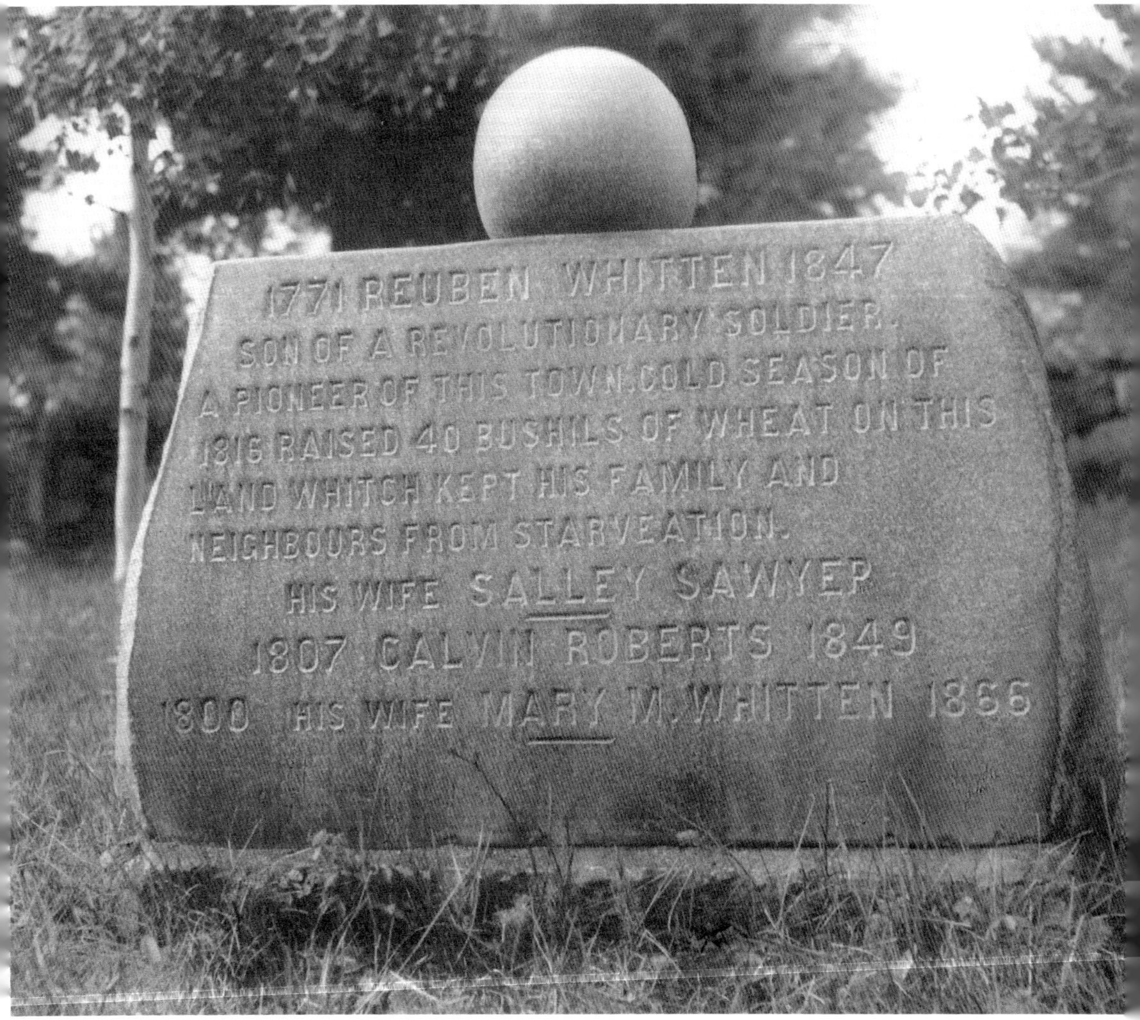

"A Cup of Water . . . Will Not Be Forgotten"
Reuben Whitten is famous for a single act of generosity. In 1816, the infamous "Year Without a Summer," apparently caused by a volcanic explosion in Indonesia that affected worldwide climate, the Ashland man managed to grow 40 bushels of wheat on his upland farm. He then carefully dried the wheat on his hearth and shared it with his neighbors. According to local history, this single action kept his family and others alive through the nonexistent growing season.

In 1911, his grandson Alfred Roberts, who was a stonecutter, carved a stone that describes Reuben's generosity for Whitten's small grave on Highland Street. The monument is one of the few physical reminders anywhere of the uncommonly cold summer and, as a result, Whitten's kindness has become widely known.

The local man's small house was recently moved to the grounds of the Whipple House Museum, where the Ashland Historical Society operates, and is now awaiting restoration. (Courtesy of Ashland Town Library.)

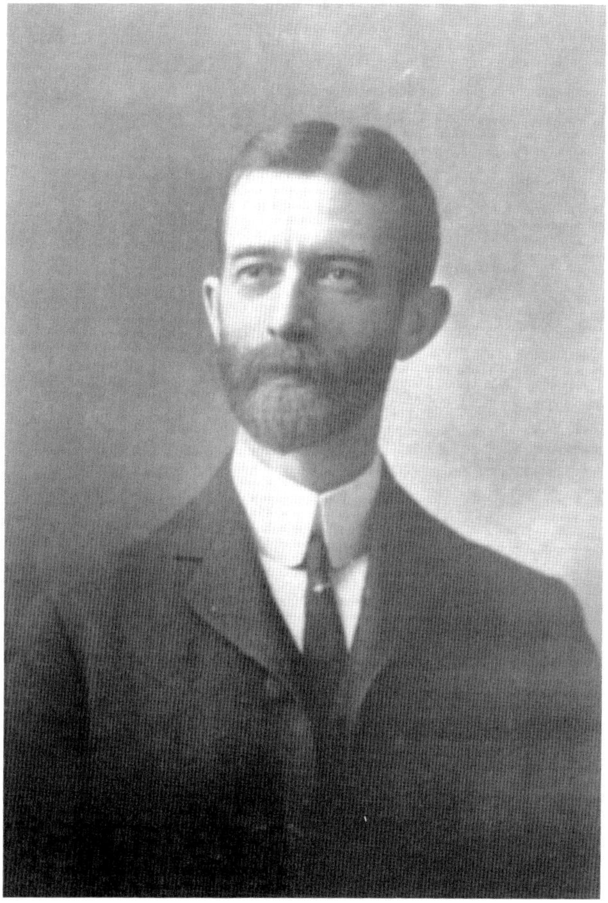

Working on the Railroad

The Robie (or Roby) family worked as farmers in the Winona Road section of Meredith and New Hampton from the early 1800s. Charles Robie, the son of William and Harriet (Chase) Robie, was born on the family farm in New Hampton in 1866.

Charles and his older brother Samuel were both interested in printing. Charles first whittled wooden alphabet letters, then made his own foot-powered scroll saw to improve their quality; he even purchased his own printing press. But it was Samuel who stayed in the field, starting the *Meredith Review* and later working as editor for Franklin's *Journal Transcript*.

Meanwhile, Charles got a job with the American Express Company office in Plymouth. The business was on the verge of prospering, as its offices, like the one in Plymouth, were set along the growing railroads. At that time, the company shipped and received all kinds of goods, from packages and freight to livestock and perishable foodstuffs.

Robie grew with the company, eventually advancing to become the route agent for the Boston & Albany Railroad, and became superintendent for the Massachusetts division in 1896. In 1906, he was named assistant general manager, and in 1923, vice president of the Railway Express Agency, a business that grew out of American Express.

Despite Robie's career advancement, he maintained strong attachments to the Lakes Region. He purchased Rock Ridge Farm overlooking Lake Waukewan and remodeled it into a large vacation home where he regularly entertained wealthy business associates. Robie built a boathouse on the lake and enjoyed being on the water. He died at the farm in 1949, not far from where his family had lived for three generations. (Courtesy of New Hampton Historical Society.)

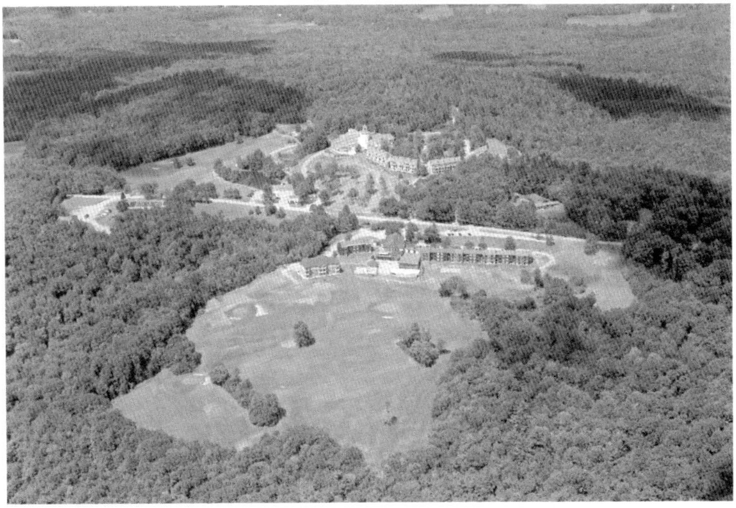

Take It from the Top

Ralph Cutillo was a former Navy pilot and fledging Providence, Rhode Island, hospitality entrepreneur when he heard about a lodging facility that reportedly included "the best piece of real estate in New Hampshire."

The old Steele Hill Farm in Sanbornton had been turned into a lodging facility in the 1930s, but it catered strictly to affluent Boston families until the mid-1960s.

In 1968, Cutillo saw the property—and its spectacular Lakes Region views—and he bought it. He hoped to turn a large part into condominiums that he could sell to folks interested in staying in the Lakes Region. But when town planners blocked his effort, he made most of Steele Hill into a timeshare operation, where buyers bought the use of a lodging unit for one or two weeks every year.

By 1976, the Steele Hill Vacation Club was growing rapidly. In the early 1990s, it became known as a premier wedding venue in the Lakes Region. At the beginning of the 21st century, Ralph's son Bill (shown below at right, with his father (center) and brother Steve) bought out his father's interest and soon began working on another round of expansion, the construction of 10 new buildings.

Today, the Steele Hill Resorts serve as an industry leader in both vacation ownership and rentals. The property is also the largest taxpaying entity in Sanbornton and a wonderful recreational resource for the Lakes Region. (Both, courtesy of Steele Hill Resorts.)

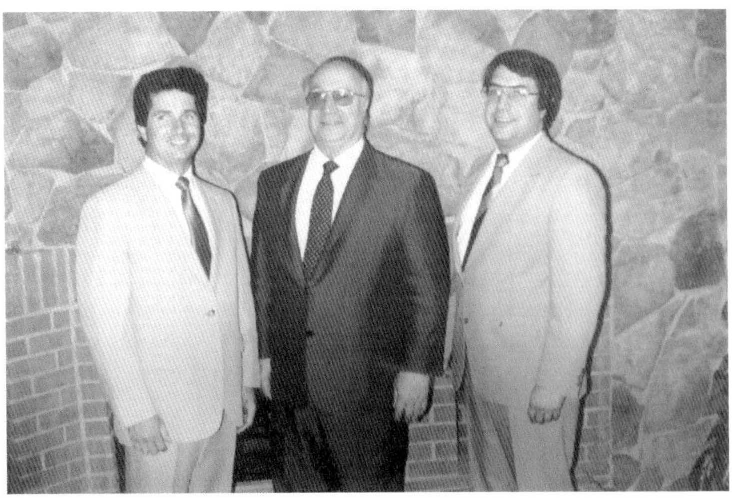

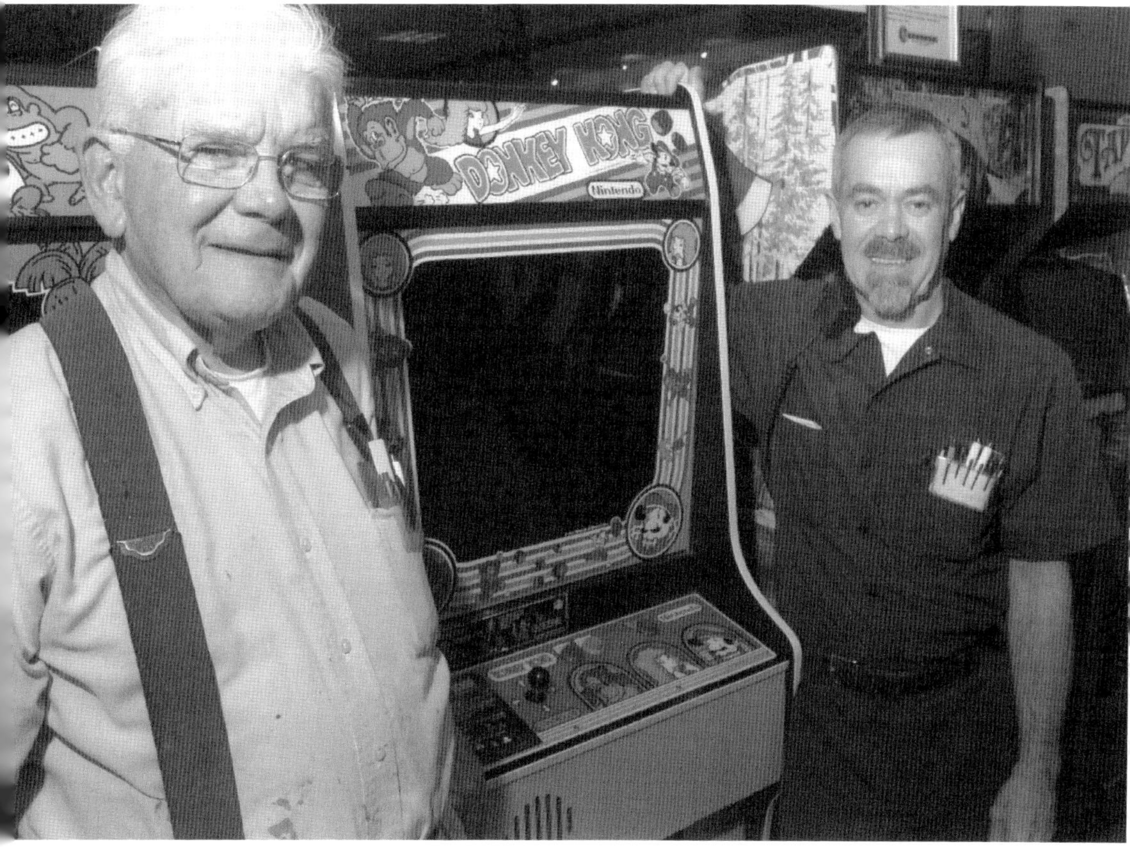

Making Big Fun

Bob Lawton (left) is a former representative to the New Hampshire legislature and a publisher of the Lakes Region's distinctive *Weirs Times*, a free weekly periodical. But his largest impact may be the creation of the Funspot Family Entertainment Center, which he began with his brother John in 1952. It is now the largest game arcade in the world and the site of the annual International Classic Video Game Tournament. Bob is seen here with Randy Lawton, one of John's sons and the longtime chief of operations at Funspot. (Courtesy of Daryl Carlson/Kamara Image Photography.)

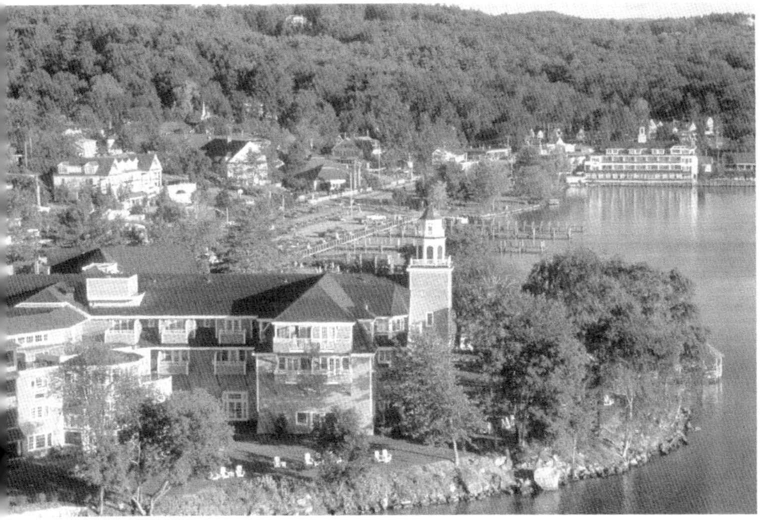

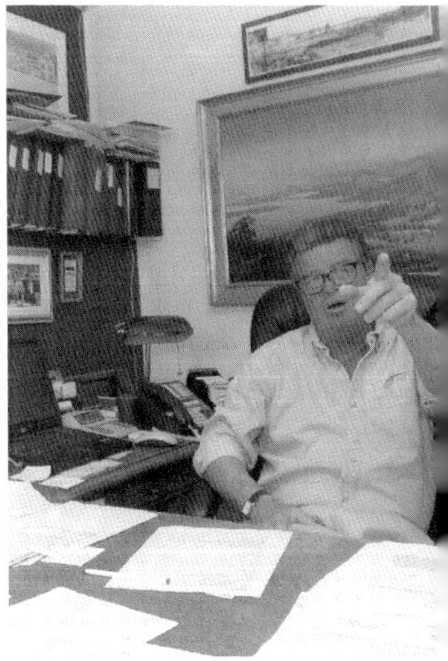

From Mill Town to Destination

In the 1980s, a local realtor named Edward "Rusty" McLear knew that Meredith was trying to find ways to revitalize without compromising its small-town charm. After talking with his neighbors, he developed a vision for reviving an old linen mill property in the center of town. Working with some partners, he had some old buildings razed but the mill preserved and reconstructed into a four-floor marketplace that maintained its historic quality.

Three decades later, Mill Falls at the Lake consists of four high-quality lakefront lodging facilities, five restaurants, 11 shops, conference facilities, an activity center, and a seasonal spa. The whole village is now a popular year-round New England destination, known for its quaint character. (Left, courtesy of Mill Falls at the Lake; right, courtesy of Daryl Carlson/Kamara Image Photography.)

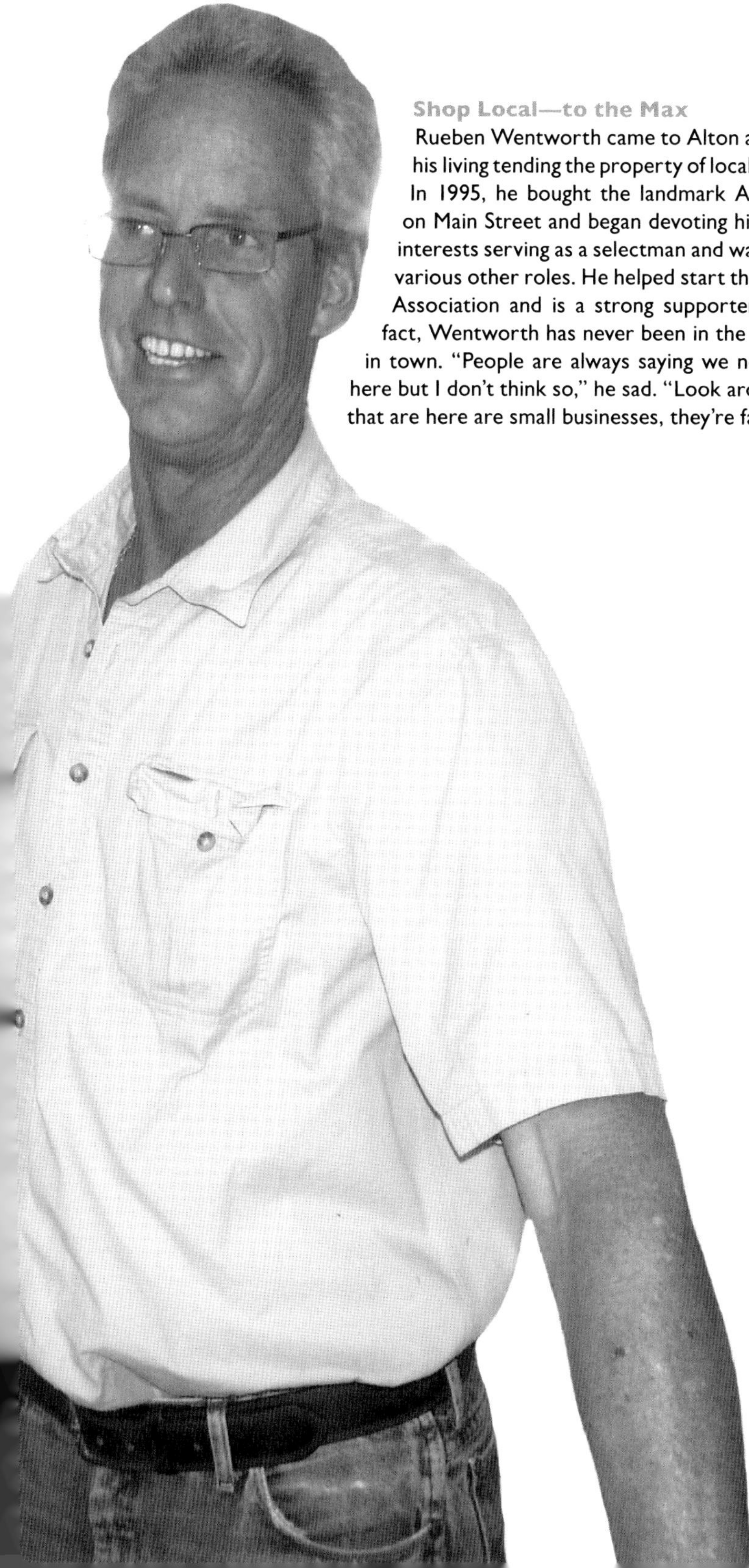

Shop Local—to the Max

Rueben Wentworth came to Alton as a young man and made his living tending the property of local senior citizens for years. In 1995, he bought the landmark Alton Home and Lumber on Main Street and began devoting himself to the town's best interests serving as a selectman and water commissioner and in various other roles. He helped start the current Alton Business Association and is a strong supporter of local businesses. In fact, Wentworth has never been in the large chain supermarket in town. "People are always saying we need 'big box' businesses here but I don't think so," he sad. "Look around—all the businesses that are here are small businesses, they're family-run businesses."

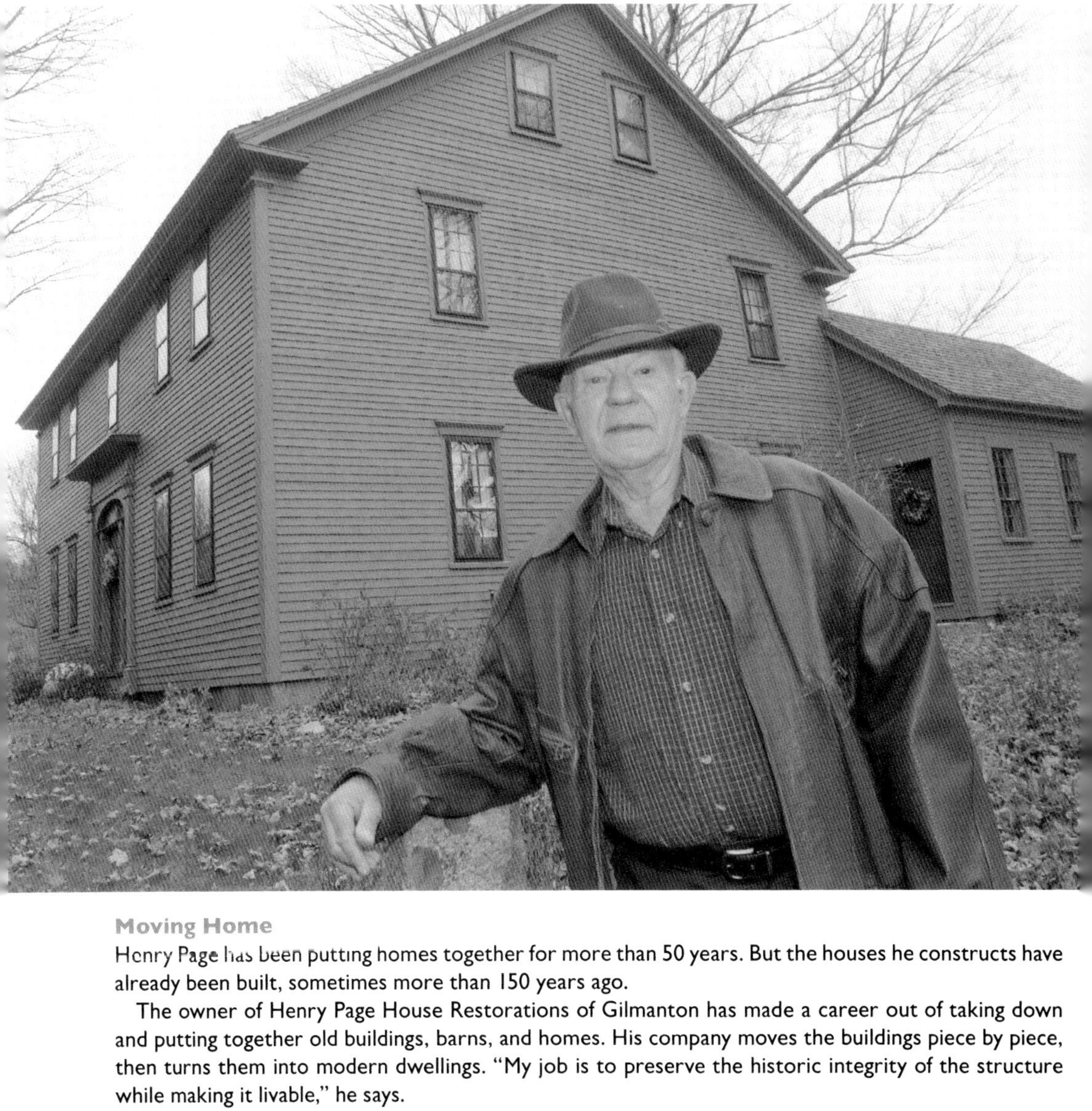

Moving Home

Henry Page has been putting homes together for more than 50 years. But the houses he constructs have already been built, sometimes more than 150 years ago.

The owner of Henry Page House Restorations of Gilmanton has made a career out of taking down and putting together old buildings, barns, and homes. His company moves the buildings piece by piece, then turns them into modern dwellings. "My job is to preserve the historic integrity of the structure while making it livable," he says.

Some of Page's work can be seen in and near Gilmanton's historic district, but he has also moved homes to (and from) New York, Massachusetts, Maine, and Texas. Page is pictured here outside his own Gilmanton home. (Courtesy of Daryl Carlson/Kamara Image Photography.)

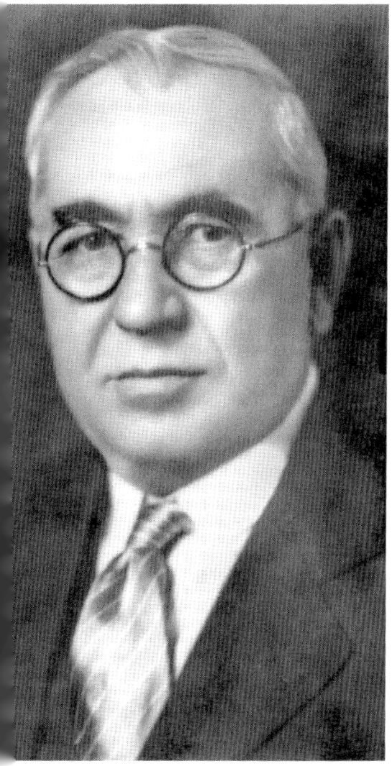

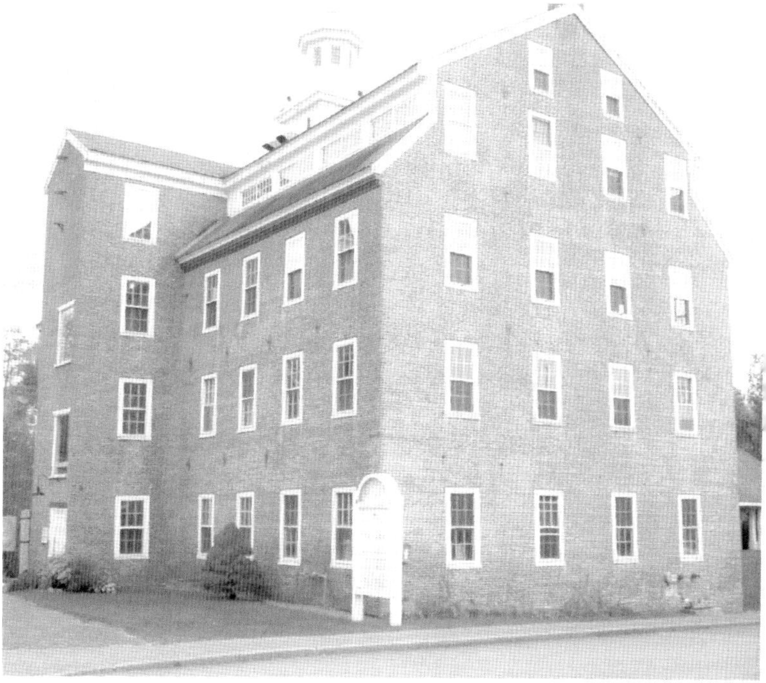

Morin's Mill

In 1895, Joseph P. Morin began operating a hosiery mill in a building that still sits alongside the Winnipesaukee River in Laconia. Morin was a French-Canadian Catholic, like most of his employees, and while workers in larger mills to the south were treated harshly during those early days of the Industrial Revolution, people were glad to be working in "Morin's Mill," the structure now known as the Belknap Mill. Morin cared about his workers and his community; he led efforts to build the Sacred Heart Catholic Church and other buildings on the campus, and lent his support to other community projects.

Today, the Belknap Mill is a community center and America's only industrial knitting museum, a place where "art and history come alive." The building is listed in the National Register of Historic Places, designated the Official Meetinghouse of the State of New Hampshire, and recognized as the oldest virtually unaltered textile mill in America, a close duplicate of the New England mill that historians say started the Industrial Revolution in the United States. (Left, courtesy of J. Paul Morin; right, author's collection.)

The Best Chinese Food

The best Chinese food is from China, naturally. That is why the China Bistro Chinese restaurant in Laconia has won the 2011 Overall Excellence Award and been ranked among the top 25 restaurants of its kind in America at the annual Top 100 Chinese Restaurant Awards in recent years. Owner Lin Bi came to the United States from China with his family when he was in his 20s. He studied business at the University of New Hampshire and opened the local eatery when he was still a senior in college. He currently owns one other restaurant—in Beijing.

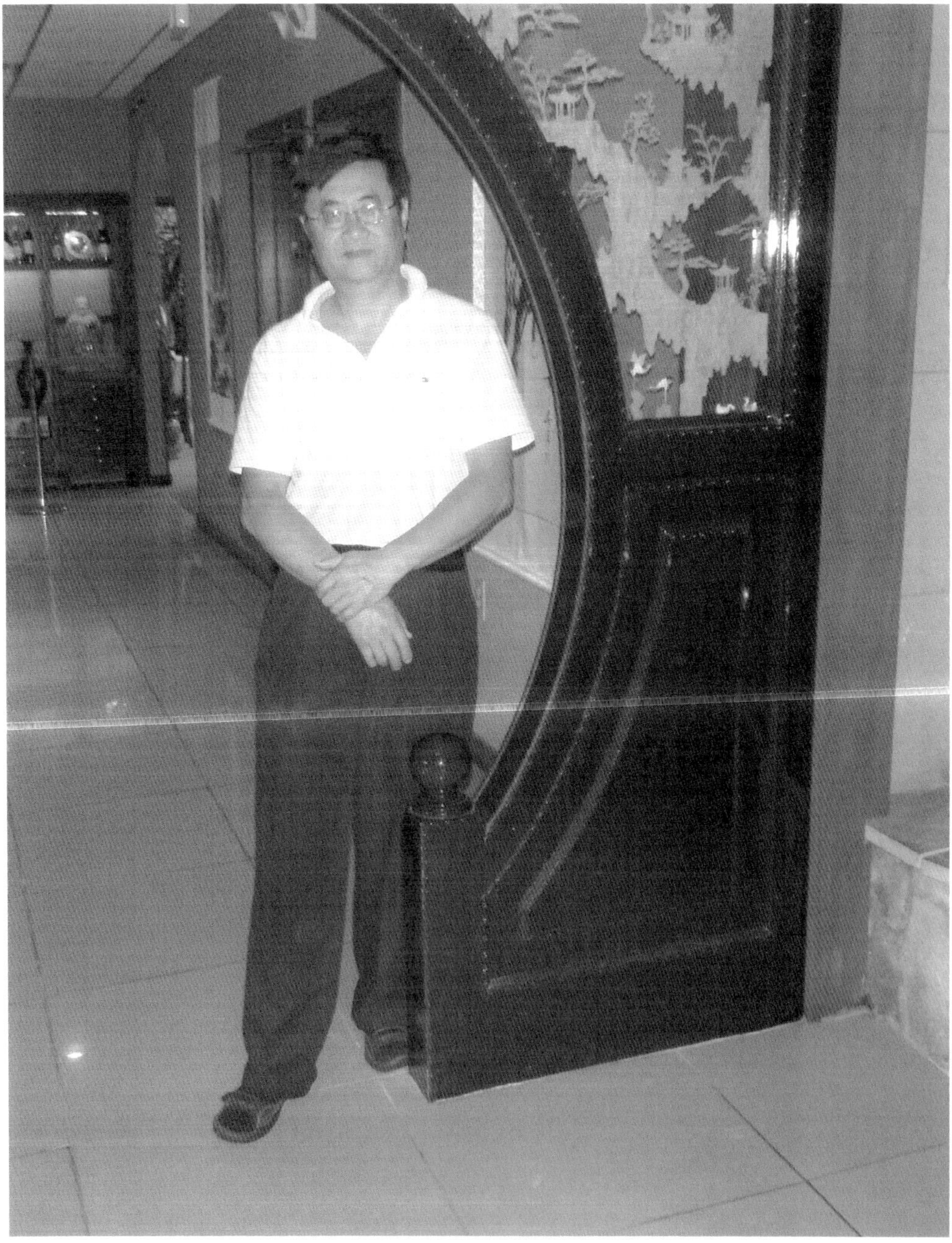

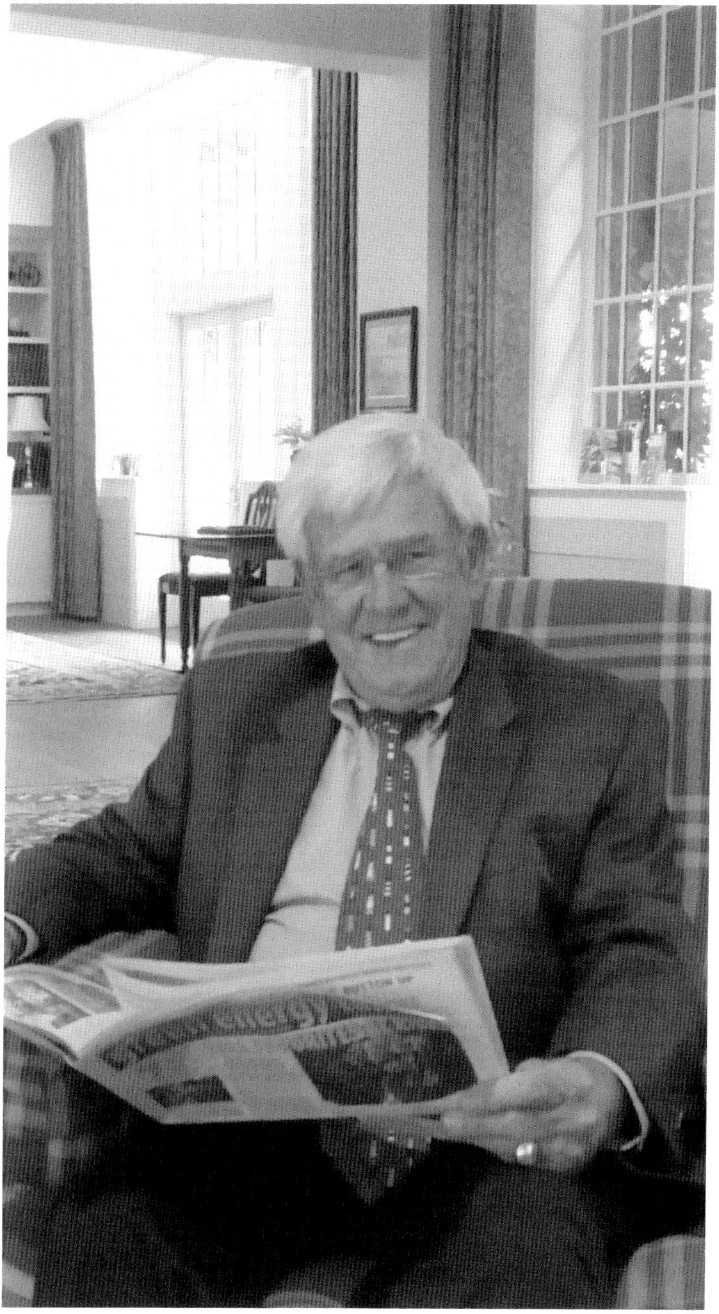

Hometown Boy Gives Back

Raymond R. Boissoneau was born and raised in Laconia but later moved to Manchester, where he built and managed a successful circuit board manufacturing company. Years later, he was riding his Harley-Davidson during Motorcycle Week when he noticed that an old manufacturing complex was for sale, and he decided to purchase it. Ray and his family restored the structure, and today the Lake Opechee Inn is a five-star waterfront lodging, spa, and function facility. (Courtesy of Michelle Boissoneau-DuPont and the Lake Opechee Inn.)

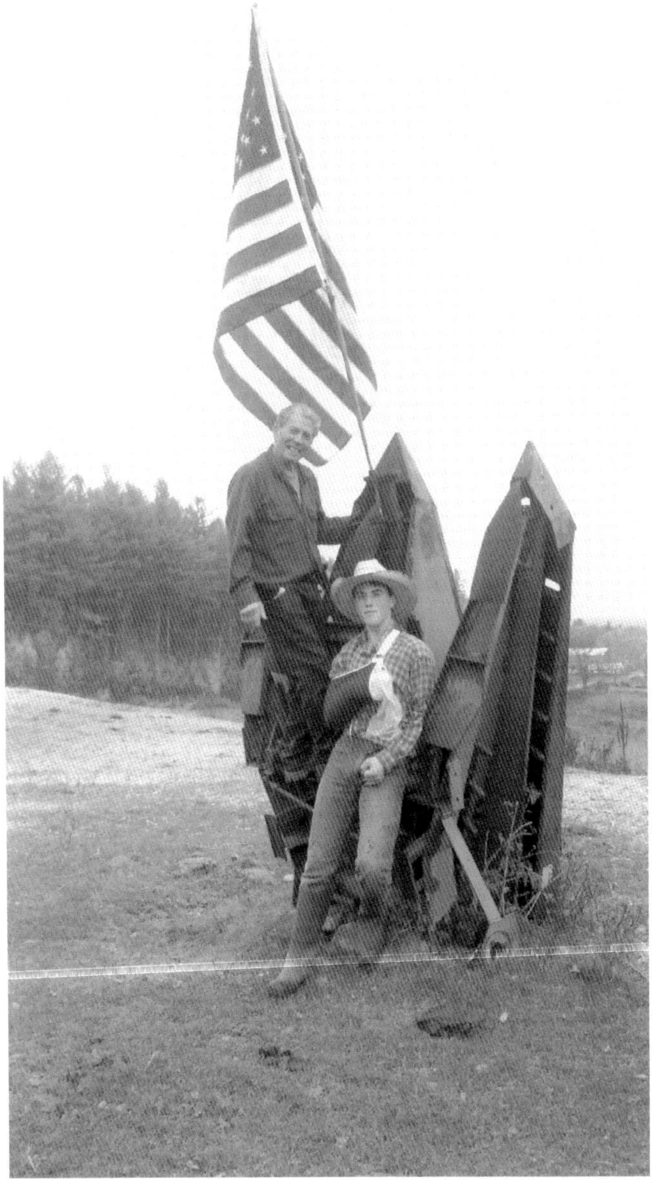

Down on the Farm

In the 1920s and 1930s, Frank Swain owned a general store in Winnisquam and married Josephine Hunkins. The Hunkins family were longtime Sanbornton farmers, so sometime later, Frank sold his business and began working the property. He loved the work and was soon adding other property. Today, the Swains own 850 acres, which they operate primarily as a dairy farm.

The Swain family is well known in the Lakes Region for their courtesy and kindness. Besides their foodstuffs, Frank's son David has connected with many local children as the "Cow Man," teaching kids about farming. Additionally, members of the family now operate the Heritage Farm property, which is open to seasonal visitors anxious to get a taste of farm living—from the bucolic surroundings to the animals roaming freely and the homemade breakfasts. Pictured here are David Swain and his grandson Tyler Matthew Swain. (Courtesy of Rachel Swain.)

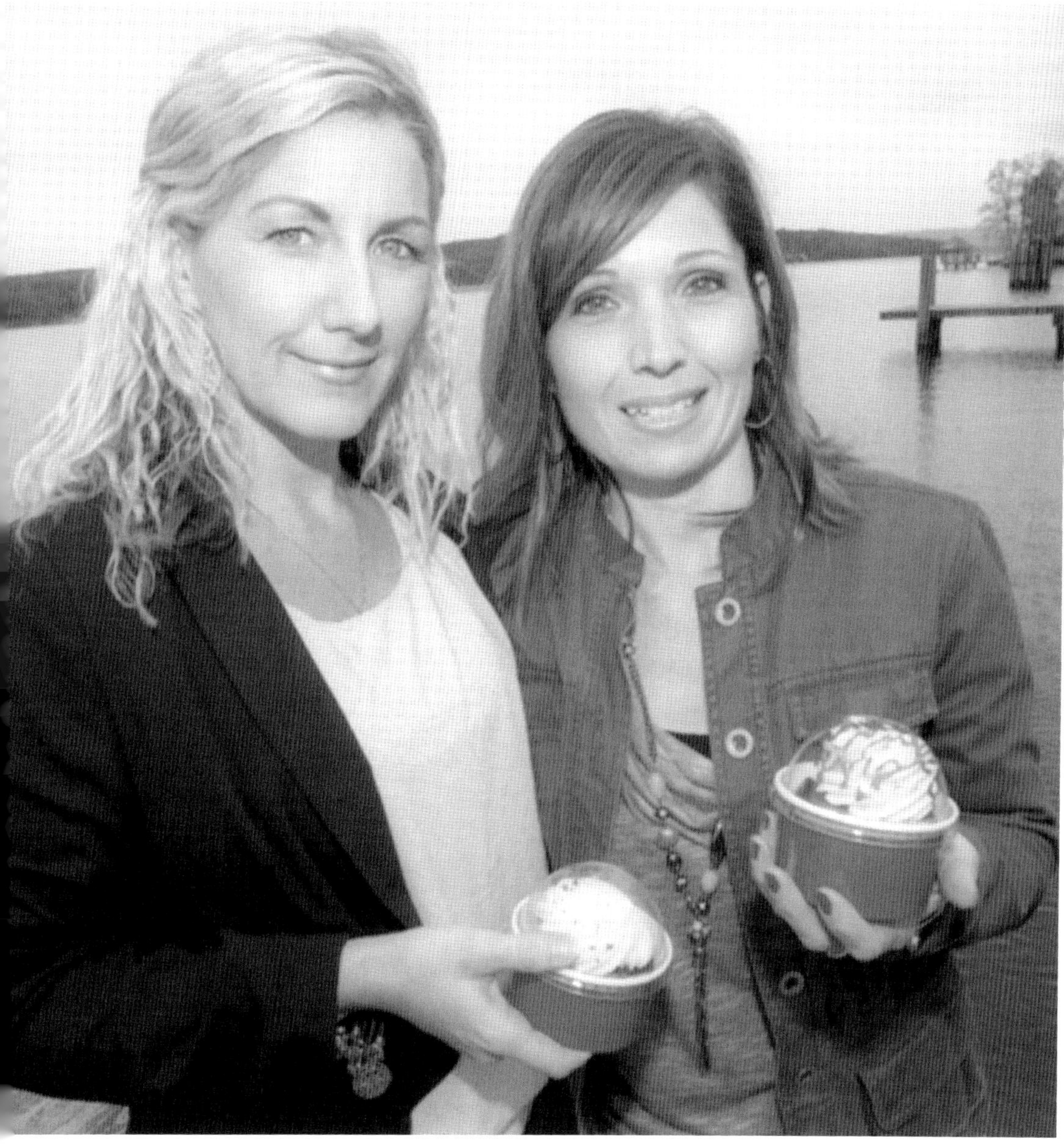

Sweet Enterprise

Stephanie McKim (left) and her sister Shelli Shumway (right) wanted to do something different. So, they opened Lakes Region Cupcakes on Main Street in Tilton, where they bake gourmet cupcakes from the freshest ingredients. Then they took things a step further by making "every day new;" that is, new, fresh-made cupcakes daily, in delicious "I-never-thought-of-that-before" flavors like Almond Joy, Thin Mint, cannoli, strawberry shortcake, and chocolate-covered bacon. One year after the shop opened, it won WMUR-TV *New Hampshire Chronicle's* "Cupcake Crown" as the best cupcake shop in the state. Since then, it has won numerous other regional awards. (Courtesy of Daryl Carlson/Kamara Image Photography.)

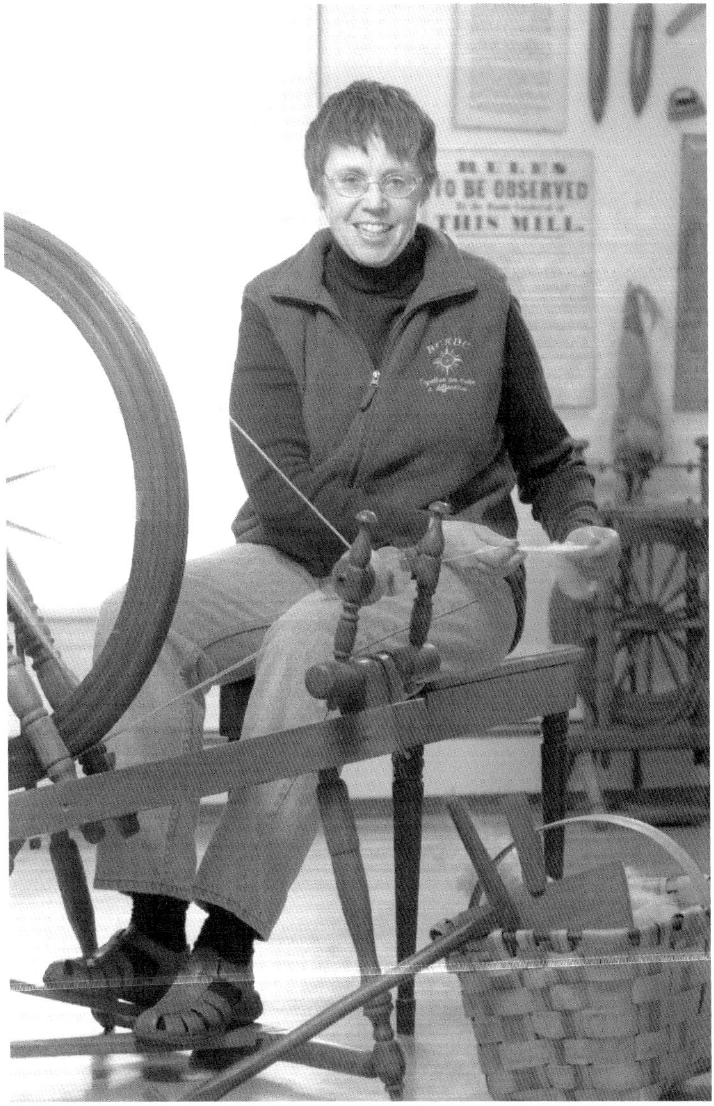

Her License Plate Reads "NHJOBS"

When Eliza Leadbeater started the Belknap County Economic Development Council in 1992, she had already had success directing both businesses and nonprofit organizations. But, here in the Lakes Region, her skills may have attained their highest levels—and when she retired to her home in New Hampton it was likely proof that she found her heart here as well.

During her 15-year tenure at the economic group, Leadbeater established a revolving loan fund that lent over $6 million to local entrepreneurs and businesses, and assisted businesses in securing millions of dollars more in conventional loans. She also helped secure some $10 million in grants for nonprofit organizations in the Lakes Region. She is known as a visionary and driving force behind the renovation of many underutilized manufacturing facilities in the area, turning them into exposition centers, condominiums, apartments, childcare centers, culinary schools, hotels, and a performing arts center.

Many local folks do not know that Leadbeater is considered a worldwide expert on spinning—the traditional art of turning fiber into yarn or thread. She has authored two books on the subject, *Handspinning* and *Spinning Wheels*. (Courtesy of John Hession.)

Locke Lake

Kent Locke's family settled in the Barnstead area in the 1600s, but in the early 1960s, he had a dream to turn his large land holdings into a modern housing colony. With the help of his three sons, including James N. Locke Sr., a banker who helped secure funding for the project, the Locke Lake Colony opened in 1965. It included lakefront property as well as other lots, beaches, a community center, two tennis courts, a ski area, a riding stable, and a golf course. The colony was completed in less than 10 years with 1,220 lots on 1,500 acres, making Locke Lake one of the largest housing developments ever built in New Hampshire. Shown here in the project's early days are, from left to right, Kent Locke Jr., Kent Locke, James Locke Sr., and Thomas G. Locke. (Courtesy of James N. Locke Sr.)

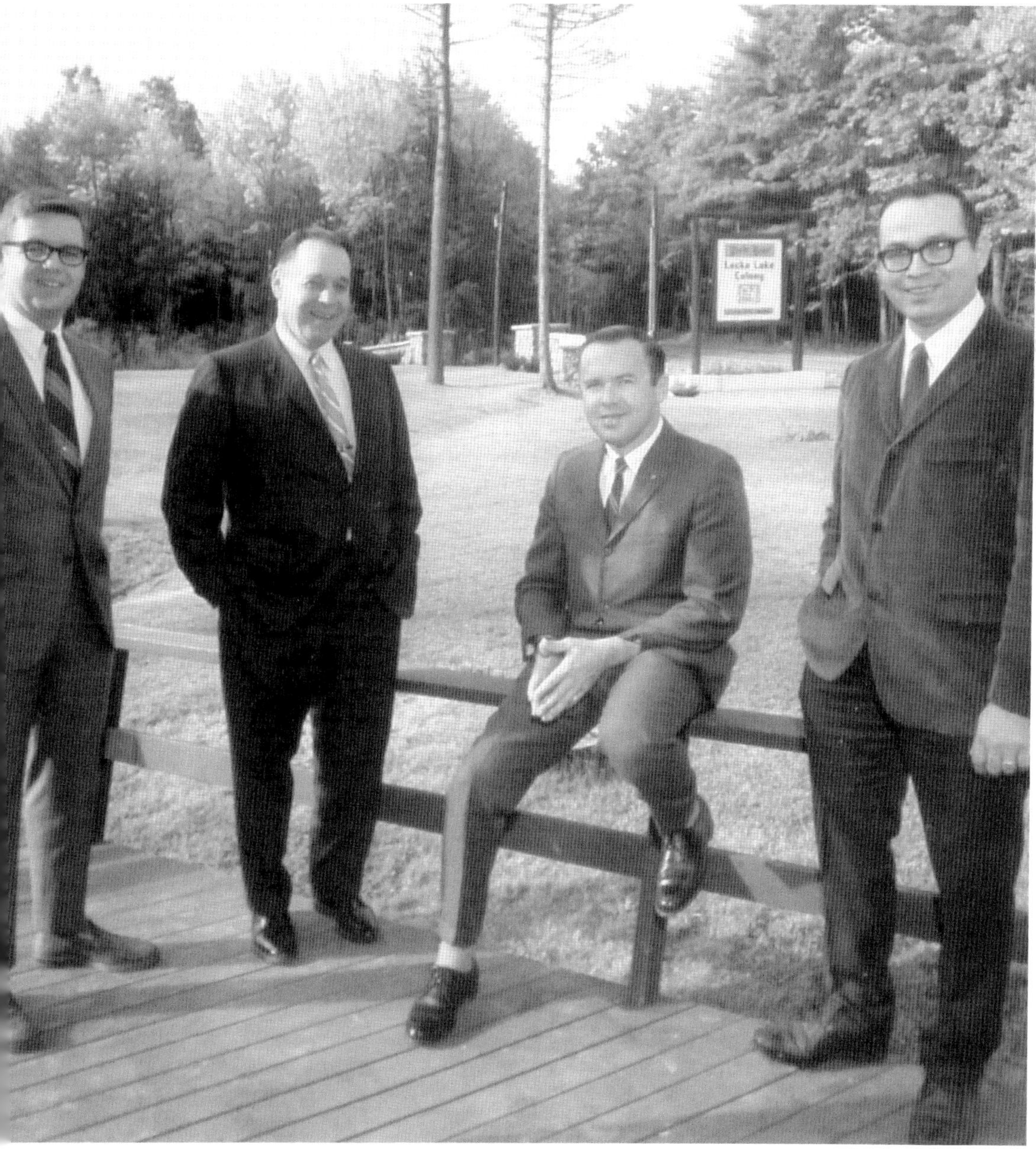

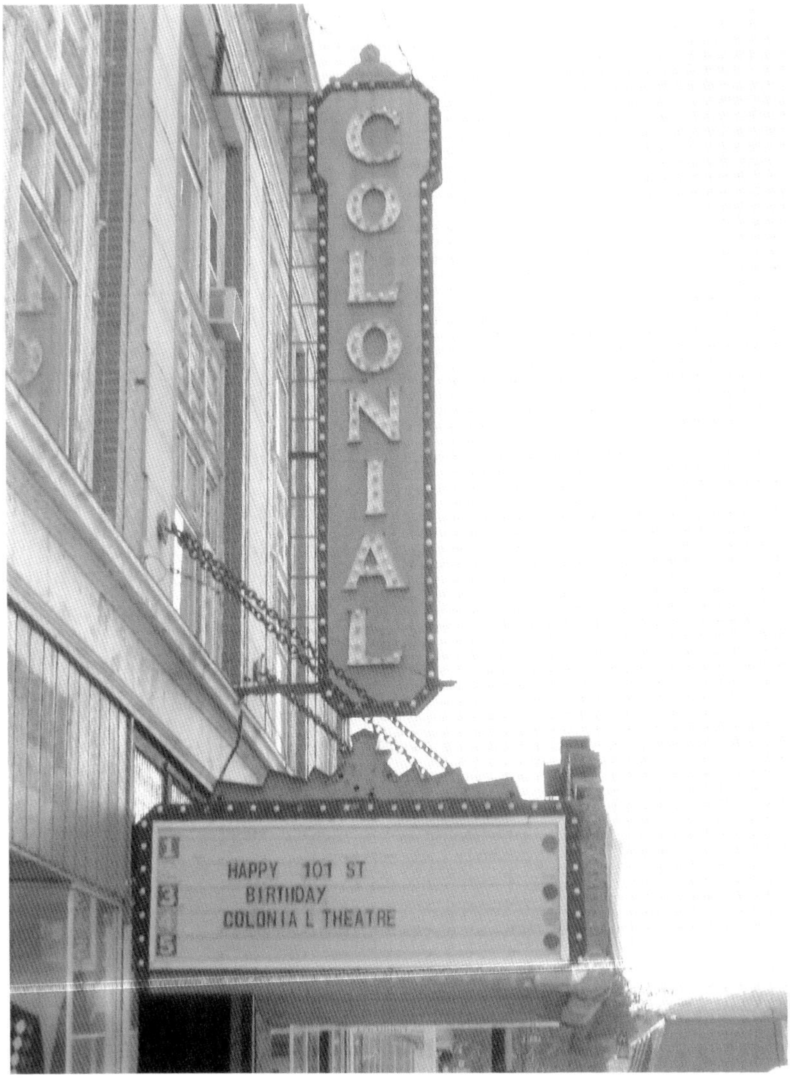

Bright Lights
Benjamin Piscopo was born in Italy and immigrated to Boston as a teenager, where he made his fortune in real estate. In the early 20th century, he moved to the Lakes Region and invested heavily in the area, building a summer home on Lake Winnisquam and the original Piscopo Block, which helped establish Laconia's Main Street as a commercial thoroughfare.

The block's Colonial Theater, which is still standing, was a local landmark and considered "one of the handsomest play-houses to be found in New England," according to a 1915 newspaper story. Vaudeville performers and motion pictures shared the stage, but the playhouse was also used for public meetings, high school graduations, recitals, and lectures. It operated primarily as a movie theater for many decades afterwards, and there are still people interested in reviving the facility.

Interestingly, Piscopo's theater manager, Ralph Morris, is credited with inventing the tiny lights now used on Christmas trees. Morris, who had worked previously for the telephone company, said he was inspired to utilize the tiny bulbs that lit up on telephone switchboards as an alternative to candles. Previously, it was not uncommon to hear of tragedies when lit candles hanging on trees started house fires.

CHAPTER THREE

Community Glimpses

Somewhere between the economic center of New England and the local town landfill is that nebulous Lakes Region entity called community.

It is not a specific term, but it captures everything seen and known about the localities, from popular coffee hangouts to dusty courtrooms, noisy town meetings to quiet barbershops.

And it includes everyone in that world, from the underpaid daycare worker to the lauded police chief, from the uncomfortable new bank president to the joyous chamber of commerce director.

The community even includes local tastes, from submarine sandwiches to gourmet pizza, country radio to quiet jazz jams, and neat mountain snow trails to a colorful cluster of sailboats lined up, waiting to get into the lake.

In a funny way, the community even speaks about who the people are—their prides and prejudices, graces and faults, humors and mean streaks.

It is in this vague area, between high-ranking government officials and a bored high school grocery cashier, that most of us live most of our lives.

That is why it is such a warm surprise when someone makes the community better—more joyful, more convenient, or just plain more pleasurable to be in on a day-to-day basis.

While prominent businesspeople have already been noted in the previous chapter and public servants are in the following, the remaining group is a delightful cast of historians, innovators, athletes, and organizers who have made—or in some cases continue to make—the Lakes Region something special with their own personal, creative touch.

It may be the upbeat personality of Moultonborough's Adele Taylor; the persistent industriousness of local housing aide Linda Harvey; the enthusiasm of Laconia's coach, Jim "Fitzy" Fitzgerald; or the creativity of Wolfeboro's wooden boat guru, George Johnson.

This is a group of people whose actions, on a daily basis, speak loudly about the pride and love they have for their community.

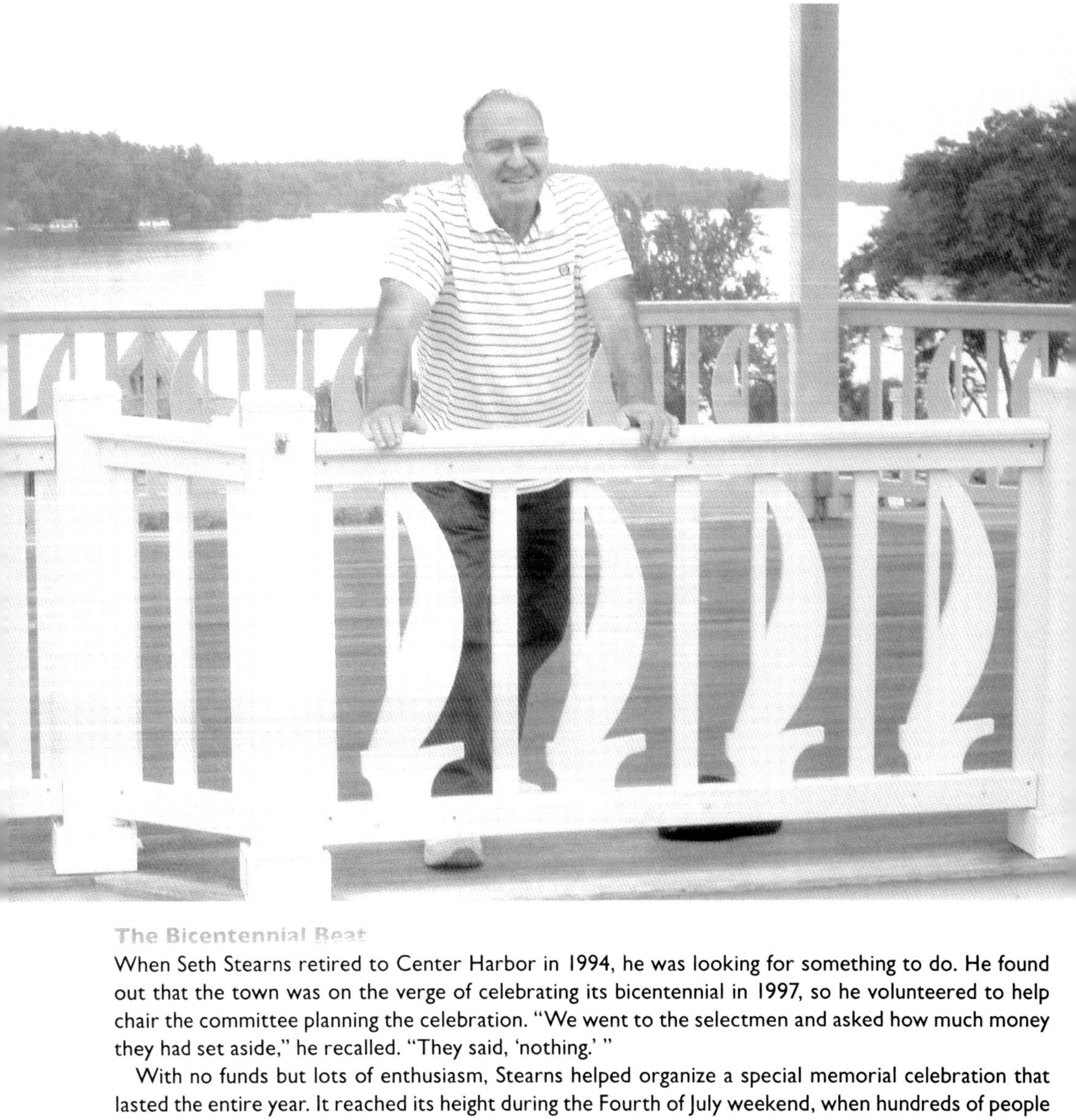

The Bicentennial Beat

When Seth Stearns retired to Center Harbor in 1994, he was looking for something to do. He found out that the town was on the verge of celebrating its bicentennial in 1997, so he volunteered to help chair the committee planning the celebration. "We went to the selectmen and asked how much money they had set aside," he recalled. "They said, 'nothing.' "

With no funds but lots of enthusiasm, Stearns helped organize a special memorial celebration that lasted the entire year. It reached its height during the Fourth of July weekend, when hundreds of people gathered around the newly constructed bicentennial bandstand on the town green. "It was the biggest party this town has ever seen," said Stearns.

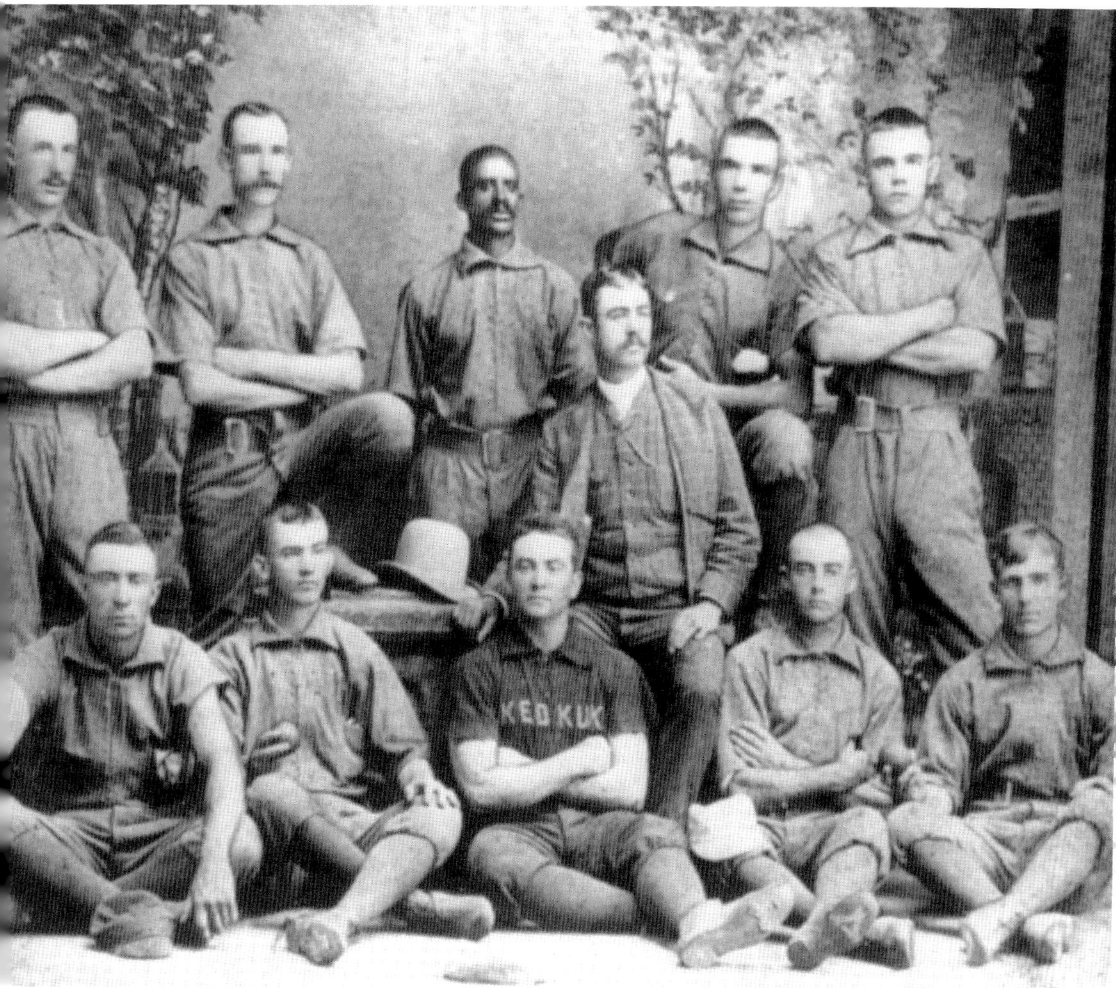

Play Ball

John W. Jackson Jr., born in 1858 and best known as John "Bud" Fowler, was one of the best baseball players of his era. In fact, historians now call Fowler one of the game's racial pioneers, as he was a black man who played well enough to be regularly added to the roster of white professional teams.

That is what happened in the Lakes Region.

Reliable history about black Americans from the era is spotty, but Fowler may have been the first black professional manager of an integrated team in America while he was with the Laconia town team. An 1885 newspaper report on a game played between the local nine and the National League team from Boston (likely nicknamed the Beaneaters) reads, "The Laconias showed up well and, in some respects, brilliantly. Fowler, the colored second baseman, made several remarkable plays and filled that position as well as it was ever cared for on the grounds."

Two years before coming to Laconia, Fowler was the star player of the Keokuk, Iowa, baseball team. He is seen here standing to the left of the unidentified manager; all other players are unidentified. (Courtesy of the National Baseball Hall of Fame Library, Cooperstown, NY.)

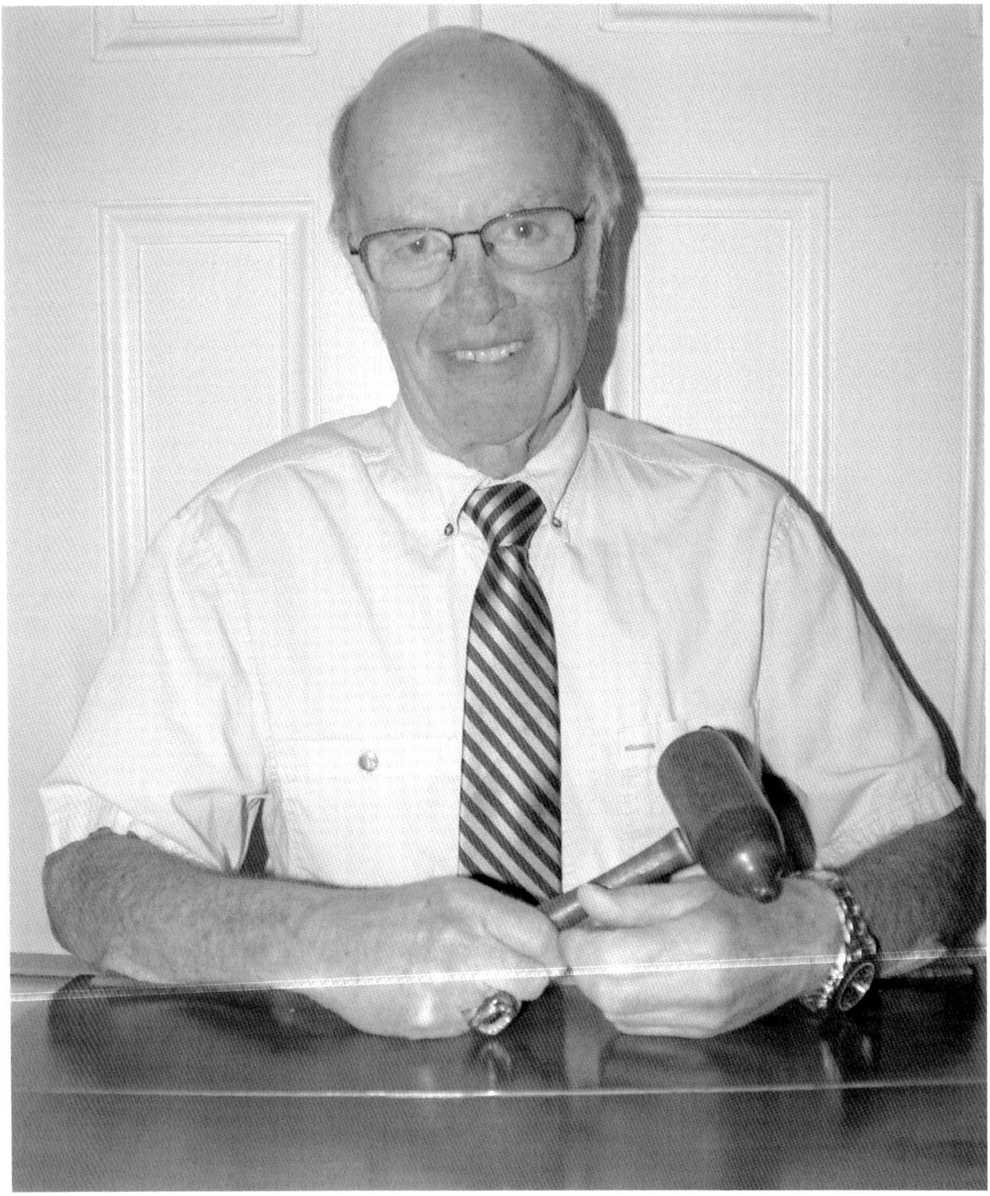

Maine Man in Sandwich

Lee Quimby was somewhat of an institution in Maine, delivering the news, sports, weather, and various announcements on WCSH-TV in Portland for 20 years. But when it came to where he would set down roots, Quimby chose the Granite State. He is now a resident of Sandwich and, just as he has done everywhere he has been, he has taken a leadership role in the Lakes Region. He has served in the New Hampshire House of Representatives and has sat on the town selectboard. He has organized Memorial Day observances and Meet the Candidate events. Quimby also stands as town moderator, school district moderator, and moderator of the Community Church of Sandwich. (Courtesy of Lee Quimby.)

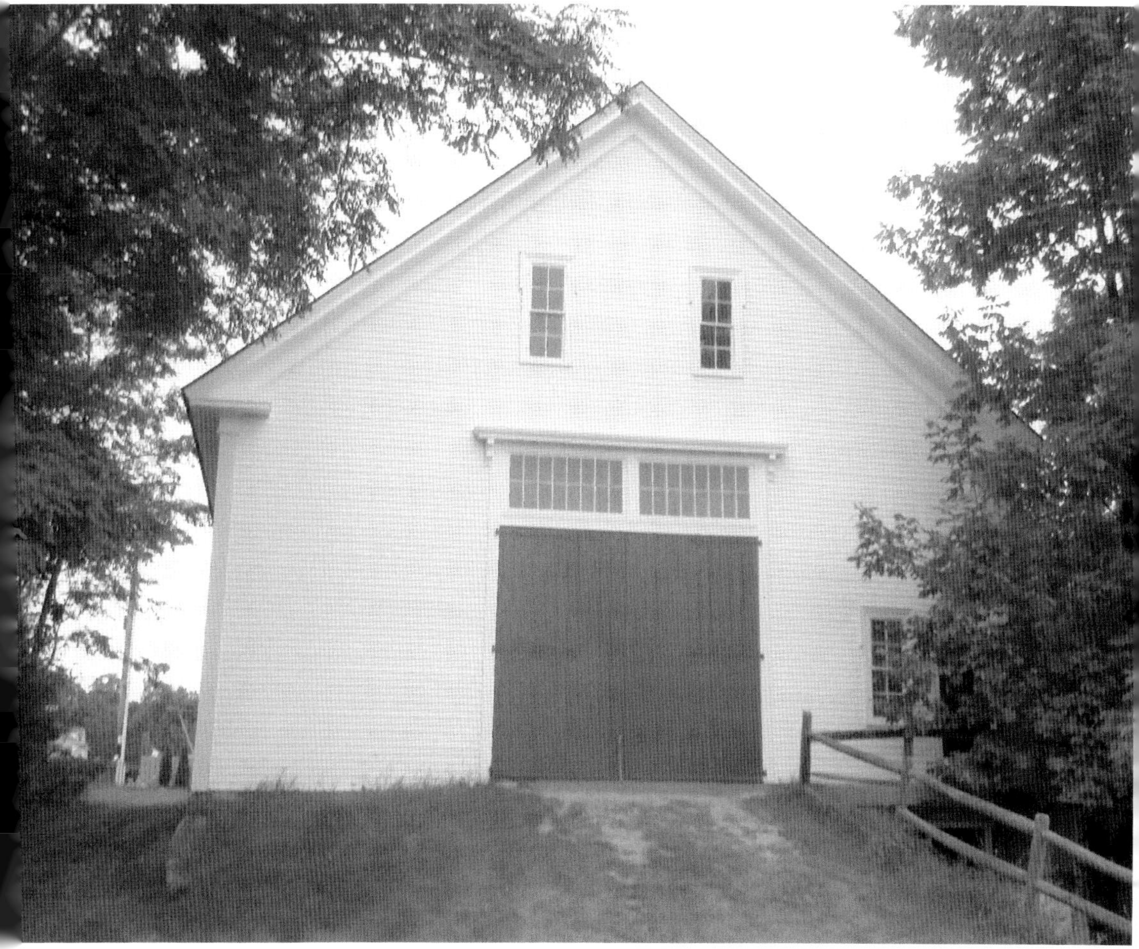

Saving a Town

Every community should have an Ernest Dane.

Dane was a banker and a philanthropist who lived in Brookline, Massachusetts. He was drawn to the Lakes Region because his wife had spent summers in Center Harbor as a youngster. Sometime in the 1920s, Dane began buying up properties in the village, and once he got started, he just kept going.

Typically, Ernest Dane would buy a farm or business and then allow the previous owner to work on it. He purchased several prominent village buildings and created a sizable dairy farm with about 100 Guernsey cows, pigs, and some Belgian workhorses. (One of the more prominent barns, now adjacent to the Canoe restaurant, is shown here.) So many townspeople worked for him at one point, Dane built a dormitory for his employees. When he passed away, Dane owned about 5,000 acres in Center Harbor, and much of it is still under conservation protection.

Interestingly, Dane never moved to Center Harbor permanently, preferring to spend his time outside Massachusetts in Maine. But, longtime residents say that Ernest Dane saved their town from the worst of the Great Depression.

Voice of the Lakes Region

Esther "Essie" Peters (right) of Gilford was at a party in early 1953 when Arthur "Roxy" Rothafel of WLNH radio overheard her voice. He approached her and asked if she would be interested in his business. Peters accepted the job offer and was soon hosting *Around Town* from the window of a store on Main Street in Laconia. Over the years, she interviewed everyone from Dwight Eisenhower to Paul Newman, Rose Kennedy, and Tallulah Bankhead.

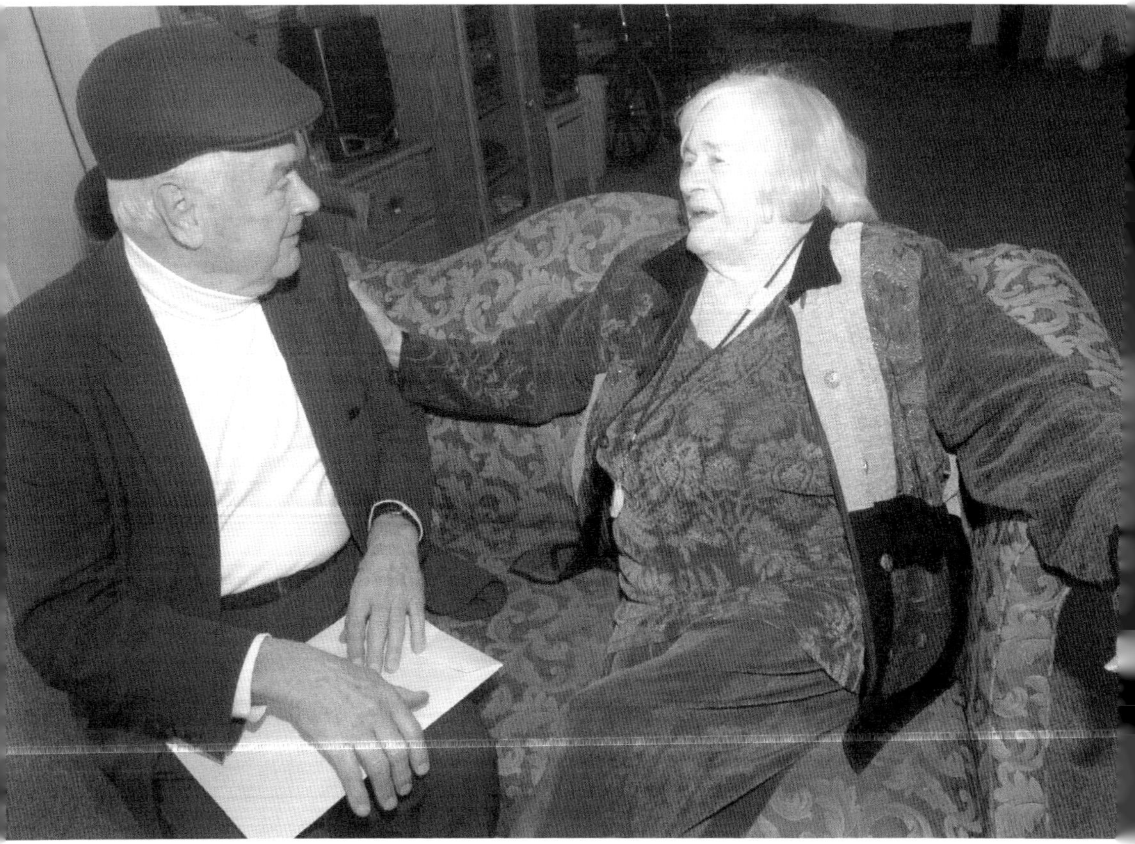

Burton for Certain

If politics is a business, then Ray Burton (left) may have been the world's greatest CEO. Businesspeople know the value of providing good service, and, to Burton, everyone who lived in his far-flung district north of Concord was his customer. His personalized service was the living embodiment of the old credo, "All politics is local."

He came to almost any kind of public meeting—from school boards to presidential debates and high school graduations—prompting the newsroom quip that Burton would "come to the opening of an envelope." But, he also listened and learned, anxious to see how he might help the people in his district make connections, find jobs, or raise their standard of living. "To Ray, no need was too small or too trivial," said former governor John Lynch.

No one has ever served a longer term on the state's Executive Council than Burton, who was there for almost 40 years before passing away in 2013. (Courtesy of Daryl Carlson/Kamara Image Photography.)

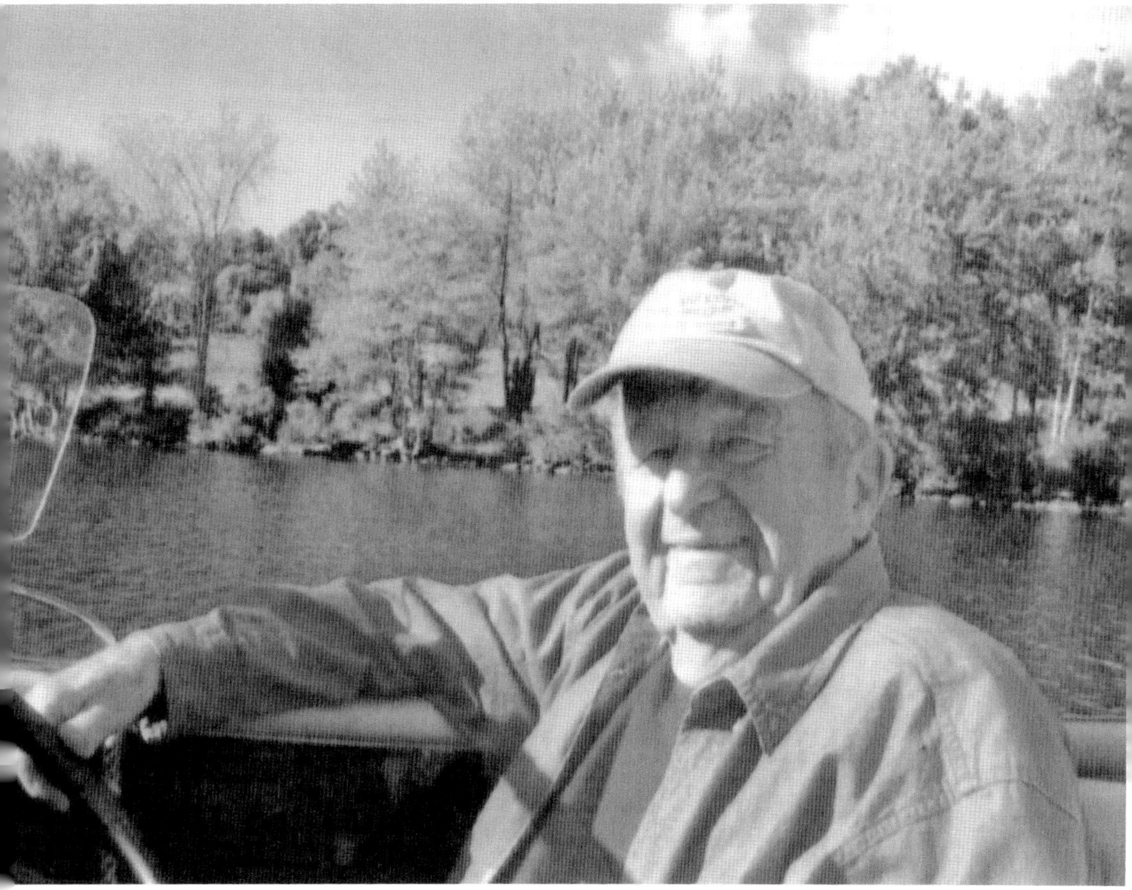

First in

If one asks people in the Wolfeboro boating community, the current romance with classic wooden boats began with local legend George Johnson. Johnson was originally in aviation, but when he retired to the Lakes Region, his fascination with mechanical things and the things they powered shifted to boats, especially the classic wooden runabouts he had seen too easily discarded. He began to restore the wooden boats and began a whole new field in the process. As the hobby grew, the need to find the right equipment for refitting the engines and renovating the topsides followed. Johnson would find the items needed, or, if they were not available, he would reproduce the screws, fixtures, varnishes, and other materials.

Johnson's Sawmill Marina on Wolfeboro Bay became a haven for people looking to find and build the classic vessels. He gathered materials, but he would also teach, advise, and sell. His yard was a virtual museum of wooden boats waiting to be adopted. He was named the "world's largest unauthorized Chris-Craft dealer in the world." In 1990, thanks to his efforts, the New Hampshire Boat Museum moved to Wolfeboro. Johnson died in 2007. (Courtesy of Rick Kourian.)

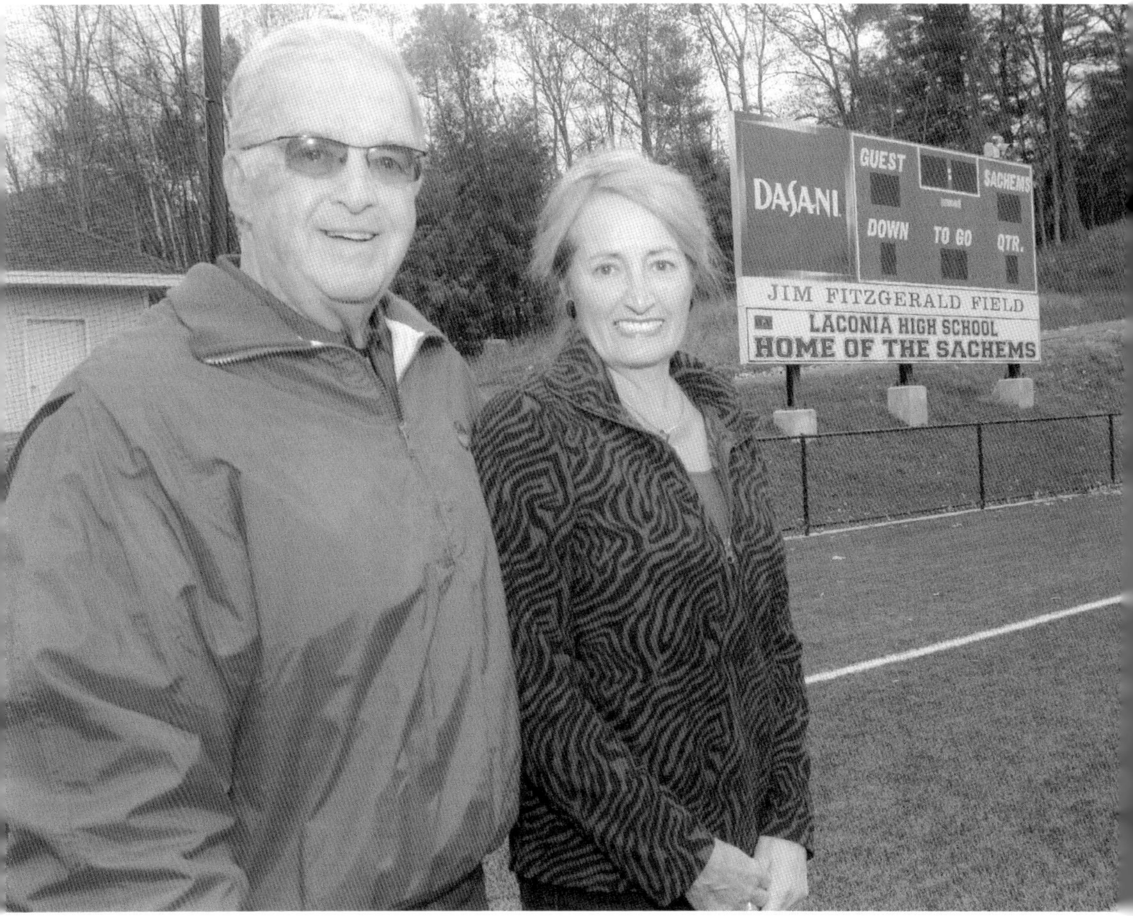

Fitzy's Goal

One of the most successful and honored school coaches in the Lakes Region, Jim "Fitzy" Fitzgerald led the Laconia High School football team for 28 years. During his tenure, the Sachems went to 19 state semifinals games and 12 finals, and were crowned state champions three times. As athletic director, Fitzgerald led the effort to boost women's sports programs and expand and improve the school's athletic facilities. Most importantly, he was loved and respected by his student athletes, who campaigned to have the school's new athletic field named in his honor in 2013.

Fitzgerald himself always said his biggest fan was his wife, Jeannine. (Courtesy of Daryl Carlson/ Kamara Image Photography.)

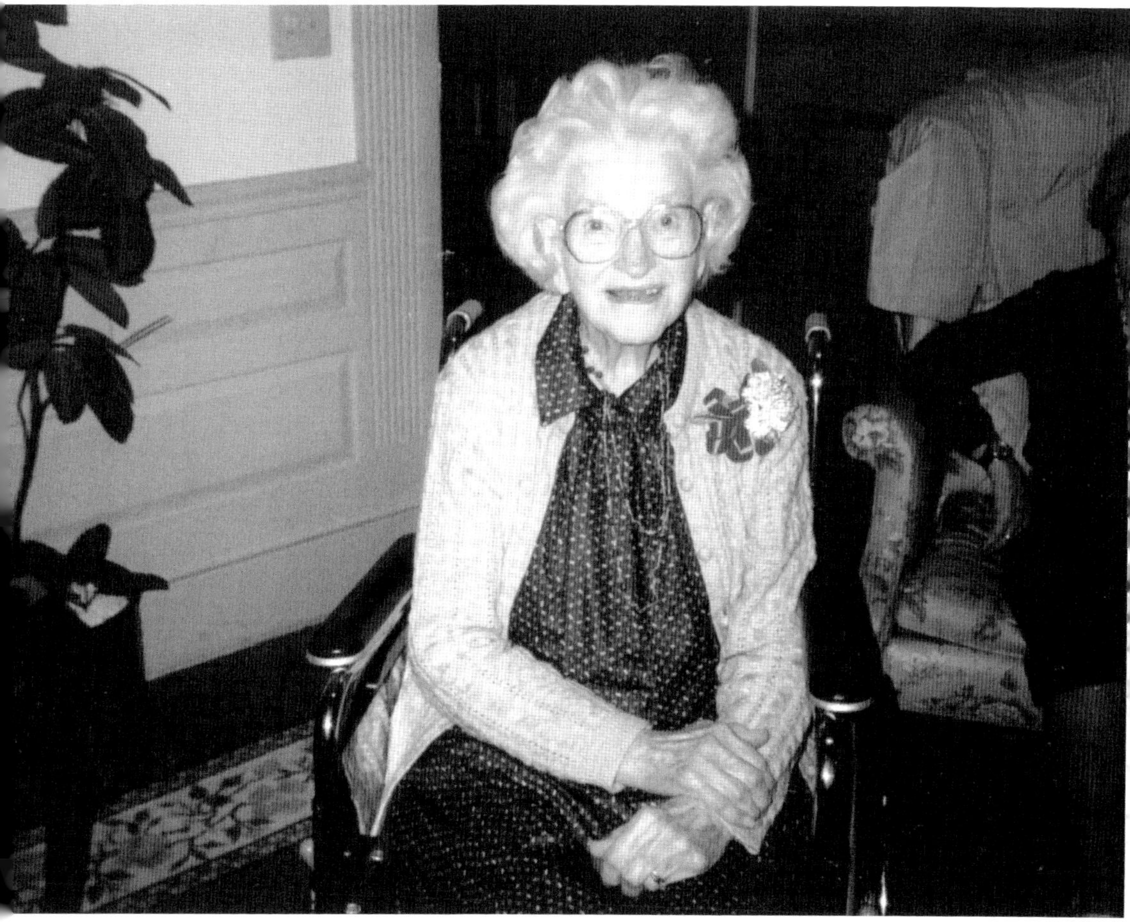

In the Middle

Marion Robie was the heart of Melvin Village. It was hard to be otherwise. For 20 years, she owned the general store, managed the local telephone exchange, and ran the post office—all in the same building. Robie was born in Melvin Village and loved the community. She served as the town clerk of Tuftonboro, was a founder of the Tuftonboro Historical Society, and sang in the Melvin Village Community Church. She passed away in 1990 at the age of 92. (Courtesy of Tuftonboro Historical Society.)

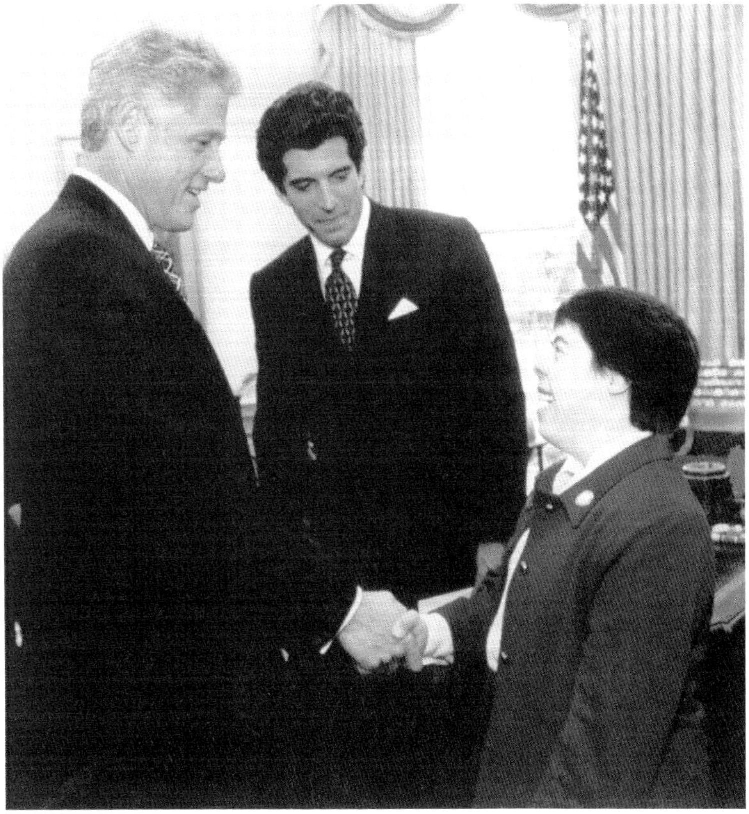

Living on the Upside of Down (ABOVE AND OPPOSITE PAGE)

When Annie Forts was born, the birth doctor told her parents she had Down syndrome and probably would never amount to much. He recommended that she be put immediately into an institution to avoid upsetting their family life.

The family certainly did not think much of the recommendation and instead took Annie home.

From the start, it was clear that Annie Forts would not be held down, either by her physical challenges or by the misconceptions of other people of what she could do or become. Her outgoing personality and positive outlook on life, with the help of family and friends, allowed her to excel far beyond expectations.

Forts likes to say that some people do not understand the "ability" part of the word disability. Today she is a vibrant, inspiring woman who devotes herself to seeing that others with Down syndrome—and those with other disabilities—are respected and included, without reservation, in their communities.

Forts is an accomplished motivational speaker and the winner of numerous prestigious honors. She was twice appointed by President Clinton to serve on his committee on mental retardation. She has also served on many other boards, including the New Hampshire Developmental Disabilities Council. Additionally, she was the first winner of the Joseph P. Kennedy Jr. Foundation International Self-Empowerment Award at the United Nations in New York City. Forts is pictured on the opposite page celebrating her image being shown over Times Square in New York, and above, accepting congratulations from President Clinton and John F. Kennedy Jr.

Annie is especially proud of her Annie Forts UP Syndrome Fund, which began in 1997. The fund provides enrichment opportunities for people with Down syndrome and awards scholarships to students committed to pursuing a career in special education. To date, the UP fund has made available more than $150,000 in scholarship and enrichment resources. (Opposite bottom, courtesy of Daryl Carlson/Kamara Image Photography; other images courtesy of Jim MacMillan.)

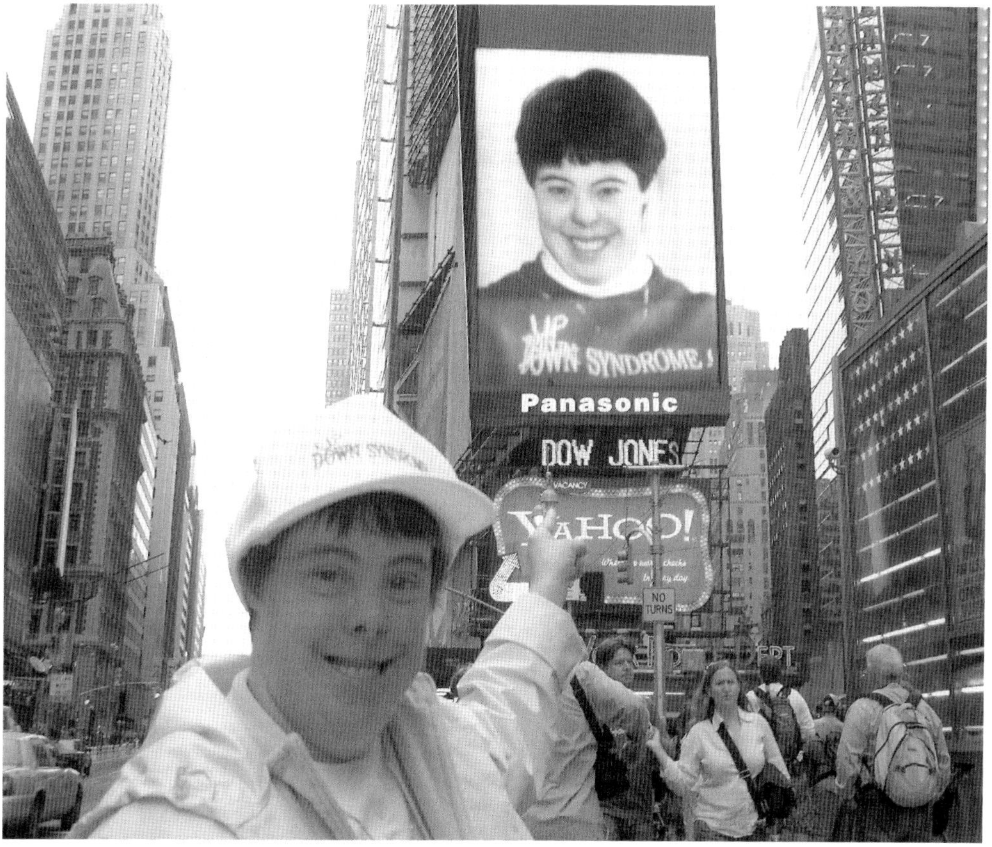
Panasonic
DOW JONES
YAHOO!
NO TURNS

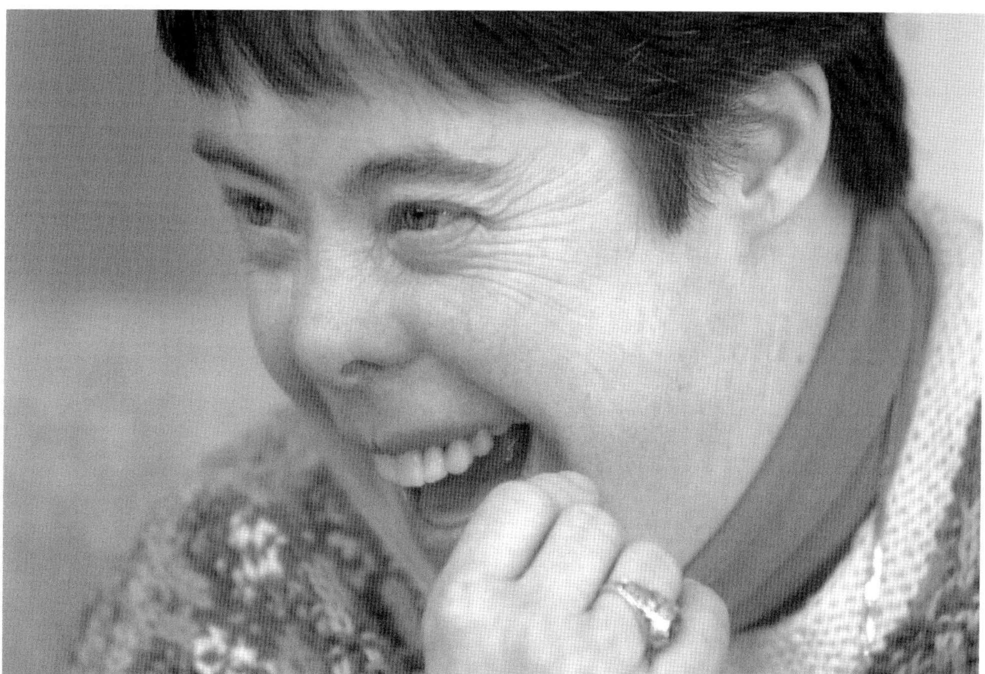

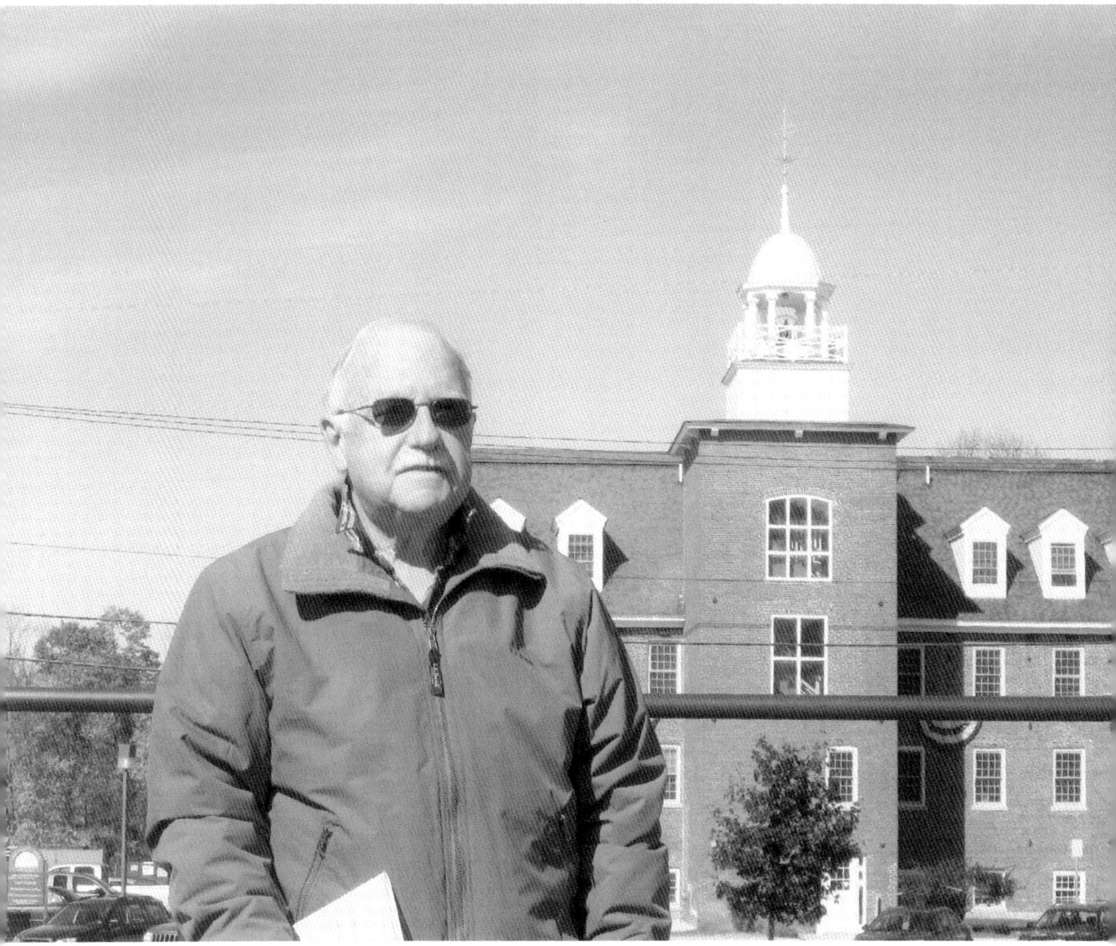

Salvation Rhodes

As Belmont's longtime town historian, Wallace Rhodes led an uphill charge in the 1990s to save the town's last historic building. The Belmont Mill, perched along the Tioga River, was built in 1833 and converted to hosiery production in 1865. (One story, perhaps apocryphal, tells of a plane flying in from Washington simply to purchase the mill's socks for Pres. Franklin Roosevelt; Roosevelt suffered from polio and was constantly looking for ways to improve blood circulation in his legs.) After a massive fire in 1992, however, the mill property was largely abandoned and dilapidated. Town officials took down all of the other structures, but Rhodes and his supporters were able to halt the planned demolition of the original mill building. The state's first PlanNH charrette and $1 million in federal grant money allowed the building to be renovated and repurposed. It is now used as a community center and offices. (Courtesy of Linda Frawley.)

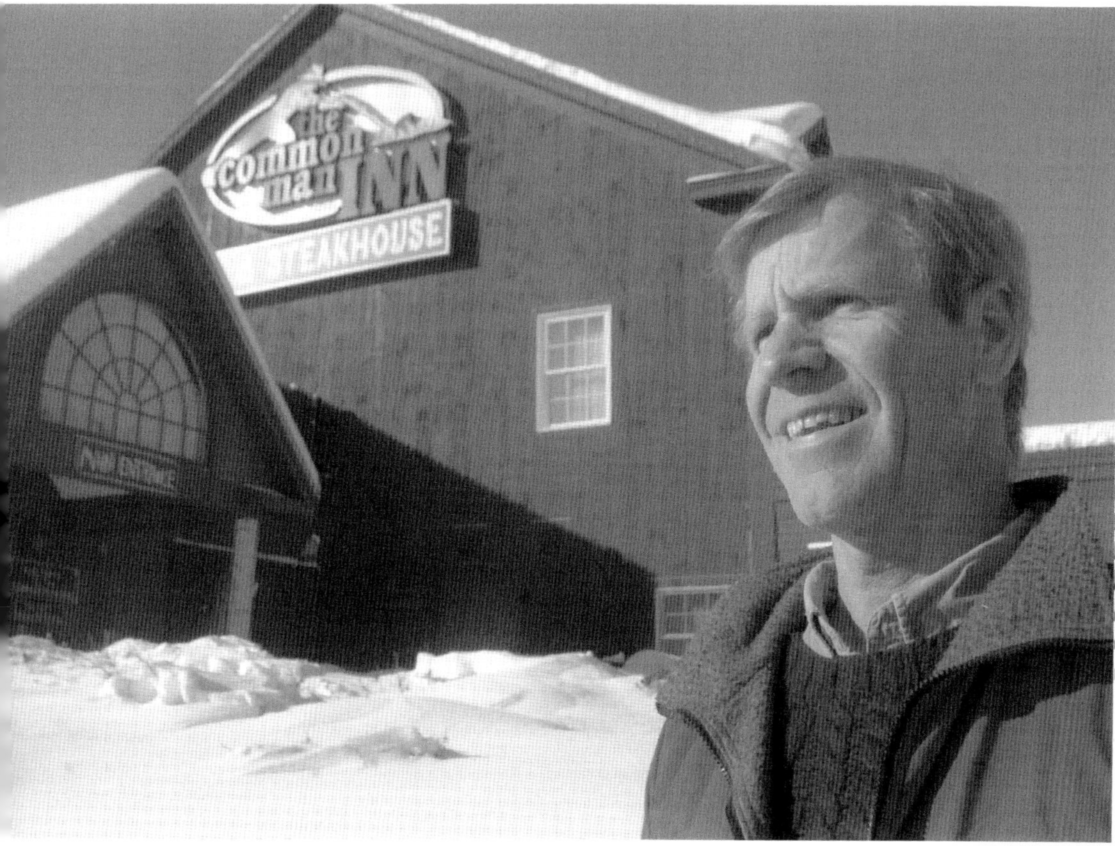

An Uncommon Experience

Alex Ray could be New Hampshire's best illustration of the simple truth that "a man reaps what he sows."

Ever since he opened the first Common Man restaurant in Ashland 45 years ago, his business has prospered due in large part to his motto, "Doing well by doing good."

It helps that Ray seems to have an unerring sense of how to create great family-style restaurants that serve good food at reasonable prices. There are now 17 eateries in the state's Common Man family of restaurants, as well as two Common Man Inns, a spa, a company store, and the Flying Monkey Movie House and Performance Center in Plymouth, which regularly draws some of America's best talent.

But, Lakes Region residents also appreciate how the company does business. Over the years, it has donated hundreds of hours of employees' "sweat equity" as well as thousands of dollars in scholarships, food, and in-kind donations to local, national, and international organizations. After the terrorist attacks on September 11, 2001, Ray himself drove a truck packed with food down to the New York City site.

The Common Man has won recognition on both a local and national level, including a national Cornerstone Humanitarian Award from the National Restaurant Association. The company has been named one of the state's Businesses of the Decade by *BusinessNH* magazine, Business of the Year by the New Hampshire Department of Resources and Economic Development, and the Best Company to Work for in the Food Service Industry by the *Griffin Report*. (Courtesy of Daryl Carlson/Kamara Image Photography.)

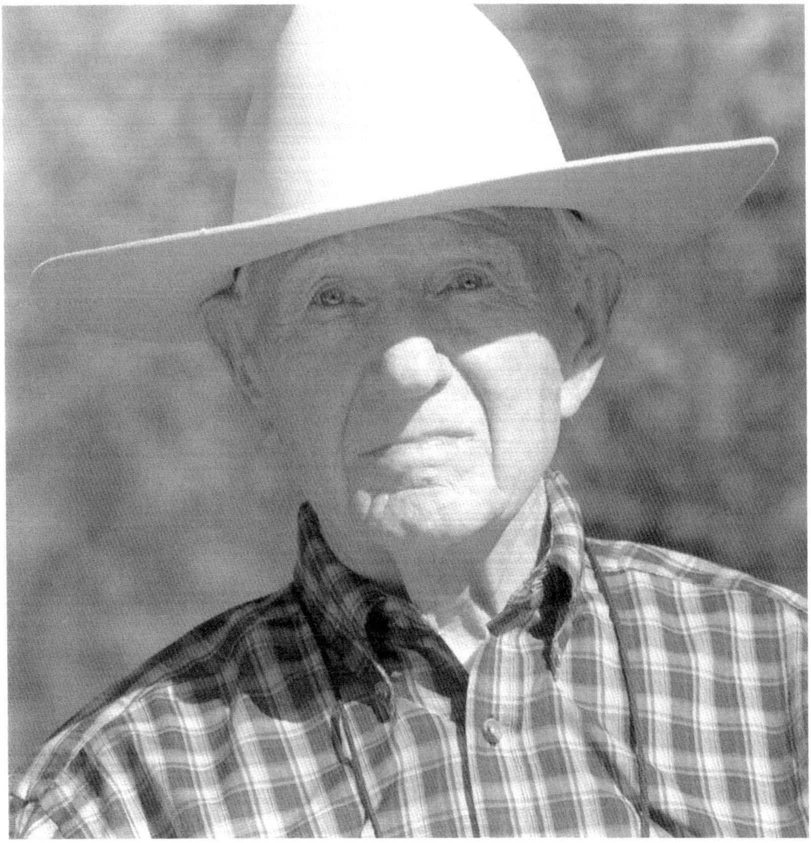

The Man in the Cowboy Hat

If someone wears a cowboy hat in the Lakes Region, he or she will attract attention. Bob Lamprey's distinctive Stetson was his calling card, but it was his real estate business acumen that led him to play a significant role in the area.

Bob and his brother Stuart formed the Lamprey & Lamprey real estate company in 1945. Their first office was in Moultonborough, in a building that now houses the town's historical society museum. But the pair soon realized they needed a more visible location, so they relocated to a cozy little building on Paugus Bay in Laconia, where Paugus Bay Sporting Goods is now housed.

After several years of successful operations, the growing business relocated to Union Avenue in Laconia. And in the late 1960s, the company moved to the P.I. Building in Meredith, now the home of the Inn at Bay Point.

Every move showed the Lampreys' appreciation for fine historical structures and the importance of understanding and appreciating how the Lakes Region developed. As they saw the increase in seasonal home sales, they developed the desire to see the Lakes Region grow in a thoughtful, careful way. So, they became involved in politics at the local and state level and worked on conservation, clean water, and preservation activities.

In the 1980s, Stewart Lamprey started New Hampshire Business Sales, and not long afterwards, Bob renovated a Victorian home at 249 Whittier Highway in Center Harbor, which he used for the new company offices. Since he loved the challenge of renovating older homes, he moved on to renovate another structure in Moultonborough that is now an attorney's office.

An icon of the real estate business, Bob Lamprey passed away in 2008 at the age of 90. His daughter Mary Lamprey Bare now owns and manages Lamprey Real Estate Associates. (Courtesy of Daryl Carlson/Kamara Image Photography.)

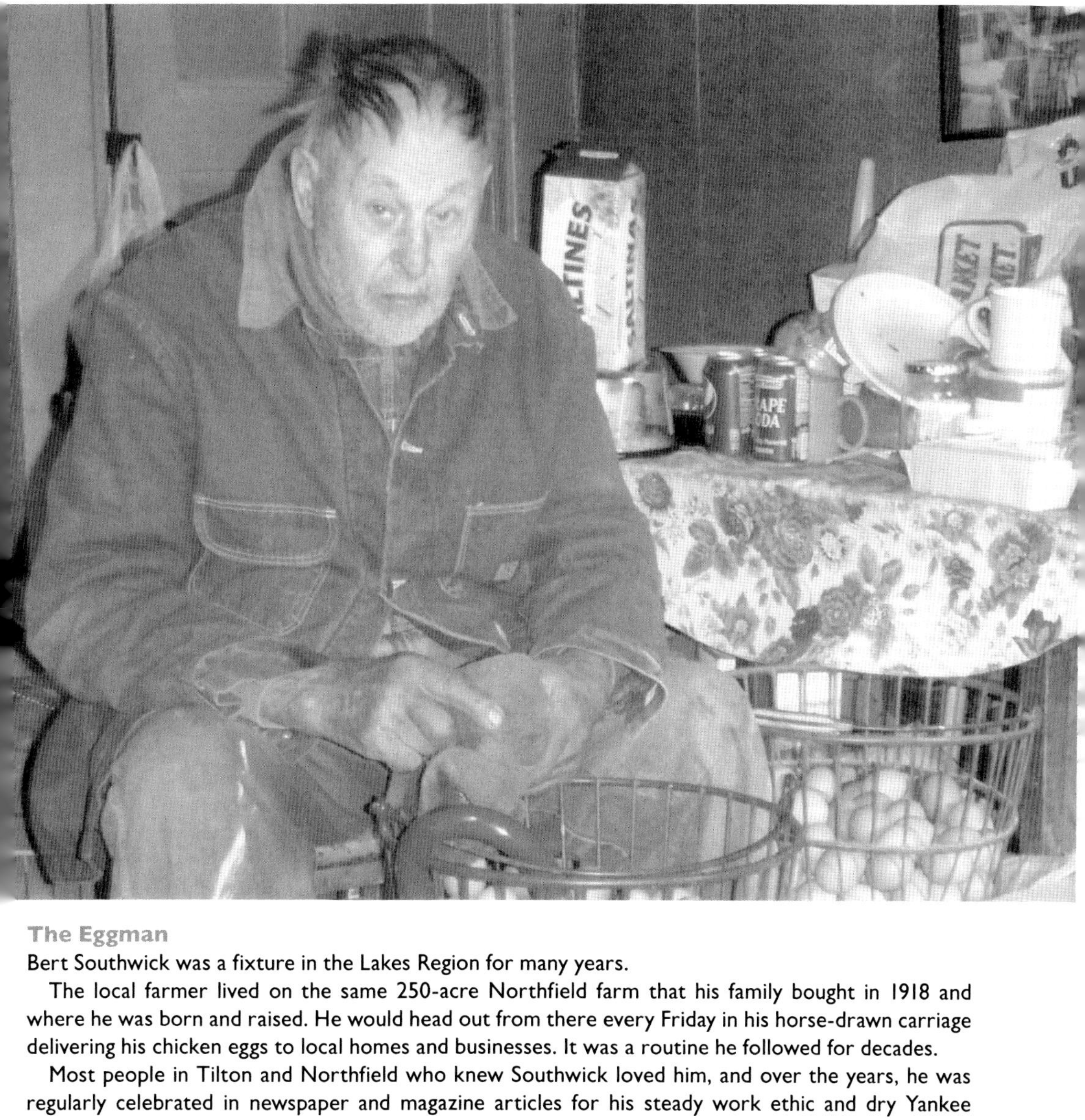

The Eggman

Bert Southwick was a fixture in the Lakes Region for many years.

The local farmer lived on the same 250-acre Northfield farm that his family bought in 1918 and where he was born and raised. He would head out from there every Friday in his horse-drawn carriage delivering his chicken eggs to local homes and businesses. It was a routine he followed for decades.

Most people in Tilton and Northfield who knew Southwick loved him, and over the years, he was regularly celebrated in newspaper and magazine articles for his steady work ethic and dry Yankee humor. He is seen here in the fall of 2014 cleaning off some eggs before selling them to his faithful customers. "Clean eggs taste better," he deadpanned.

"Bert Southwick may well be the only horse-and-buggy egg man left in the nation," wrote *Yankee* magazine in 2008. He was 91 years old when he died in early 2015.

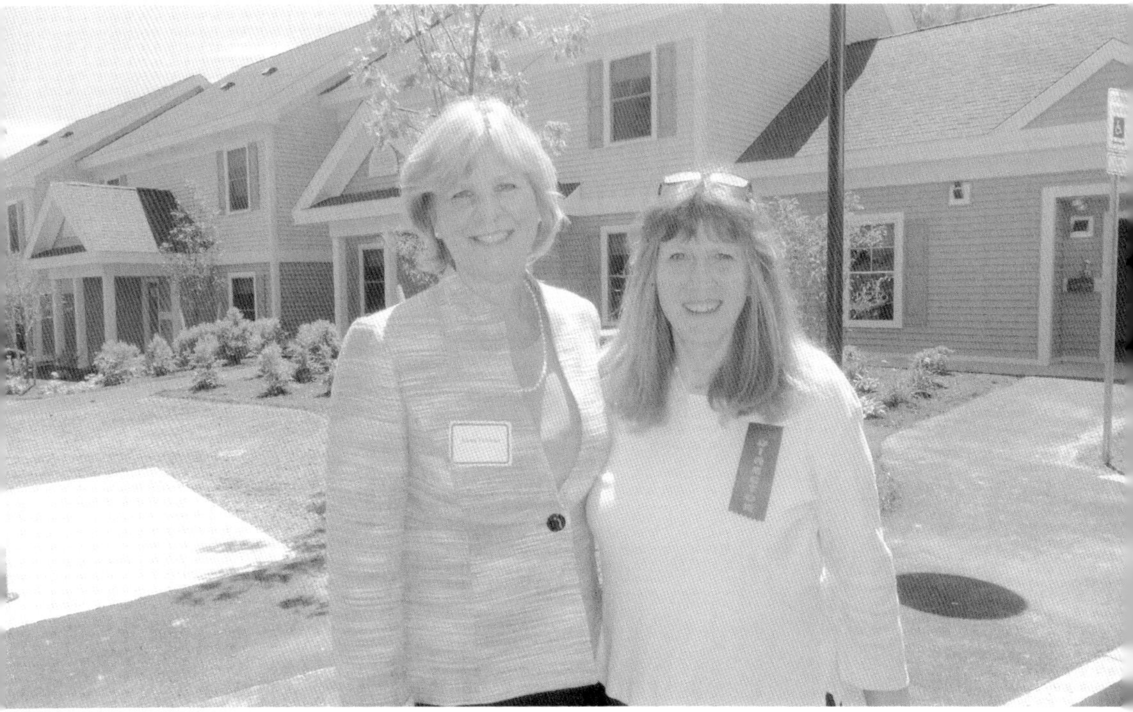

Home is Sweet

When Linda Harvey was appointed founding director of the Laconia Area Community Land Trust (LACLT) more than 20 years ago, she had a folding chair and the promise of $20,000 to get the organization going. Fortunately, Harvey has a knack for getting people behind LACLT's efforts to improve local housing. Her group has grown from a small fledgling start-up to a nationally recognized organization of strength and success, with almost 300 local housing units in five Lakes Region towns. Harvey (right) is pictured here with state senator Jeanne Forrester at the Lochmere project ribbon cutting in 2013. (Courtesy of Laconia Area Community Land Trust.)

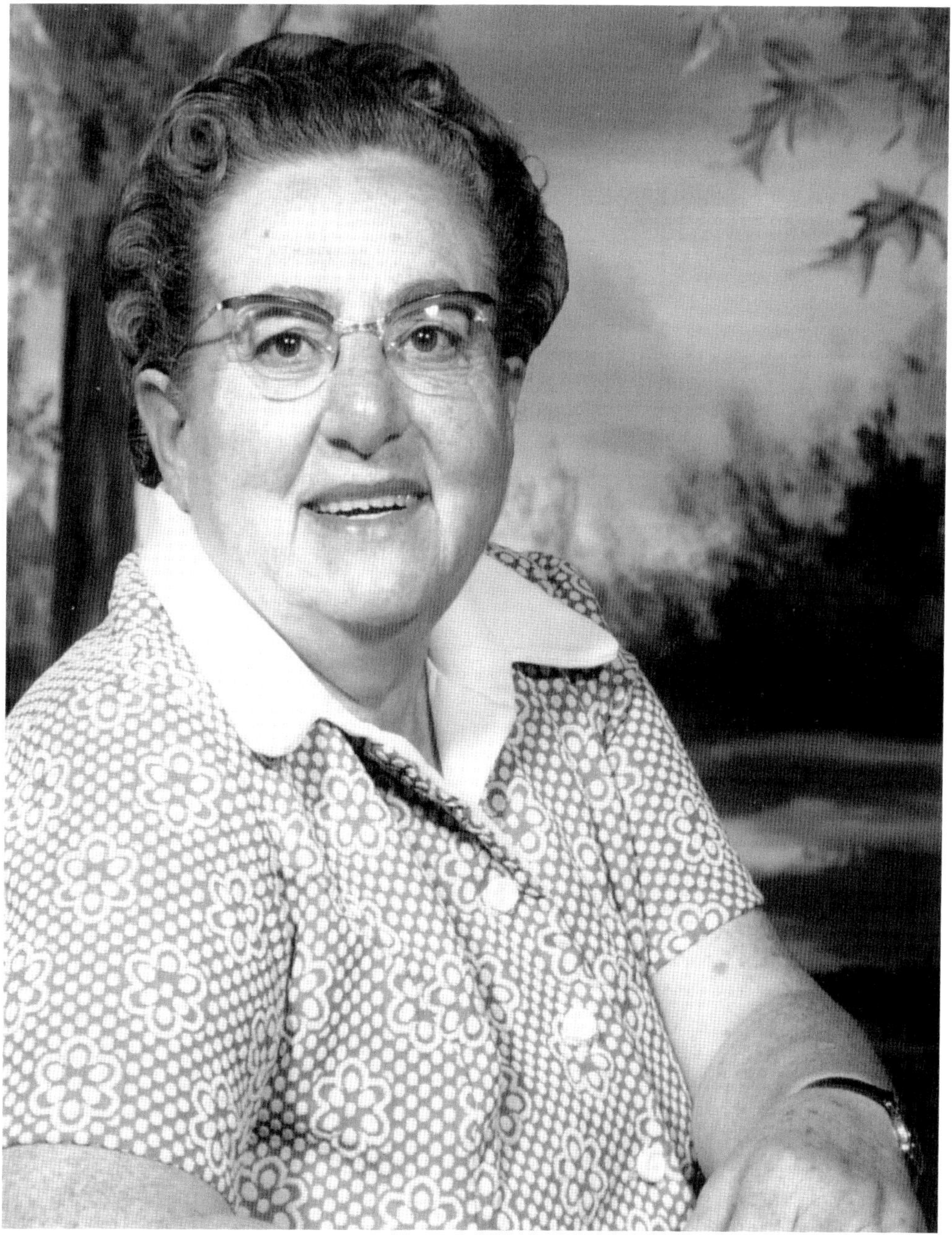

Word of Mouth

Adele Taylor never traveled far from her hometown of Moultonborough. Maybe it was because she loved the community, and her neighbors loved her.

Taylor was born in her grandparents' village home in 1913; it sat where the Moultonborough Library is now. She grew up and worked at the library for about 50 years, and also worked at the town post office for more than 20 years. Taylor knew virtually everyone in Moultonborough, and was the right person to write a weekly column about the community in the *Meredith News* for 20 years. She died in 2005. (Courtesy of the Taylor family.)

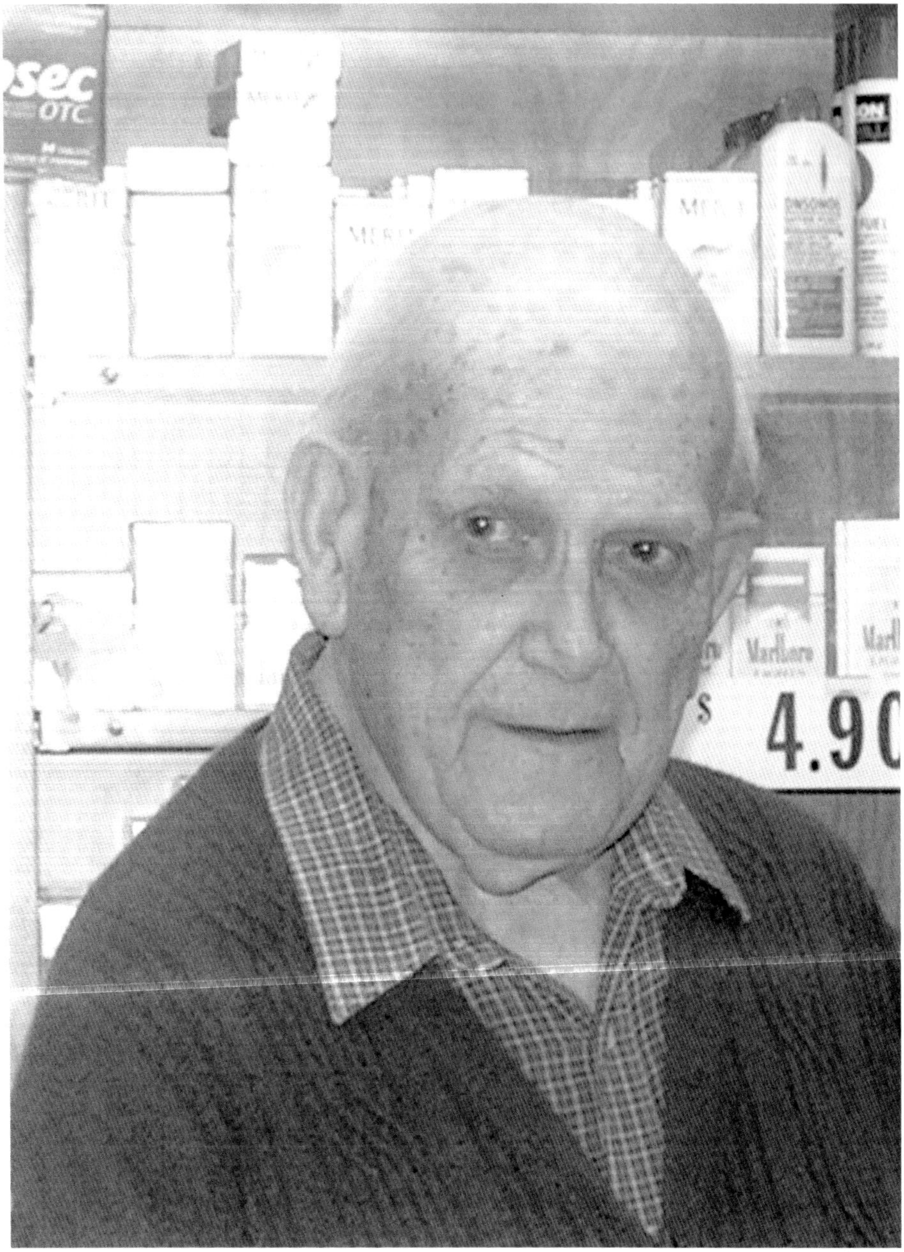

Town Representative

For 69 years, Barnard "Bun" McBride was the face of Wolfeboro village to generations of people. He began working at Black's Paper Store as a teenager, when his parents owned the business, and stayed through five owners. "Ironically, each time the business changed hands, the purchase and sales agreement included the inventory, the name, the goodwill and the building, but never once was the most priceless asset, Bun McBride, ever mentioned," said Cindy Patten, who now owns Black's with her husband, Chris.

Bun McBride was a true Yankee gentleman—steadfast, honest, and helpful. He died in his Wolfeboro home in 2010, at the age of 87. (Courtesy of *Granite State News*.)

CHAPTER FOUR

Artists and Craftsmen

If businesses make things and governments control things, then artists and craftsmen design the space where time, design, and function meet.

It is not always a material image. Sometimes the artist lets an audience simply reflect on what is good, wholesome, and pure about life.

"The goal of art is delight," said the late Jules Olitski, the world-famous painter who, late in his life, spent his summers on Bear Island in Lake Winnipesaukee; Olitski was quoting the 17th-century French painter Nicolas Poussin.

But, he may well have been speaking of a myriad of artists like himself who have added delight, color, and form to life in the Lakes Region.

There is the soft, poignant music of the late folksinger Bill Morrissey of Ossipee; the wild, exuberant accordion playing of Sandwich's Franz Nicolay; the mellow blue-white snow of Gilford painter Loren Percy; the piercing, humorous dialogue of New Hampton's Ernest Thompson; the creative combinations of Belmont's Jon Lorenz, who is both a musician and the originator of the NH Jazz series.

It is inevitable that the artists who have made a home here have brought invention and inspiration to the community.

More importantly, they help to create an open-minded atmosphere where respect and honesty are prized. Their impact ripples out throughout the area, encouraging creativity, freedom of expression, and grace.

After all, beauty is not just well-designed colors on a piece of canvas, but a sweet freedom to express thoughts and emotions in a way that is sometimes more real than day-to-day life.

Can the positive influence of a children's play produced by the Winnipesaukee Playhouse in Meredith be calculated? Can the joy of hearing a favorite artist sing a signature song from Meadowbrook's outdoor stage be measured? Can the influence of the League of New Hampshire Craftsmen be reckoned—even now, more than 80 years after its founding?

God has blessed us with artists and craftsmen. God bless them.

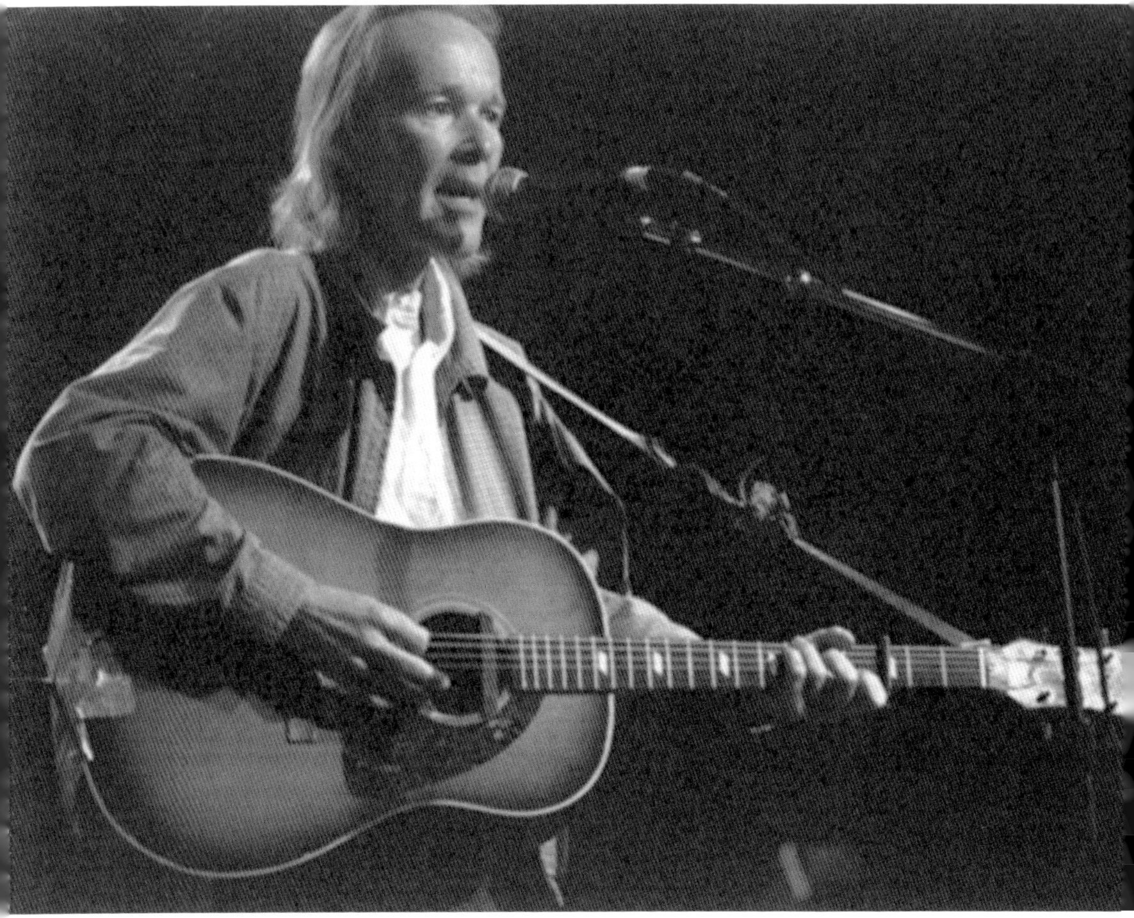

Stilled Voice

Bill Morrissey of Ossipee was a folksinger-songwriter whose hardscrabble tales of New England life struck a universal chord with people all over the world. Critics sometimes compared his lyrics to the works of writers John Steinbeck and Raymond Carver, and fans loved his deep soft growl of a voice. Morrissey, who was twice nominated for Grammy awards, died of heart disease at the age of 59 in 2011. (Courtesy of Daryl Carlson/Kamara Image Photography.)

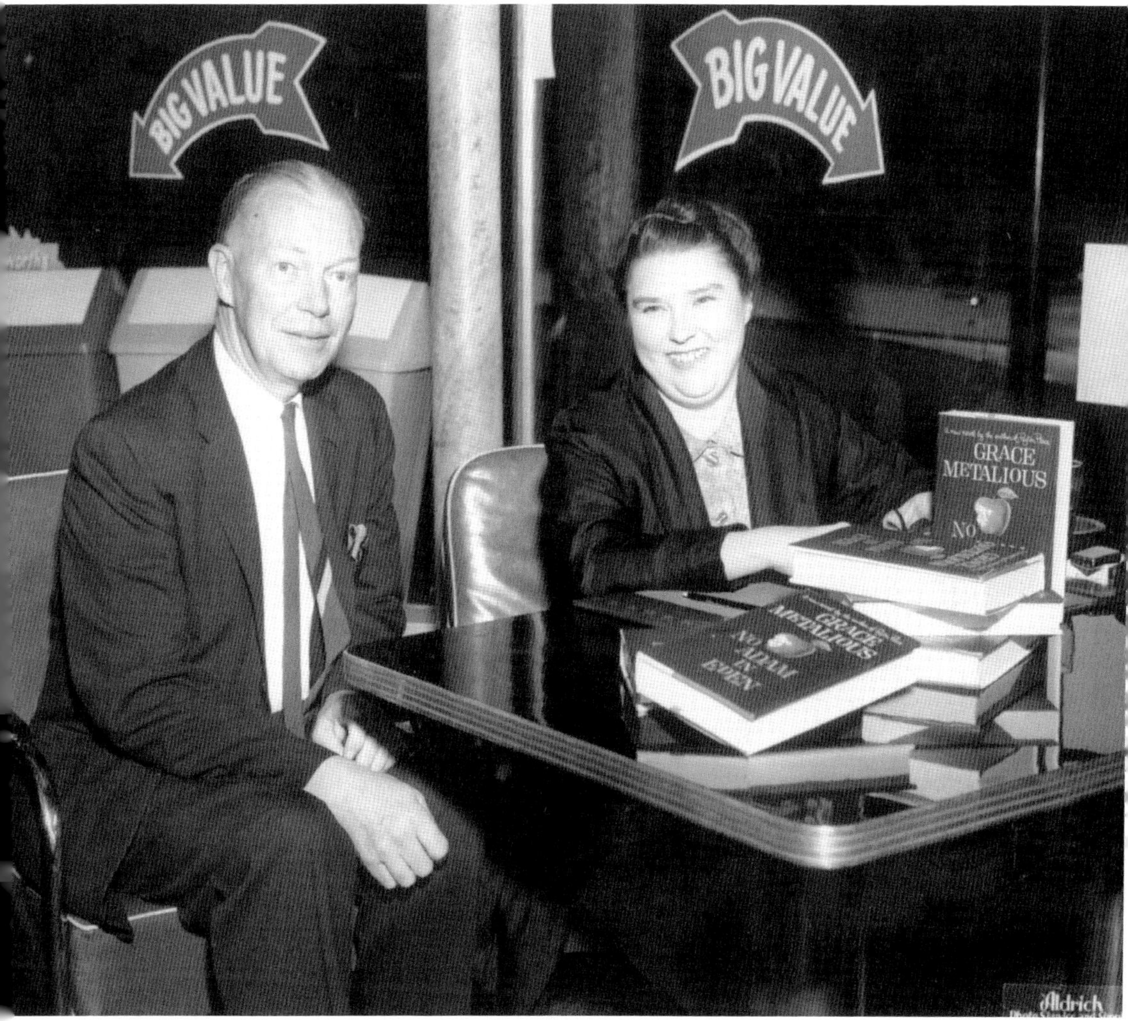

Pandora in Blue Jeans

Grace Metalious of Gilmanton shocked America when her novel *Peyton Place* was published in 1956. The then-scandalous portrait of the secrets behind the placid façade of a small New England town (not unlike Gilmanton) made for a haunting tale and turned the book into one of the most popular of the 20th century, spawning sequels, movies, and a long-running television series. Metalious is seen here with Norvin Laubenstein, the manager of Laconia's Woolworth's store, at a book-signing event for her later novel *No Adam in Eden*. An earlier photograph of Metalious, sitting casually on the floor and typing, was taken by *Laconia Evening Citizen* editor Larry Smith; the image, which appeared on the original *Peyton Place* book jacket, led to Metalious being dubbed "Pandora in Blue Jeans." (Courtesy of Laconia Historical and Museum Society.)

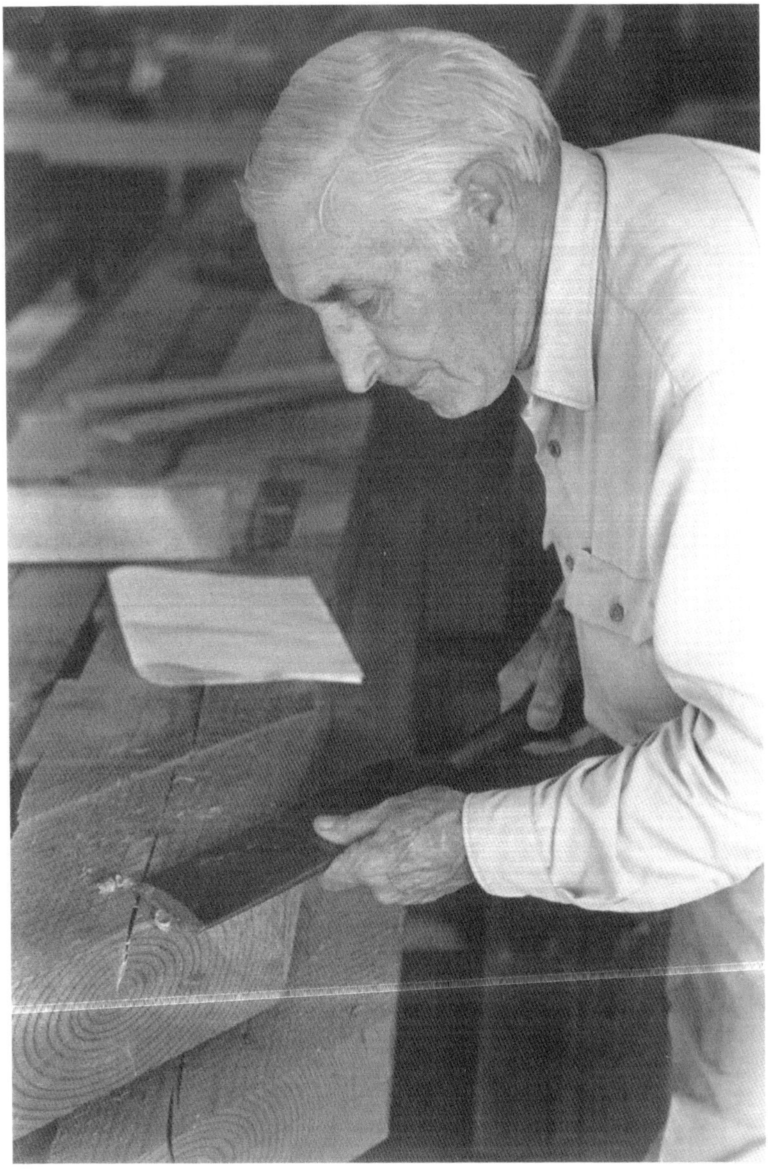

Master Bridge Builder

Milton Graton of Ashland was a nationally known builder and restorer of covered bridges. The son of a master carpenter, he became interested in the structures while he was salvaging an old covered bridge that had collapsed in 1954. Impressed by its workmanship, he began studying and working on the iconic New England structures.

Graton became the "dean of covered bridges," restoring them and constructing new ones in traditional styles, working on more than 35 in New Hampshire, Vermont, Massachusetts, New York, North Carolina, Michigan, and California.

Locally, he restored the Blair Bridge in Campton, the Durgin Bridge in Sandwich, and the Whittier Bridge in Ossipee. Graton's last project was building the Squam River covered bridge at the outlet of Little Squam Lake, less than a mile from his home. He died in 1994 at the age of 85. (Courtesy of Christine Randall.)

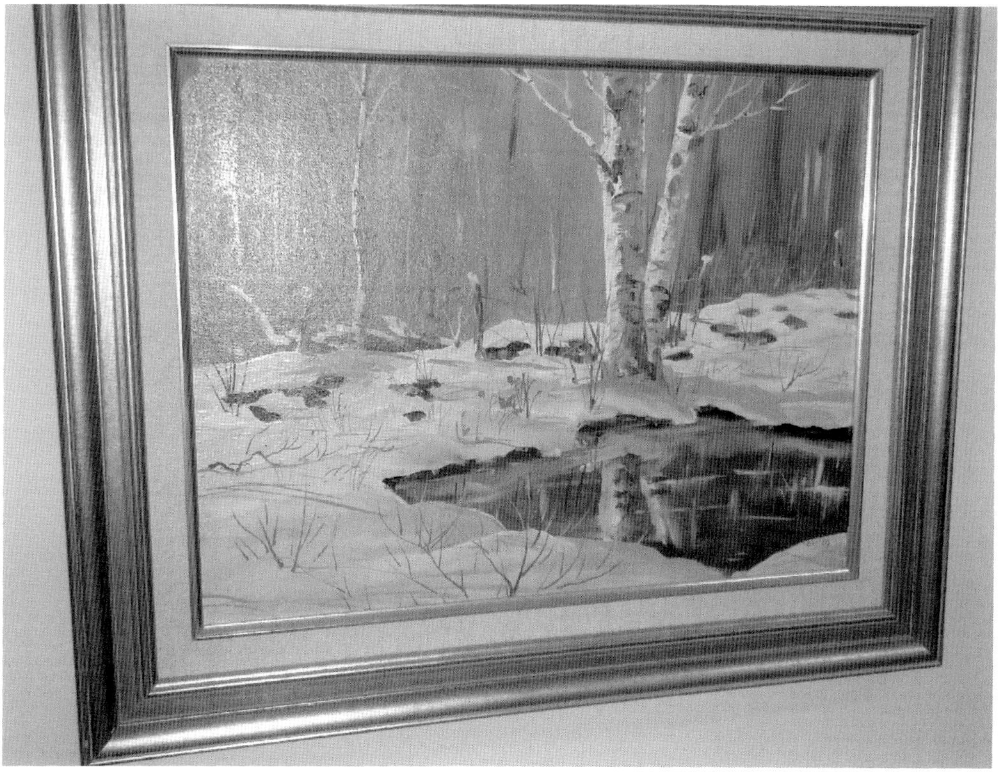

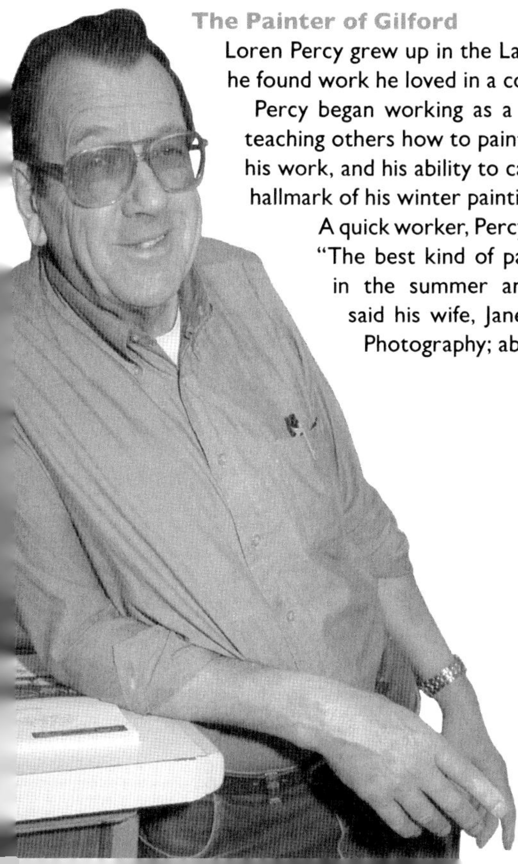

The Painter of Gilford

Loren Percy grew up in the Lakes Region, and when he started painting the area, he found work he loved in a community he enjoyed serving.

Percy began working as a photographer but eventually started painting and teaching others how to paint, mostly local landscapes. The distinctive quality of his work, and his ability to capture the area—his unique blue-white snow was a hallmark of his winter paintings—made his work extremely popular.

A quick worker, Percy sold a considerable number of paintings every year. "The best kind of paintings he did—his subjects were Winnipesaukee in the summer and Gunstock (Mountain Resort) in the winter," said his wife, Jane. (Left, courtesy of Daryl Carlson/Kamara Image Photography; above, courtesy of Jane Percy.)

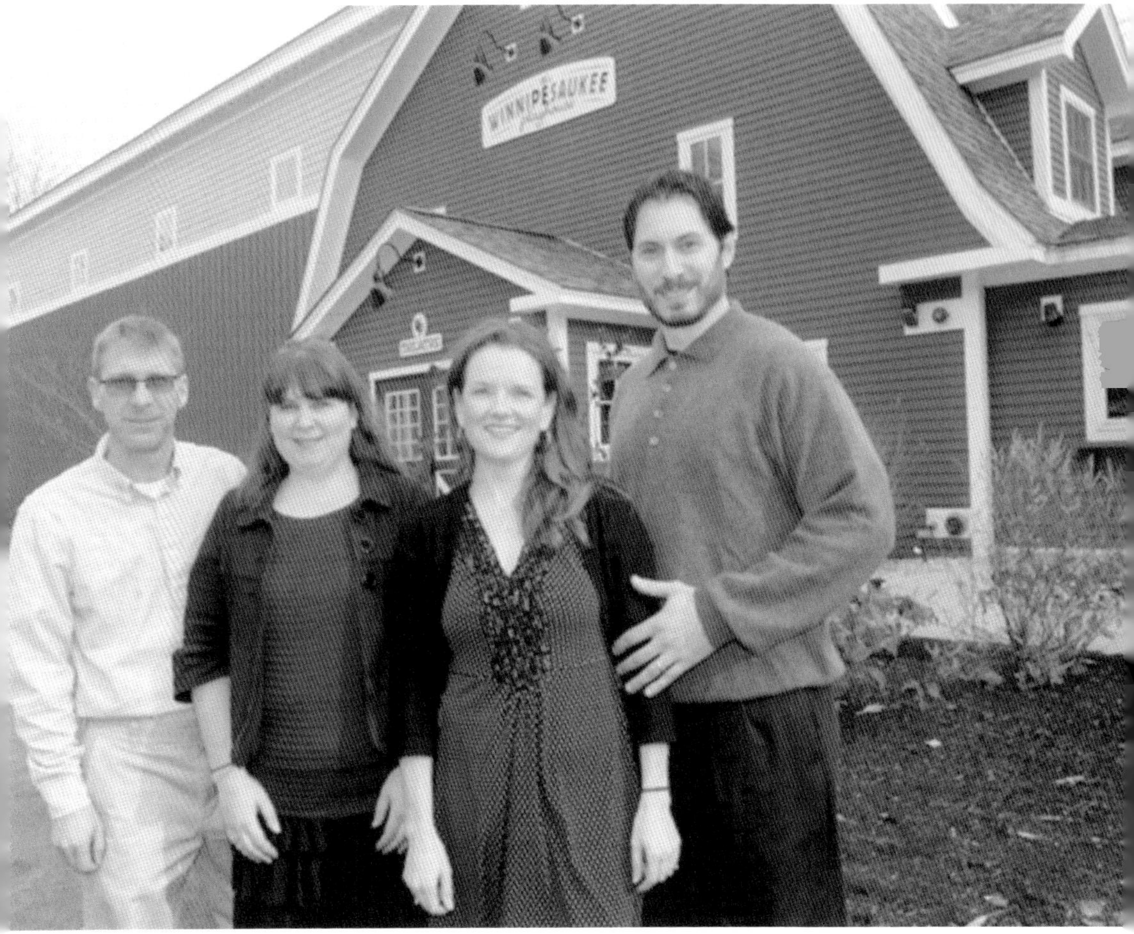

On with the Show
Four young family members came to the Lakes Region about 10 years ago, with the vision of bringing high-quality theatrical arts to the area. Siblings Lesley Pankhurst and Bryan Halperin and their respective spouses, Neil and Johanna, rented out a storefront space in Weirs Beach and began producing plays and teaching theatrical skills to adults and children.

It was not long before their modest little company began gaining recognition from the New England theater community, winning both acclaim and awards. In 2013, the Winnipesaukee Playhouse opened a new 194-seat theater on its campus in Meredith (the former site of the Annalee Mobilitee Doll Company).

The playhouse now operates year-round, providing both theatrical and educational opportunities to the community. Pictured here are, from left to right, Neil and Lesley Pankhurst and Johanna and Bryan Halperin. (Courtesy of Daryl Carlson/Kamara Image Photography.)

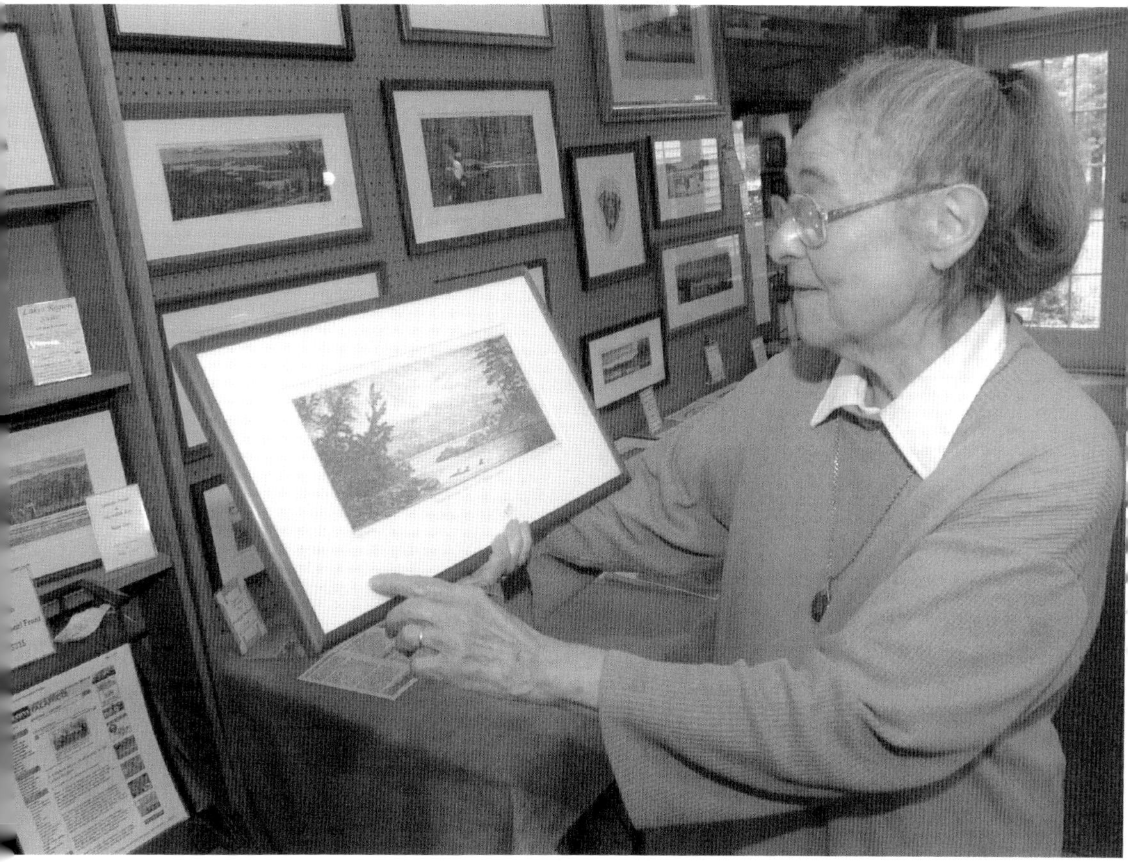

Art for The Ages

For many years, art lovers of all kinds—from international collectors to amateur Lakes Region buffs—found a haven at the Old Print Barn in New Hampton.

Owners Charles and Sophia Lane had retired from their teaching careers and indulged their love of travel and art. When they finally settled down at their Winona Road property, they opened a small seasonal gallery. But, their superior tastes drew the attention of the best critics, and before long, they were operating year-round out of a totally renovated Civil War–era barn.

Their stellar collection included thousands of pieces, primarily works on paper—watercolors, photography, illustrations, and a wide variety of prints (some made from processes dating back to the 1500s). Eventually, the couple published an internationally recognized periodical called the *Journal of the Print World*. Charles Lane died in 2009, and Sophia passed in 2014. (Courtesy of Daryl Carlson/Kamara Image Photography.)

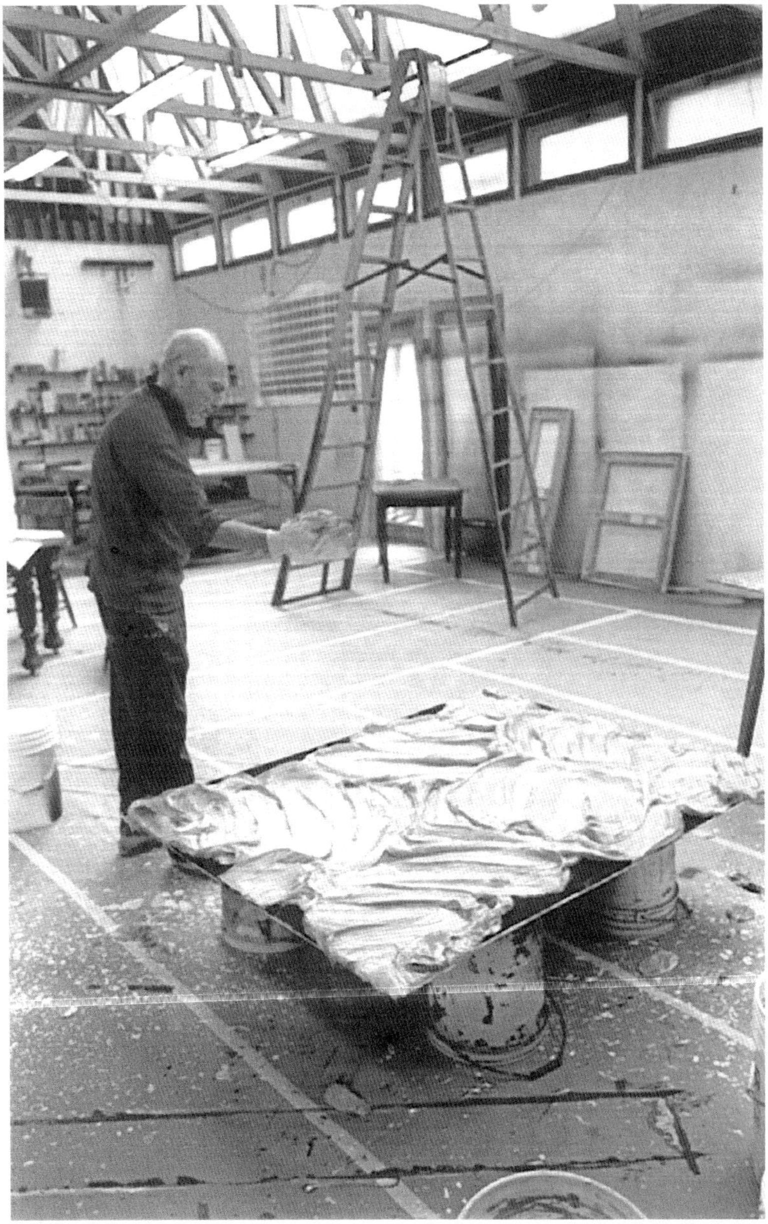

"I Believe in Beauty"
Not many people know that for the last few decades of his life, world-famous artist Jules Olitski spent several months a year working in his studio on Bear Island in Lake Winnipesaukee. Olitski, one of the seminal modern abstract artists, was once called "the best painter alive" by prominent art critic Clement Greenberg.

He was best known for his abstract paintings, which are represented in the finest museums and galleries in the world. In the Lakes Region, Olitski was regularly inspired by the natural world, drawing from what he saw out his studio window in Meredith.

"I believe in beauty," he said during one visit. "It's like a radical thing to say today but I believe in high art, I believe in excellence." (Courtesy of the Estate of Jules and Kristin Olitski.)

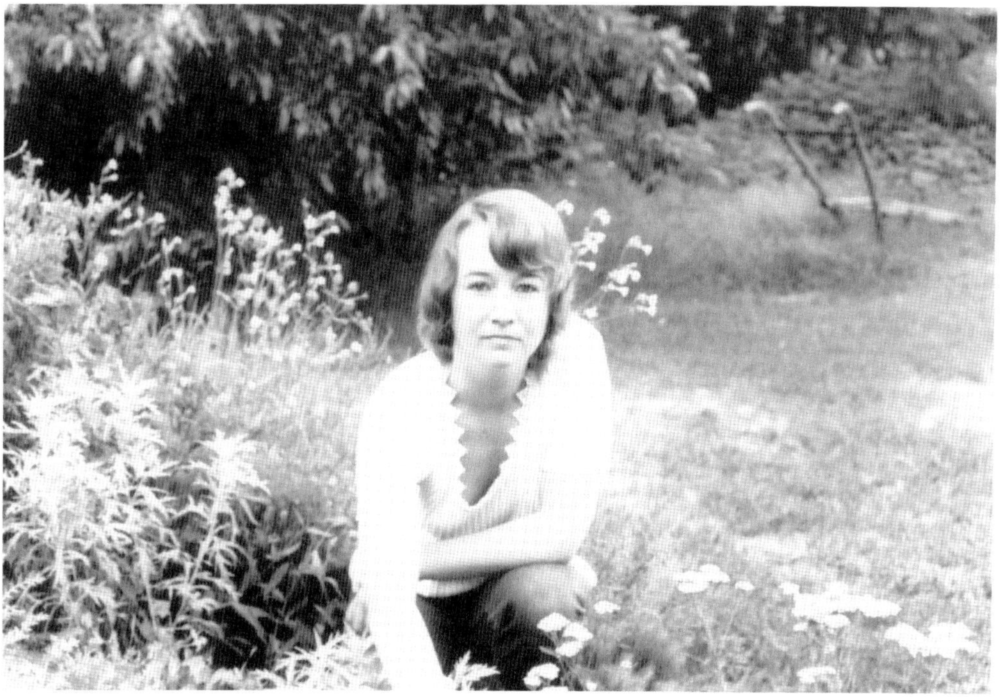

The Classic Cheerleader
In 1973, Laconia native Ruth Doan MacDougall had her fourth novel published, *The Cheerleader.* The story of Henrietta "Snowy" Snow growing into an independent young woman in a place much like MacDougall's hometown became a national bestseller and is considered a classic coming-of-age story in mid-20th-century America. MacDougall now lives in Center Sandwich and has since written several other books. (Courtesy of Ruth Doan MacDougall.)

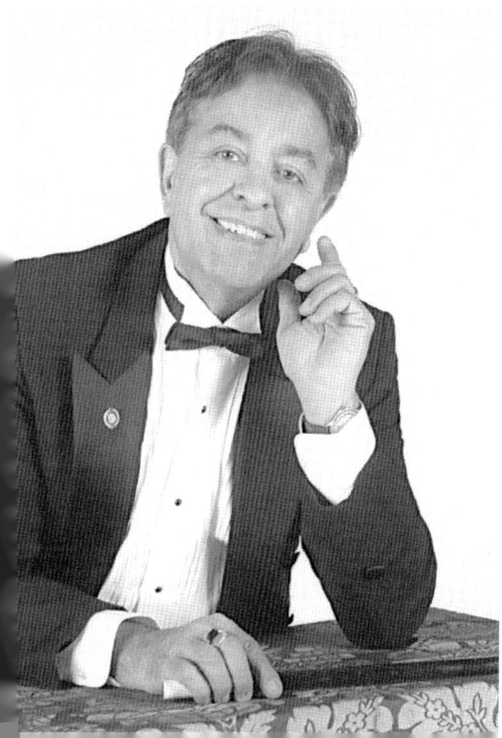

Frates Creates.
Larry Frates of Gilmanton has been working as a professional artist and performer for 40 years. His work is exhibited in museums around the world, but his biggest impact may be on the hundreds of local children and adults who have learned to express themselves artistically through the Frates Creative Arts Center in Laconia. Frates is also a serious educator, teaching at Plymouth State University and other educational institutions. (Courtesy of Tekla Frates/Tekla Photography.)

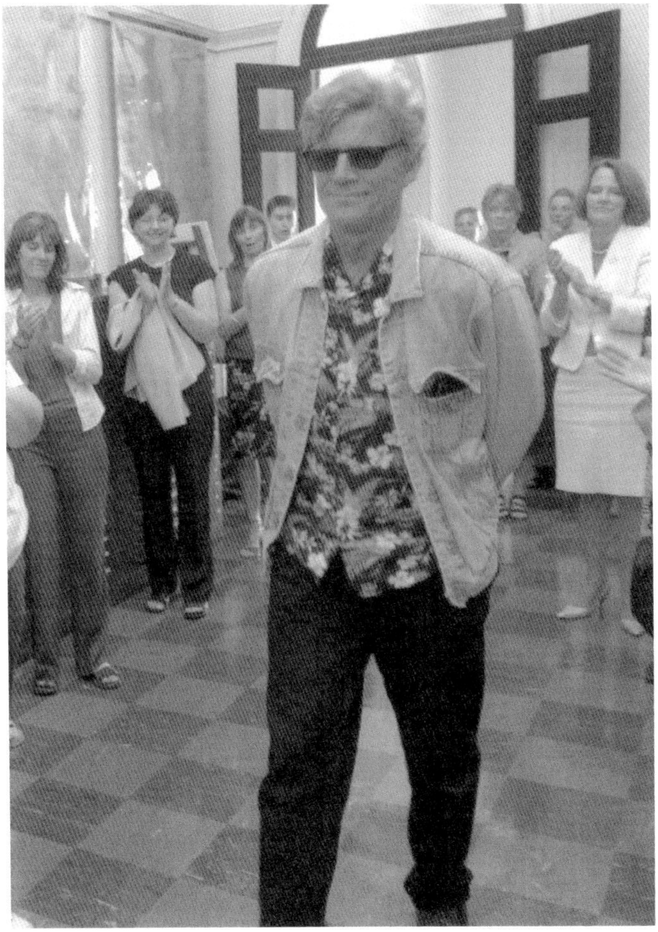

"The Loons! They're Welcoming Us Back." (ABOVE AND OPPOSITE PAGE)
Ernest Thompson was a 28-year-old actor when he wrote *On Golden Pond*, inspired by a childhood of fishing, boating, games, and reading at his family's lake house in Maine. Funny and moving, the play, now translated into more than 30 languages and produced on six continents, continues to be an international success, touching on universal themes of relationship, conflict, abiding love, and forgiveness, all the while echoing the special charms of summer life in New England.

A stellar cast was assembled for the 1981 film. Topping its 10 Academy Award nominations (including Best Picture and Best Supporting Actress for Jane Fonda), Katharine Hepburn and Henry Fonda won Oscars, as did Thompson for his screenplay adaptation. Thompson is pictured here accepting congratulations at a Concord screening of the film during its 25th anniversary.

But, perhaps most significantly for Thompson, a New Hampshire native, the film was shot in the Lakes Region, principally in and around Squam Lake. A decade later, he returned to the area to raise his children, and with partners Morgan Murphy and Lori Gigliotti Murphy (pictured opposite, bottom), founded Whitebridge Farm Productions. The outfit has since created two new films, *Time And Charges* and *Heavenly Angle*, and offers workshops for writers and actors. Thompson is seen opposite, top directing a scene in *Heavenly Angle*.

Incidentally, Thompson's professional acting debut was in a tour of *The Pleasure of His Company*, starring Cyril Ritchard and Maureen O'Sullivan; the first stop was the old Lakes Region Playhouse in Gilford. (Opposite top, courtesy of Whitebridge Farm Productions; others courtesy of Daryl Carlson/ Kamara Image Photography.)

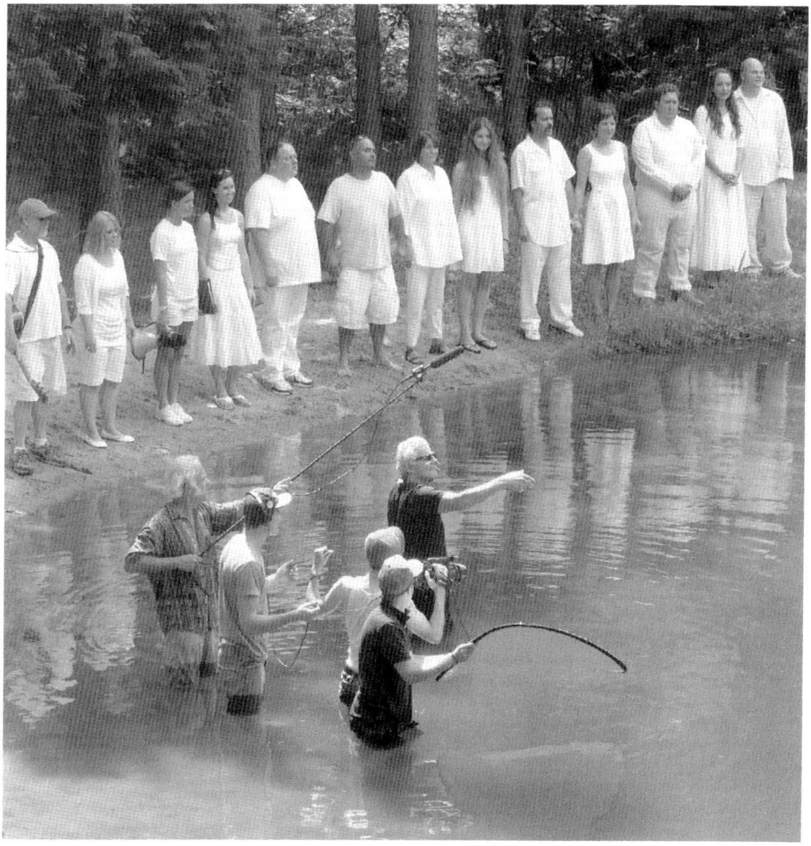

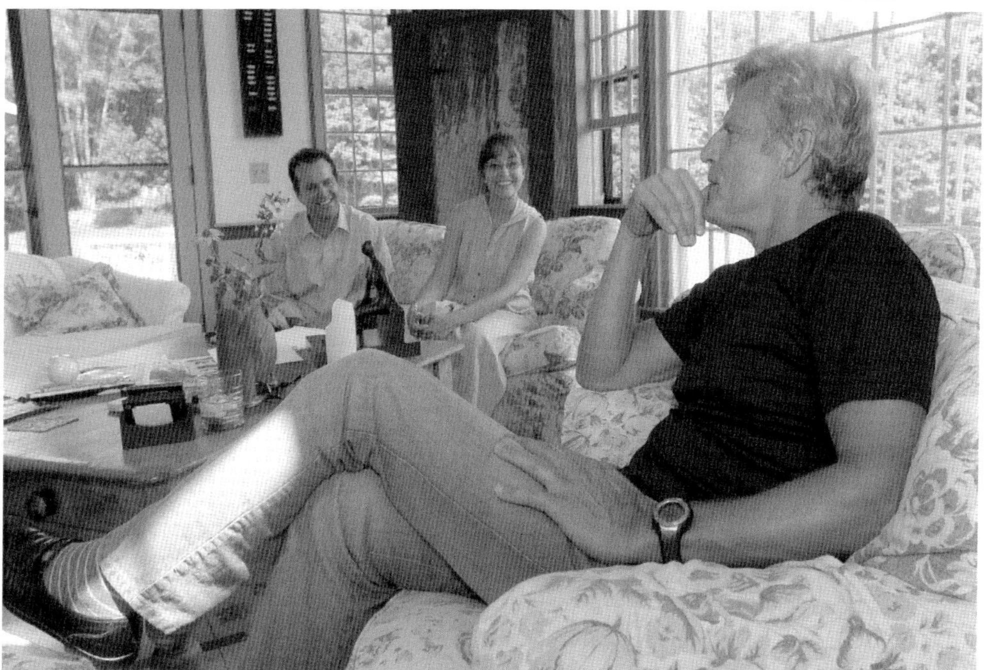

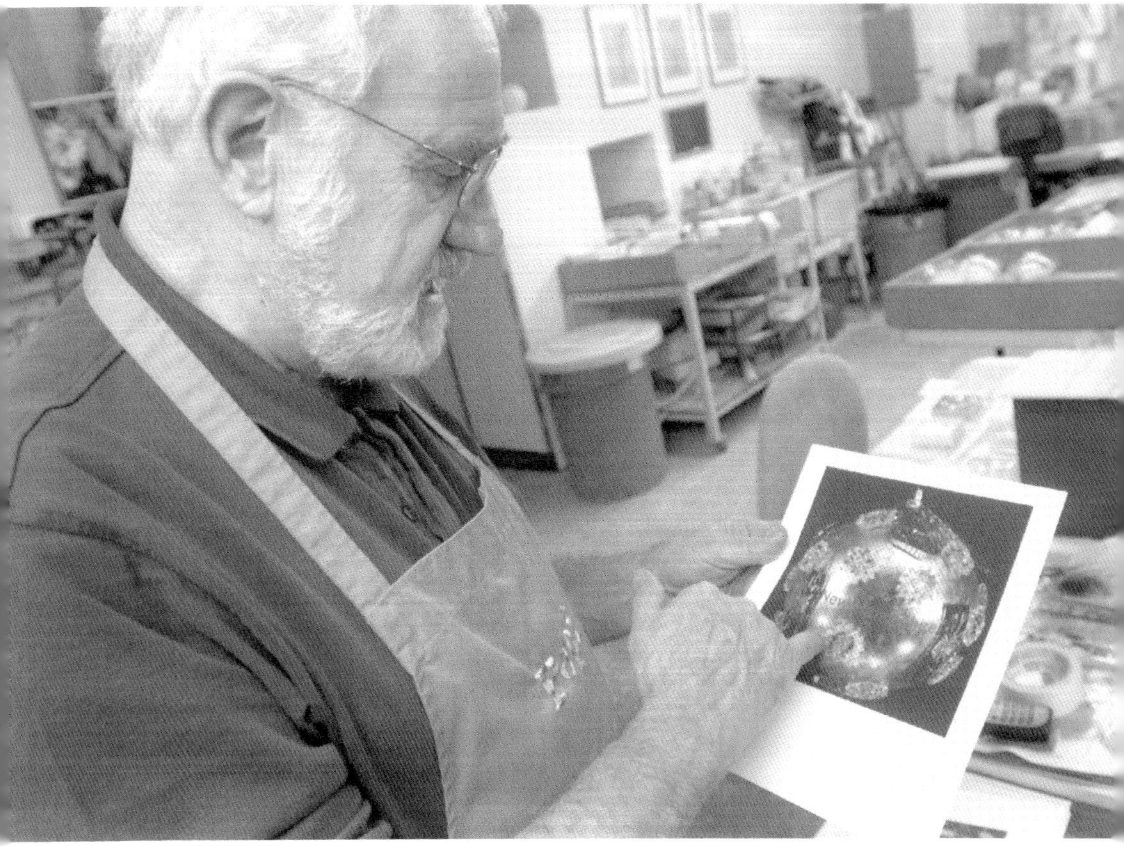

Seeing Art Glass

When Pepi Herrmann came to America from Austria in 1968, he wanted to revive the nearly lost art of Brilliant Period–cut glass, a thoroughly American style that represented cutting at its finest. He opened his shop in Lakes Region in 1974 and has become known as a pioneer in this unique style. One of only a handful of master crystal cutters in the country, his skills have been used to create radiant one-of-a-kind artistic objects of all kinds, from family heirlooms to major league sports awards. (Courtesy of Daryl Carlson/Kamara Image Photography.)

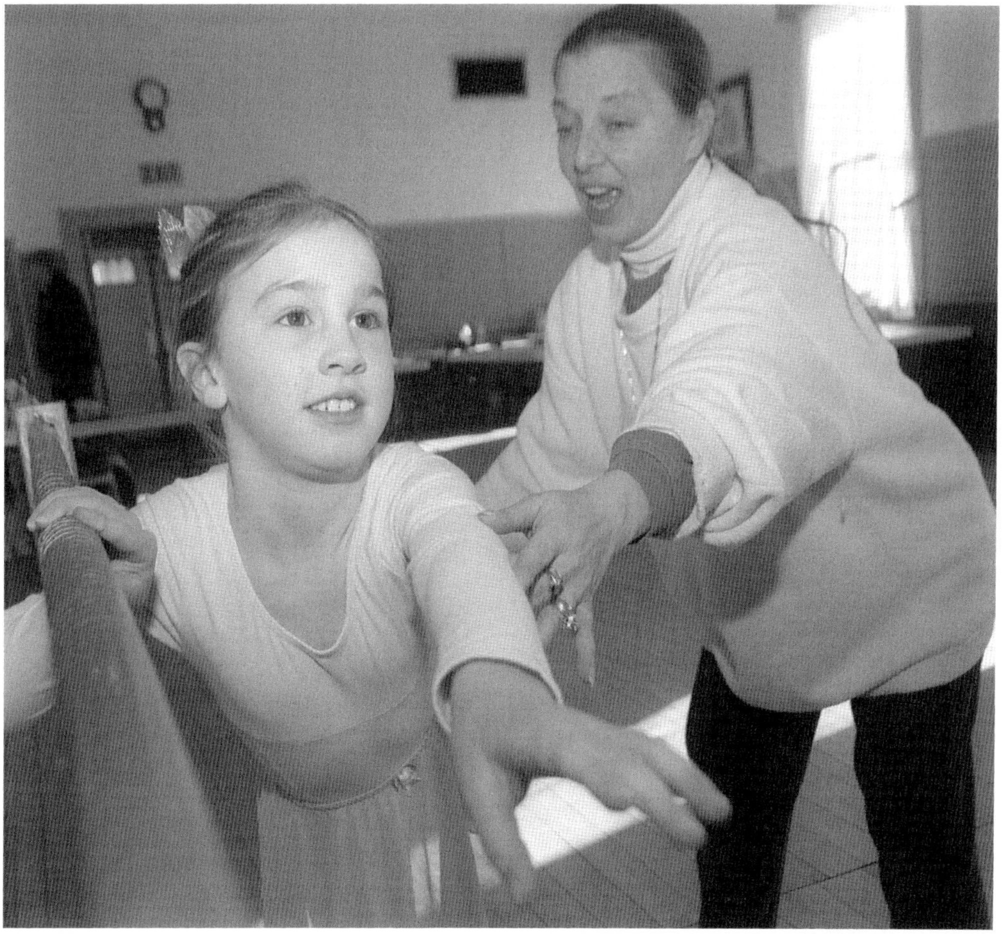

The Dance of a Life

Edra Toth was born in Hungary in 1952, when the country was under the oppressive rule of Soviet Russia. Her family escaped to Austria during the revolution in 1956 and then came to the United States.

They were poor but content, living in a tenement attic apartment in Boston. One day, the landlady asked the Toths if she could sponsor dance lessons for young Edra, as her own daughter, who was very shy, wanted to be in the class.

Toth's innate talent was quickly recognized. Before long, she was enrolled in classes with the Boston Ballet. She first danced onstage at 13 years of age and was the company's prima ballerina three years later.

Toth continued to dance professionally for another 30 years, traveling around the world and working with some of the most famous dancers of her generation, including Rudolf Nureyev, Ivan Nagy, and Edward Villella. She had begun teaching earlier in her career, so she easily transferred into fulltime teaching when she stopped dancing.

Her studio was first in Boston, but she moved it to Wolfeboro in 1999; she later opened a second studio in Dover, New Hampshire. Her endearing grace teaching classical ballet has blessed scores of New Hampshire youngsters and their families. (Courtesy of Daryl Carlson/Kamara Image Photography.)

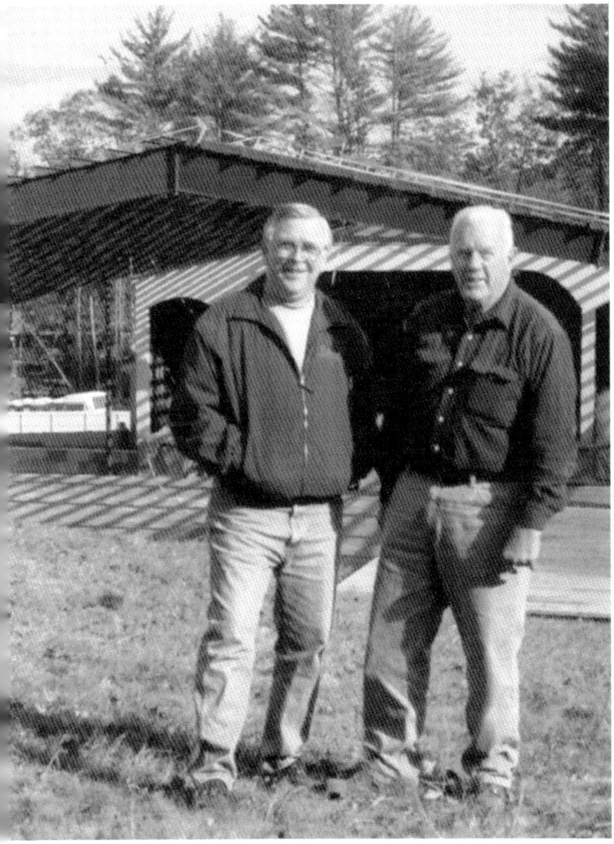

From Field to Fame

Bob Harding (left), Bill Gelotte (right), and their partners owned a Gilford hotel when they learned that a large farm adjacent to their property was for sale in 1994. Concerned that the 100-acre parcel could get turned into a business that would have an adverse effect on their operations, they bought it without much thought about what they would do with it. "Our original thought was that there was nothing to do here at night," Harding said.

Then, the general manager of a local oldies radio station asked about staging a Beatles tribute band on the farm property. Harding quickly added two more acts, and the Meadowbrook Farm Performing Center was born.

Over the last 20 years, Meadowbrook—now called the Bank of New Hampshire Pavilion at Meadowbrook—has grown into a first-class, state-of-the-art outdoor entertainment venue. In 2014, Meadowbrook was named one of the Top 10 Music Venues in America by *USA Today*; it has also been nominated as Venue of the Year by the Academy of Country Music Association five times. (Both, courtesy of Bank of New Hampshire Pavilion at Meadowbrook.)

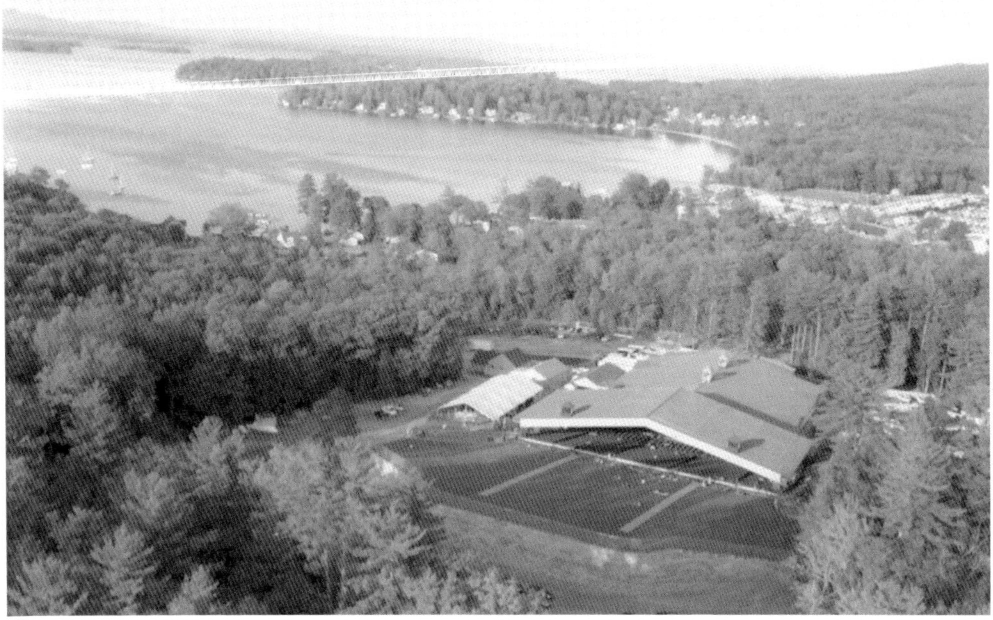

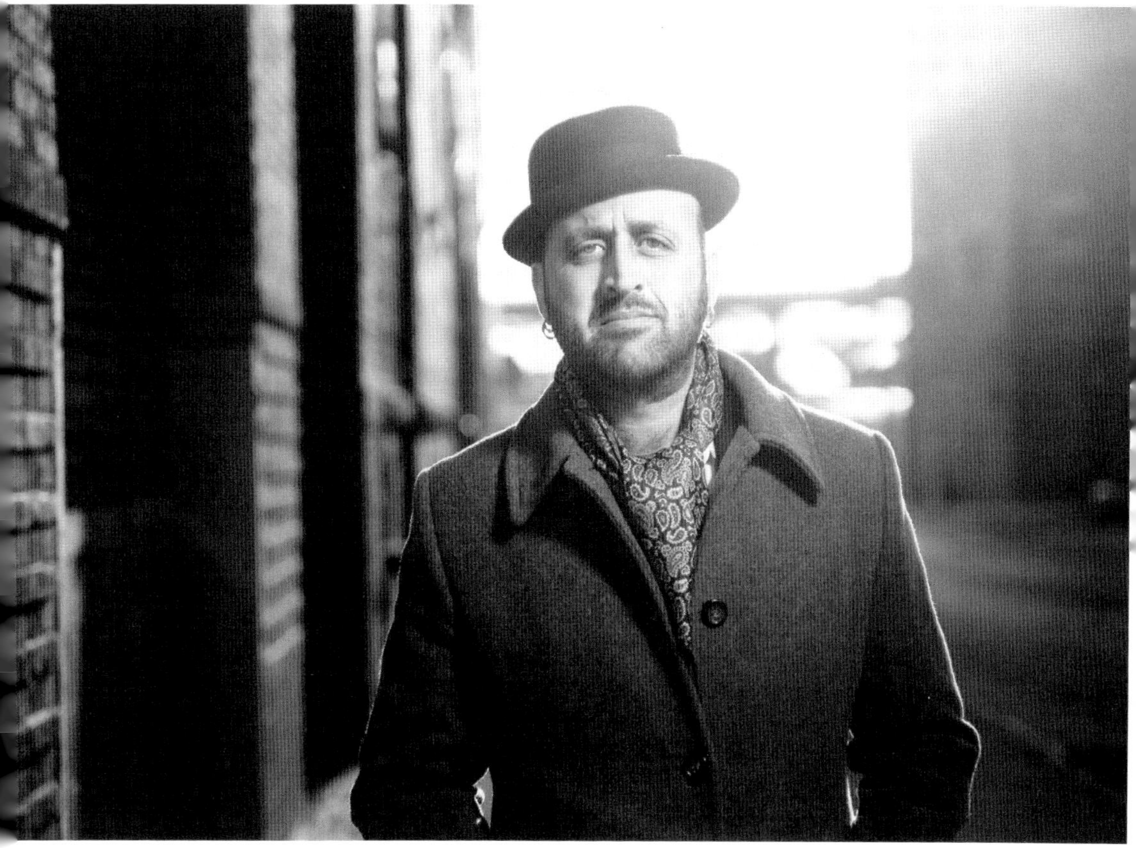

From Quiet Sandwich to Punk's Best Accordionist

Franz Nicolay of Center Sandwich has carved out a distinctive career for himself as a modern musician and writer. Primarily a pianist and accordion player, Nicolay has played or performed with all kinds of popular music performers, from Bruce Springsteen to the Dresden Dolls, a New England–based dark cabaret group. Named first on the list of Punk's 10 Best Accordion Players, he was a member of the cabaret-punk circus World/Inferno Friendship Society that *Rolling Stone* called "the world's best bar band." He has also worked as a touring member of agit-punk artists Against Me! and played with The Hold Steady and the Balkan jazz group Guignol. (Courtesy of Franz Nicolay.)

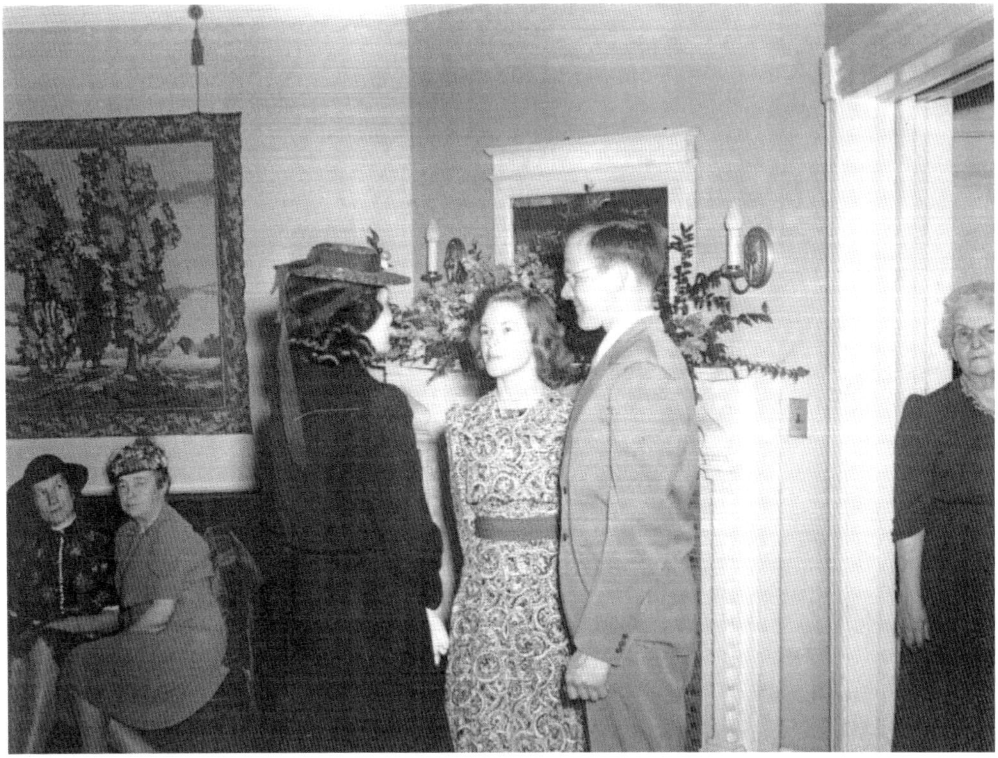

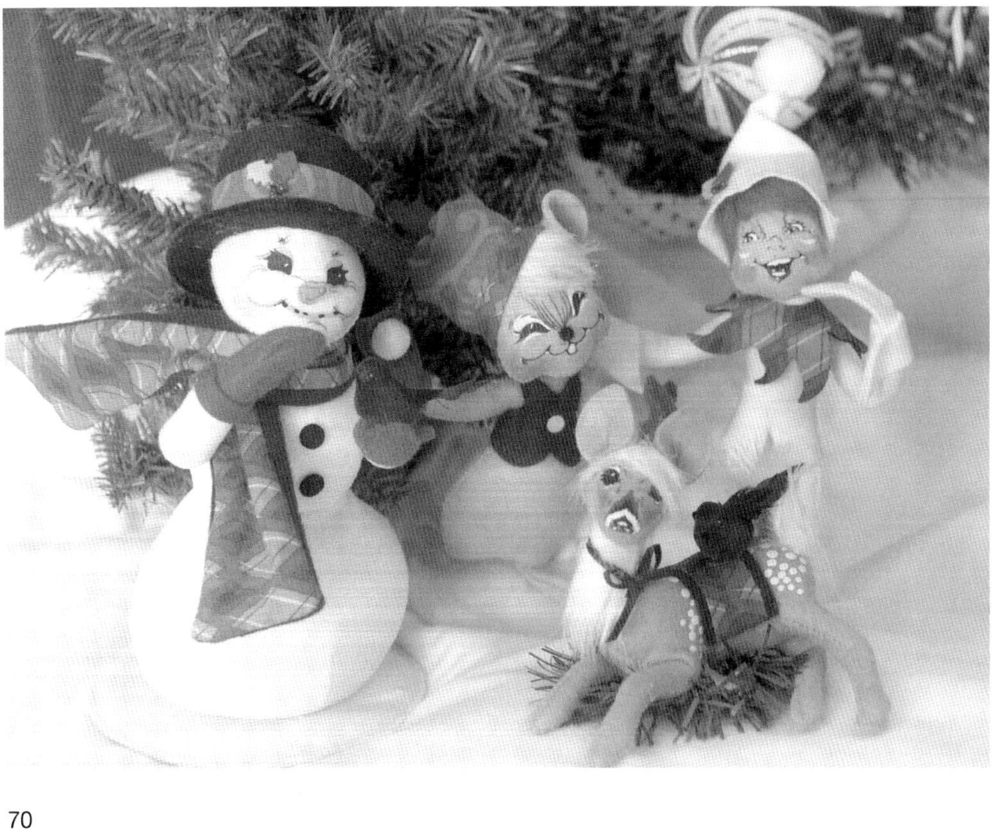

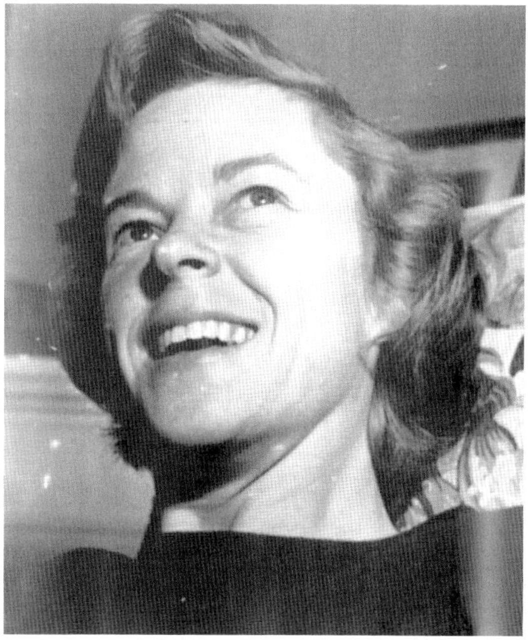

The Romance of Annalee (ABOVE AND OPPOSITE PAGE)
When one looks at an Annalee doll, there is a sense of whimsy and charm—the smiling eyes, round, rosy cheeks, and delicate cloth body all speak of light, sunny days and bright skies ahead.

It is also a reflection of how Barbara Annalee Davis Thorndike saw her world in Meredith.

Annalee began creating dolls—marionettes, really—as a young child growing up in Concord. She soon started making changeable clothes for her creations and putting the figures in set positions. To Annalee, these dolls were not toys; they were tiny works of art, light and airy figures in the midst of action, expressing the joy of life.

Annalee sold some dolls through the New Hampshire League of Arts and Crafts (now the League of New Hampshire Craftsmen). But, in 1941, she married Charles "Chip" Thorndike and moved to the Lakes Region to operate a chicken farm with him. The young couple is pictured opposite, top, at a social event. When the farm began to run into financial difficulties in the early 1950s, the family decided to see if they could make a living selling Annalee's dolls.

She started the enterprise in her home, filling every available space with doll parts, scraps of cloth for clothing, and bits of wire for the frames. Chip crafted the wire frames as well as small props like wooden skis, boats, and so forth. Local women were hired to help out.

In the 1950s, Annalee's dolls began appearing in store window promotion displays of department stores in Manchester and Boston. The State of New Hampshire hired her to create dolls to help promote tourism to the state. Annalee dolls were seen skiing, fishing, and hunting at the Eastern States Exposition in Springfield, Massachusetts, and at Rockefeller Center in New York City.

The success of the promotional programs launched Annalee Dolls into national popularity. In 1955, the company was incorporated as Annalee Mobilitee Dolls, and by 1960, the dolls were being sold at retail outlets throughout the country. In 1964, the Thorndikes moved operations out of their house and into a "factory in the woods."

For several decades, the company continued to grow, pioneering collectible dolls and winning fans all over the world. Then in 2002, Annalee died, and the company passed to her two sons. But, family tensions arose, and six years later, Annalee's company was purchased by three partners, including current manufacturer Imagine Company of Hong Kong.

Today the dolls are still designed in Meredith, based on Annalee's original designs and ideas. The company also operates a retail store in Meredith. (All, courtesy of Annalee Dolls.)

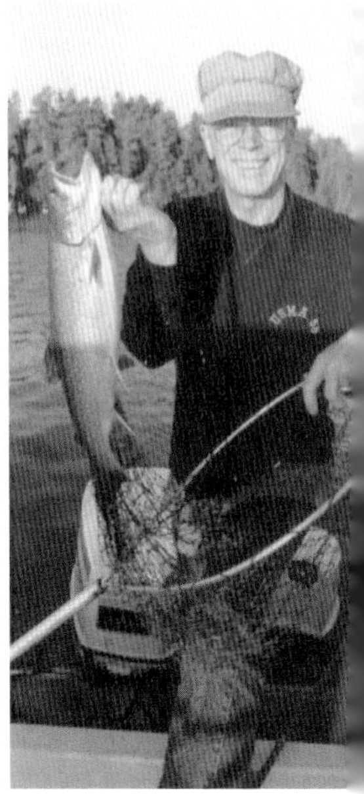

Fishing for Life's Answers

If fishing is a universal activity, than fishing on Lake Winnipesaukee produces both the greatest and the worst aspects of the human condition.

That seems to be one idea behind Hal Lyon's popular book *Angling in the Smile of the Great Spirit, Six Centuries of Wisdom from the Master Anglers of Lake Winnipesaukee*. The Meredith resident's book was named Best Book of the Year by the New England Outdoor Writers Association because it deftly weaves the experiences of 15 colorful Lakes Region fishermen into a read that is both entertaining and instructive.

Lyon himself is somewhat of an instructive read. He has served in high positions in government and the academic world, on the faculties of Georgetown University, Dartmouth Medical School, and the University of Munich, Germany (where he is a guest professor of medical education). Lyon is a West Point graduate, a former Army Ranger Paratrooper officer, a key figure in developing *Sesame Street*, and won the Gold Medal in the 1990 International Film & TV Festival of New York. He also authored six other books before writing the first and only definitive book about fishing on Winnipesaukee. (Courtesy of Deep Waters Press.)

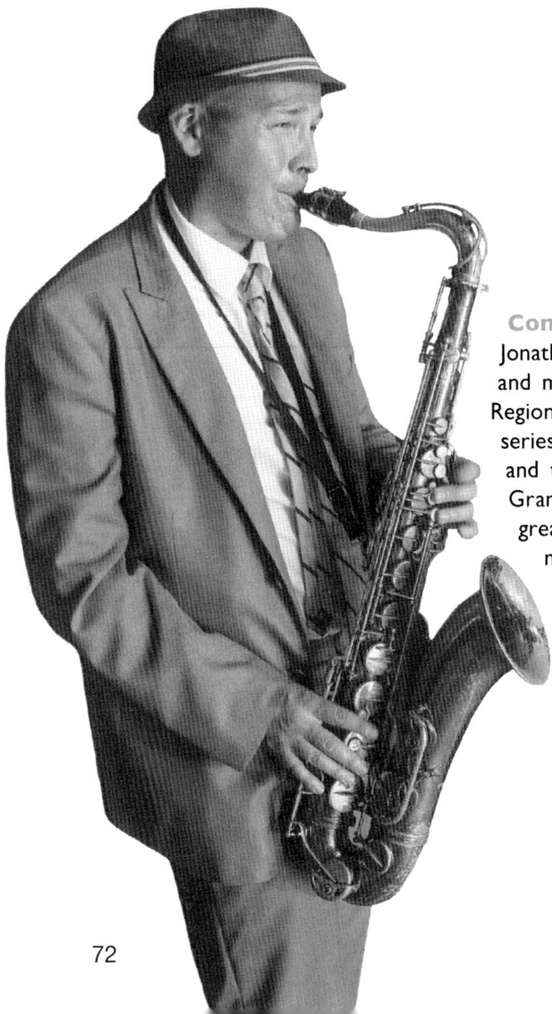

Coming up to Get Down

Jonathan Lorentz of Belmont is a saxophonist, disc jockey, and music event organizer. Since relocating to the Lakes Region from New York in 2011, he has originated a concert series of accomplished jazz artists at Pitman's Freight Room and the Margate Resort in Laconia, as well as at other Granite State locations. His NH Jazz initiative has created great listening venues, and his concert productions—more than 200 so far, featuring artists typically seen only in New York and Boston—have garnered praise from *Downbeat* magazine and other media outlets. (Courtesy of NH Jazz.)

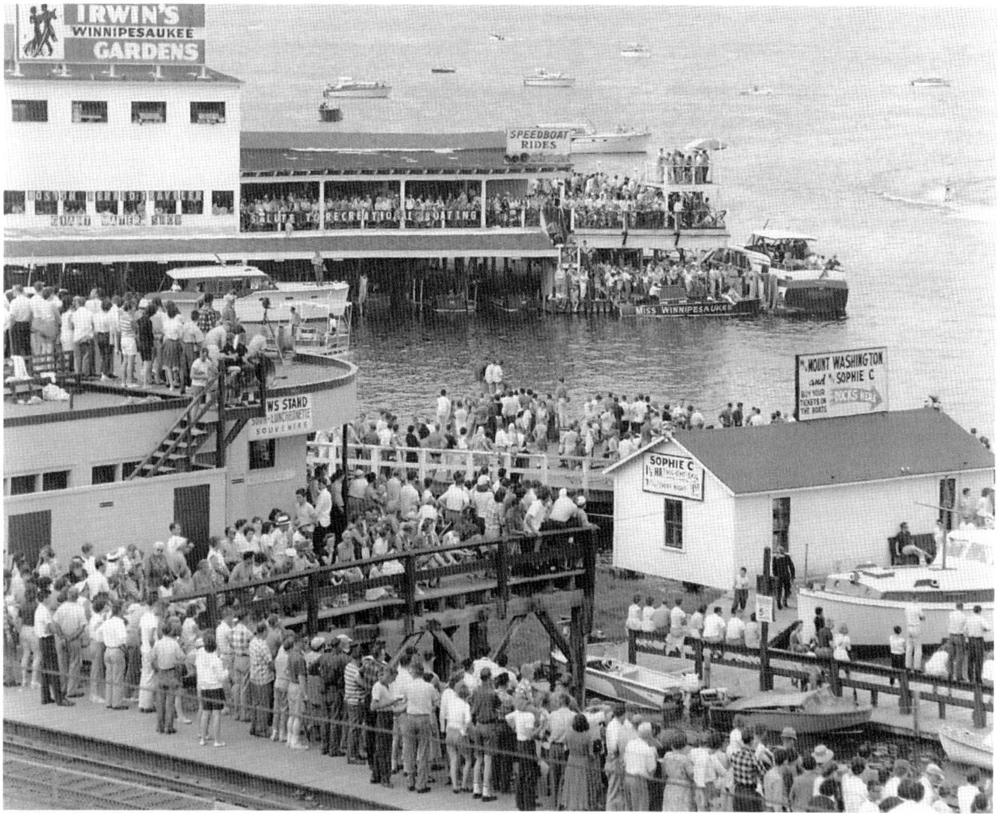

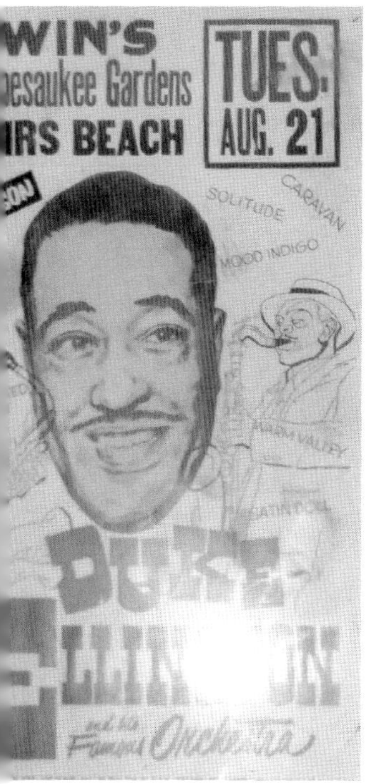

Sweet Weirs Beach Sounds

Jim Irwin was a young man with a trumpet when he first came from Boston to Weirs Beach in 1914. But, he had a dream and a drive, and developed a new music venue called the Winnipesaukee Gardens, on the Weirs dock.

It was not long before it was drawing in superior entertainers, from Duke Ellington (left) and Lionel Hampton to the Beach Boys and the Kingsmen. People loved it, filling the Weirs boardwalk summer night after summer night. Pictured above is a typical evening crowd waiting to get into the venue.

After World War II, Irwin began focusing on the boating business he had started in 1919. As a result, Irwin Marine has been America's premier Chris-Craft dealer for the last 66 years and a major Sea Ray dealer since 1983. The third generation, family-owned and operated business has also been named a Top 100 national boat dealer and is recognized in the boating industry as a leader. (Above, courtesy of Irwin Marine; left, courtesy of Lake Winnipesaukee Historical Society.)

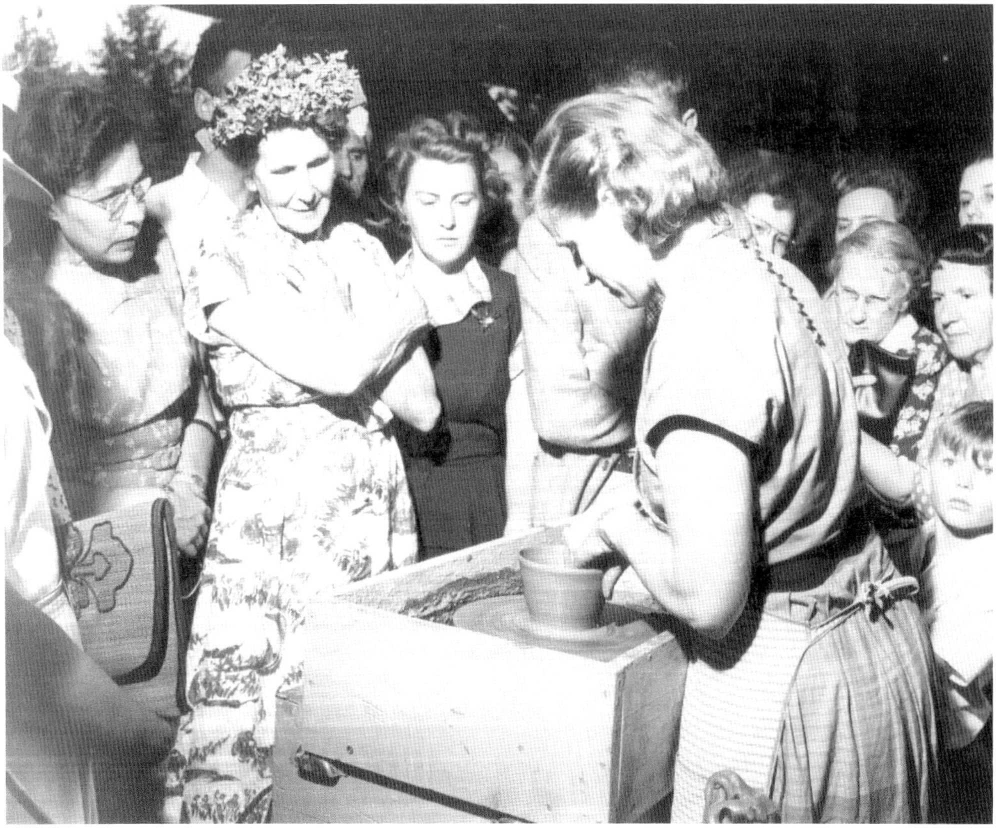

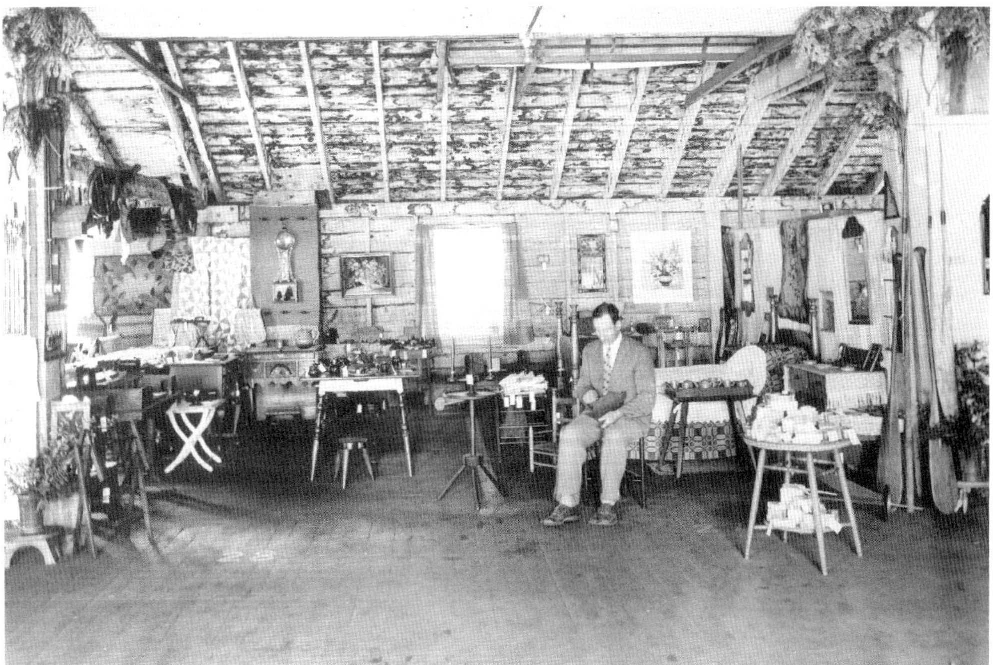

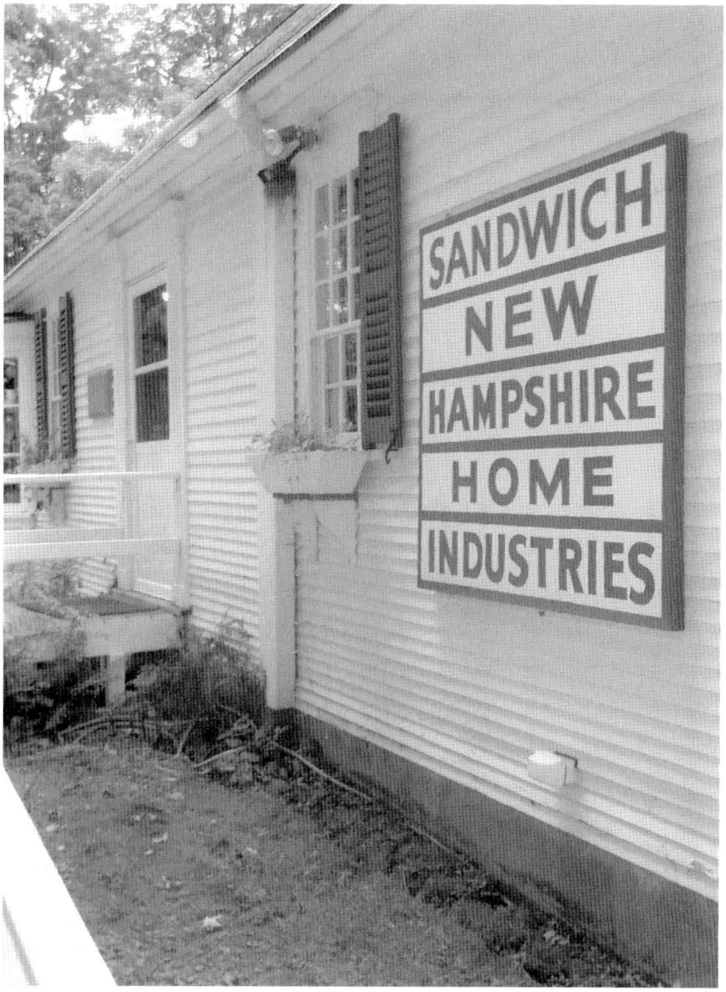

Crafting Home Goods (ABOVE AND OPPOSITE PAGE)
Small Lakes Region towns were often particularly hard hit by economic changes. For instance, when railroads resulted in the loss of business traffic along the Sandwich Notch Road in the mid-1800s, Sandwich faced severe difficulties. The town reinvented itself as a tourist mecca, opening lodging facilities and other businesses to serve city folks looking for a rest and the fresh summer air of the Lakes Region.

Another boost came when Mary Coolidge, a summer resident, noticed the fine work being done by local women gifted in handmade crafts such as hooked rugs, woolen knit sweaters, and pottery. Coolidge put some of their items on display, and the wealthier summer visitors bought them.

As time went on, Sandwich Home Industries, as the trade was called, grew in popularity. Eventually, Coolidge teamed up with A. Cooper Ballantine of Wolfeboro, who taught crafts, to form what is known today as the League of New Hampshire Craftsmen, made up of juried craftsmen from the region. Shown opposite, bottom, is an unidentified craftsman working at the organization's first annual fair, held in 1933 at the Crawford House in Crawford Notch, and (at top) a demonstration by popular potter Mary Scheier at a event in the 1950s.

The league still operates around the state, selling handmade goods at its affiliated fine craft galleries and stores, including one in Meredith and one (above) that sits very near to its original site in Center Sandwich. (Opposite, both courtesy of League of New Hampshire Craftsmen; above, author's collection.)

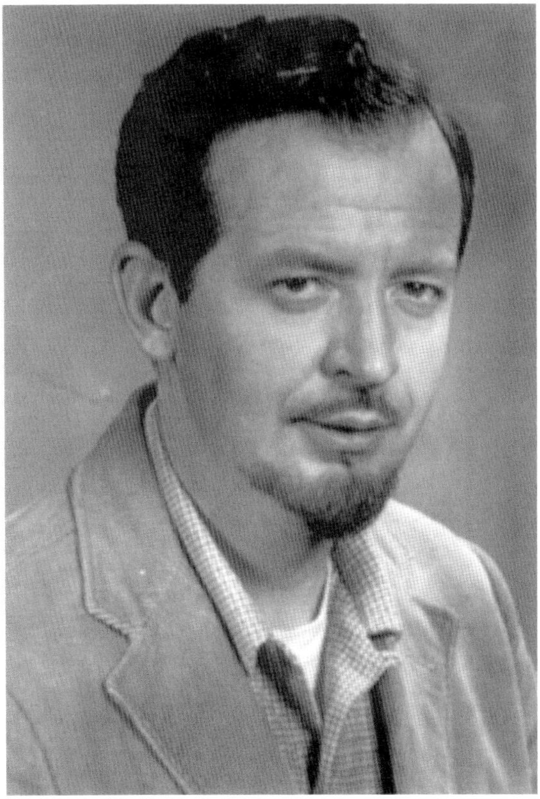

The Mirth of a Nation

In 1942, a young cartoonist named Bob Montana rented a cottage on Lake Waukewan in Meredith and spent time drawing up a comic strip featuring a new character—a teenage boy named Archie Andrews. Archie, Jughead, Betty, Veronica, and Reggie quickly became cultural icons, creating a cottage industry of comic books, memorabilia, and spin-off comic characters. After World War II, Montana moved permanently to Meredith, where he drew the popular daily *Archie* comic strips. (Both, courtesy of Lynn Montana. TM & © Archie Comic Publications, Inc. Used with permission.)

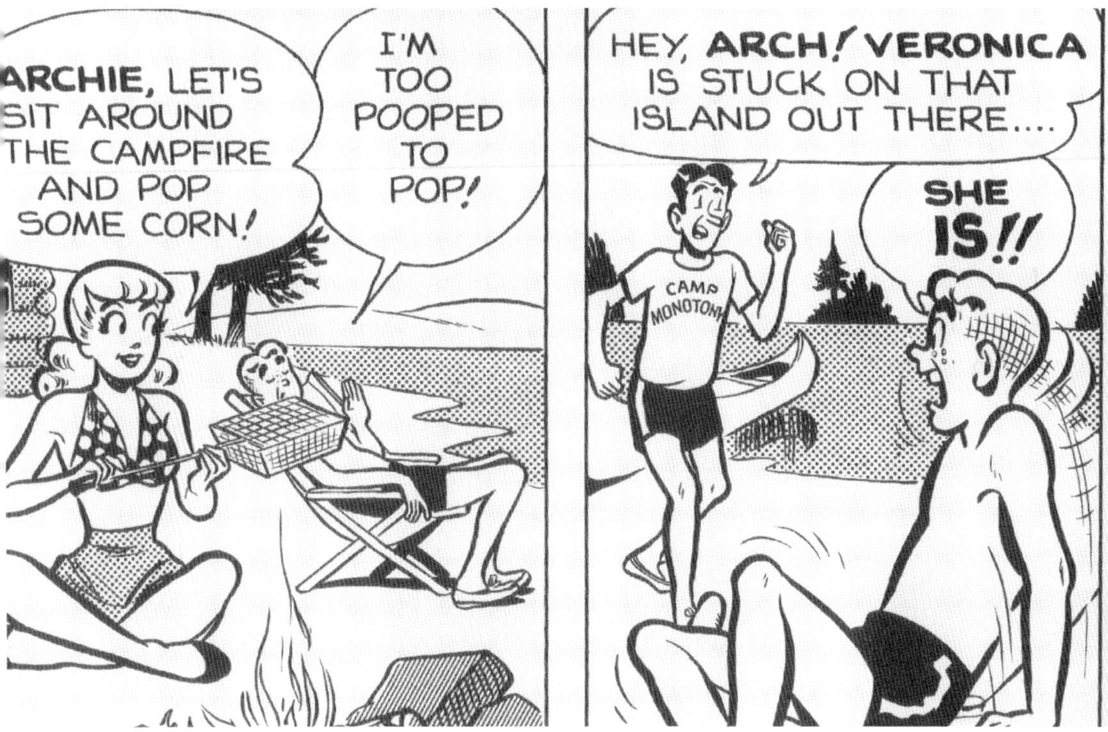

CHAPTER FIVE

Tourism Then and Now

As noted earlier, people have been coming to the Lakes Region for summertime recreation and relaxation since the 1700s, when Gov. John Wentworth set up his summer home in Wolfeboro.

But along the way, there are certain markers—individuals and groups who have made a significant impact on the development of tourism in the area.

Some seem almost accidental, like the emergence of the *Mount Washington* as a tourist vessel on Lake Winnipesaukee.

Others are more forthright, like the development of the Rockywold and Deephaven seasonal camps on Squam Lake.

Still others seem to be a fortuitous blending of opportunity and personality, as evidenced by the prominence of the late Sid Ames and his family in Weirs Beach.

However it comes about, the success reflects a deep truth about the region—bring frazzled, bedraggled, city-weary bodies and spirits, and the Lakes Region's crisp mountain air and clear blue lake waters will find a way to invigorate and restore them.

There is undoubtedly something innately refreshing here. Maybe it is that perfect blend of quiet and things to do, still mornings coupled with live music in a local restaurant, and children's beachside activities and the artistic options that adults can take advantage of. The region's attraction seems to harmonize into a mellifluous complement of ease and action, quiet and sound, new and old.

As time has moved on, the options for refreshment have grown. Now, hundreds of thousands of motorcyclists visit the area to attend the annual Laconia Motorcycle Week. Anglers by the thousands take part in the Winni Derby started by Rick Davis of Moultonborough, and Rockywold and Deephaven continue to draw campers.

Whether it is the water, the fishing, the games, or the roads, the Lakes Region is rich in the kind of off-the-beaten-path experiences that revive the human soul.

Thanks to those who have helped make it happen.

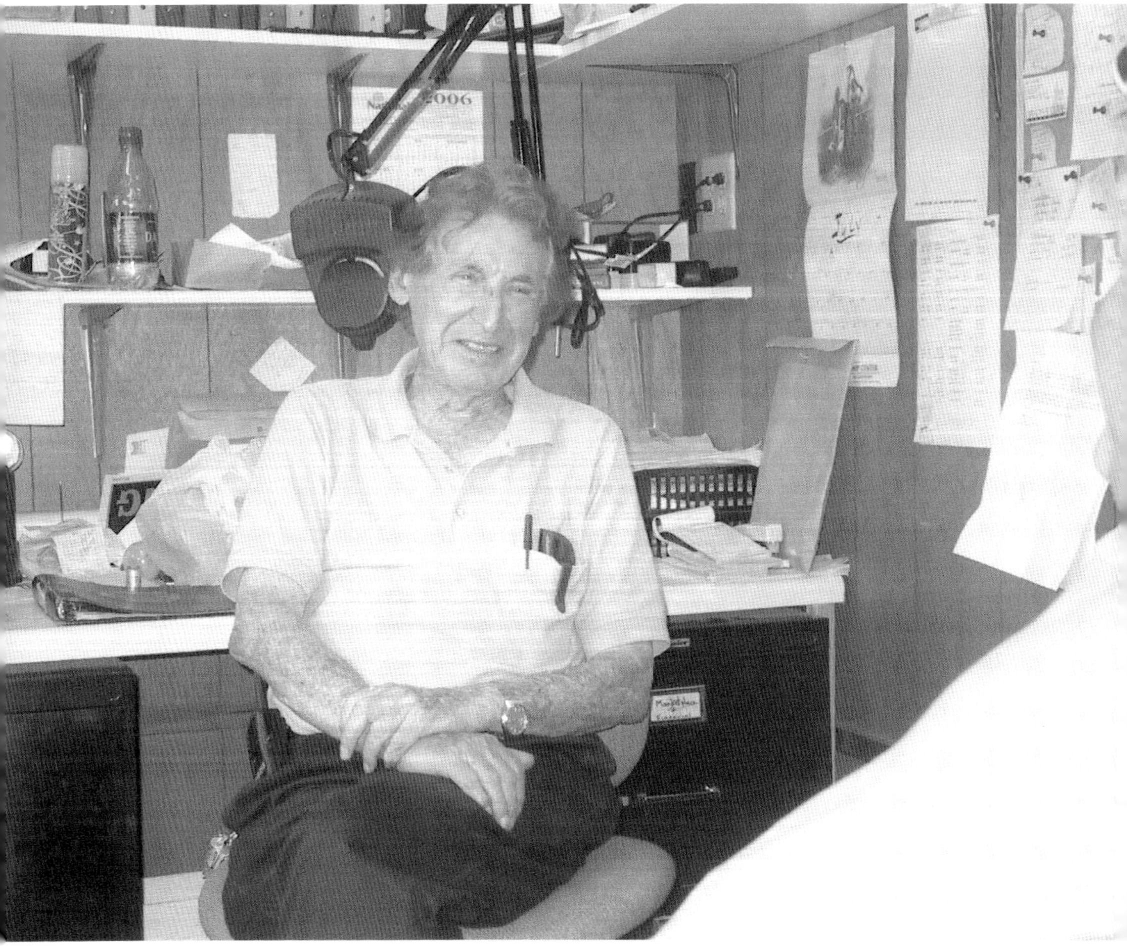

Mr. Weirs Beach

To many people, Sid Ames was the heart of Weirs Beach. He moved to the area with his family in 1950 and soon began building and developing entertainment businesses. In 1956, Ames was responsible for the iconic neon Weirs Beach sign, which still points drivers onto Lakeside Avenue. Today, Sid's three sons run the businesses, including the Half-Moon Arcade their father started. Sid Ames died in 2009. (Courtesy of Robert Ames.)

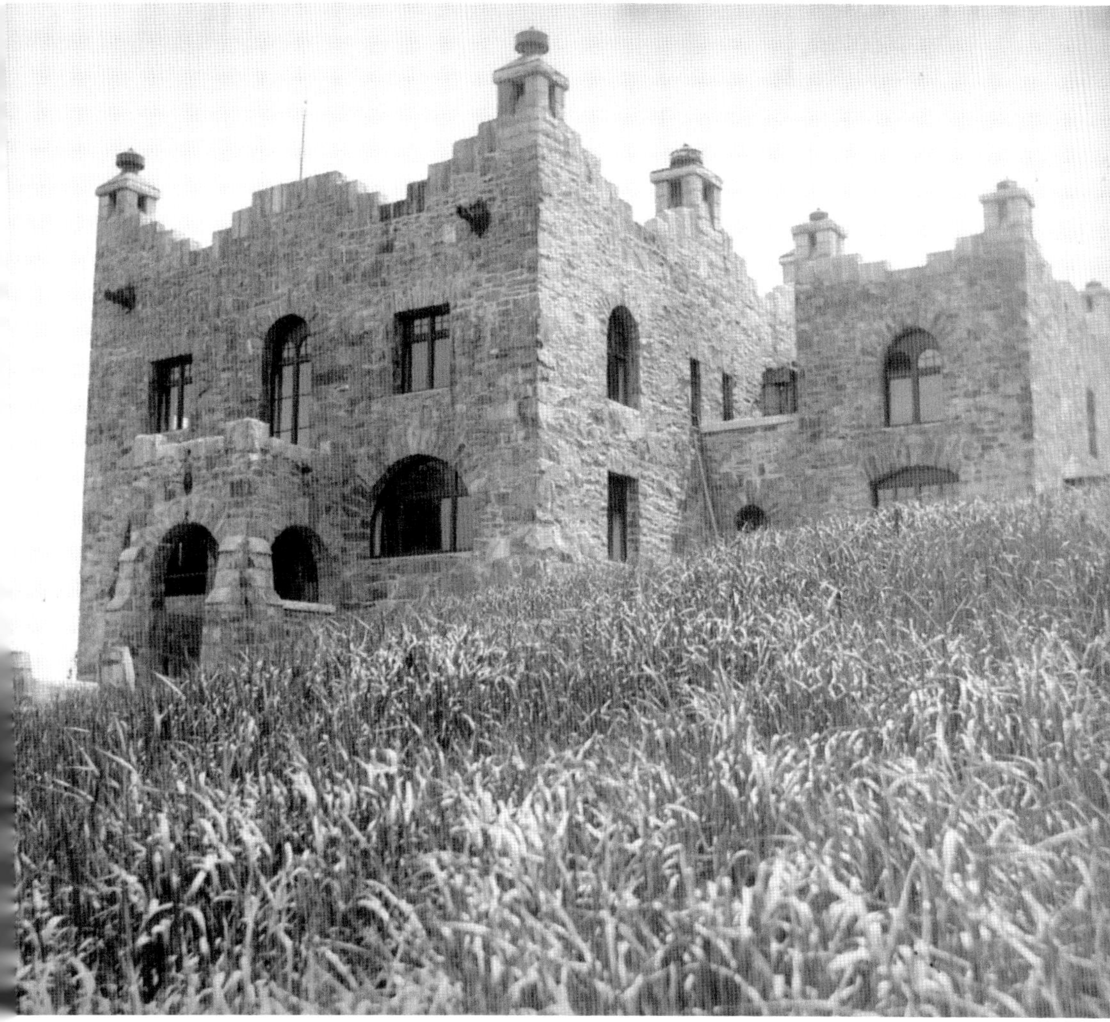

Castle is Home

Benjamin Ames Kimball was New Hampshire's 19th-century railroad baron. As president of the Concord & Montreal Railroad, he had authority over virtually all rail service in the Lakes Region, and he loved the area. In 1893, he traveled to Germany and was impressed by its hilltop castles. When he returned, he began work on a similar structure on top of Locke's Hill in Gilford. The castle overlooks the Broads section of Lake Winnipesaukee and was considered one of New Hampshire's finest seasonal residences for decades. It has been abandoned since the 1960s but is currently for sale. (Courtesy of Laconia Historical and Museum Society.)

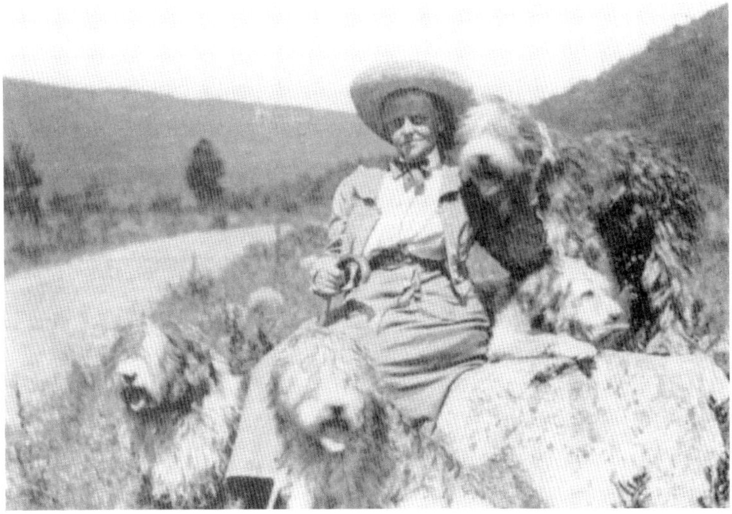

A World Apart

Lakefront summer camps built in the 19th century hold a special place in history. Created to serve as escapes from hot cities, they were places where family, faith, fun, and freedom were celebrated in a cool summer.

While most of these facilities have disappeared, the Rockywold and Deephaven camps in Holderness stand as great examples of a time when quietude and physical exertion were paramount in seasonal living. The two camps have somehow resisted changes to the basic philosophies of their founders: two women, Alice Mabel Bacon, who started Deephaven in 1897, and Mary Alice Armstrong (née Ford, see page 81), who founded Rockywold in 1901.

Deephaven was the inspiration of Bacon—a teacher, author, philanthropist, patriot, and Christian. "Build me a lodge and a road, that people may come hither and have rest," she wrote. Bacon is pictured above with her dogs, sitting on a stone wall.

Bacon loved the spirit of restfulness and friendliness her camp provided. "My camp is me," she said shortly before she died in 1917, "and I think of it, with its beauty and rational life, as one of the most worthwhile things I have ever done." (Both, courtesy of Rockywold-Deephaven Camps.)

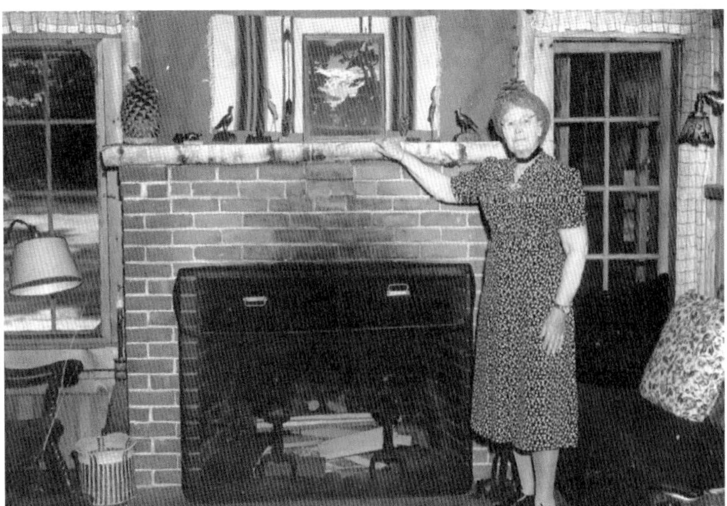

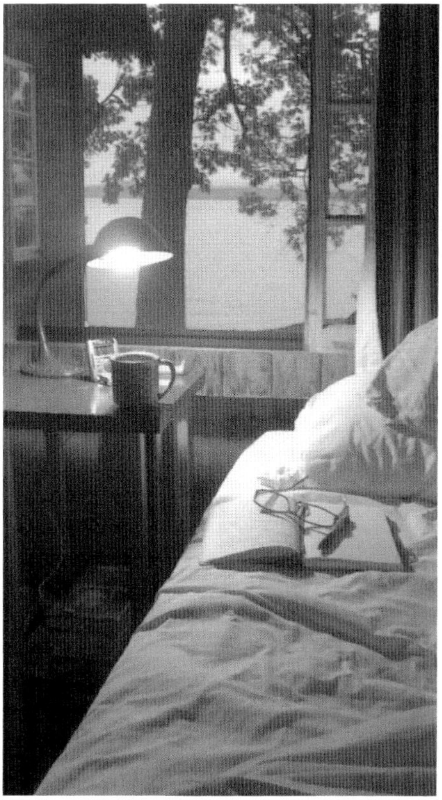

A Second World Nearby

In the early 1880s, Mary Alice Ford graduated from Plymouth Normal School (now Plymouth State University) as a teacher. Her first assignment was in Center Harbor, but she soon left to teach at the Hampton Institute in Hampton, Virginia. Hampton was one of the first colleges in America to accept former slaves, who were freed during the Civil War.

Ford eventually married Hampton's president, Gen. Samuel Chapman Armstrong, and they honeymooned on Asquam, as Squam Lake was sometimes known then.

The general died in 1893, and Alice Mabel Bacon (see page 80), who had come to know the Armstrong family, invited the widow to come to Deephaven for the summer. Later, in 1900, Bacon decided to travel abroad and asked Armstrong to manage Deephaven for a couple of years.

The replacement was so moved by the experience that in 1901 she bought land adjacent to Deephaven and opened Rockywold. Mary Alice Ford Armstrong is pictured on the preceding page, standing by a fireplace on her camp property, which is pictured on this page.

In 1918, the two camps joined together as a single operation. Today, they continue to host family and social gatherings of all kinds on the quiet shores of Squam Lake. (Both, courtesy of Rockywold-Deephaven Camps.)

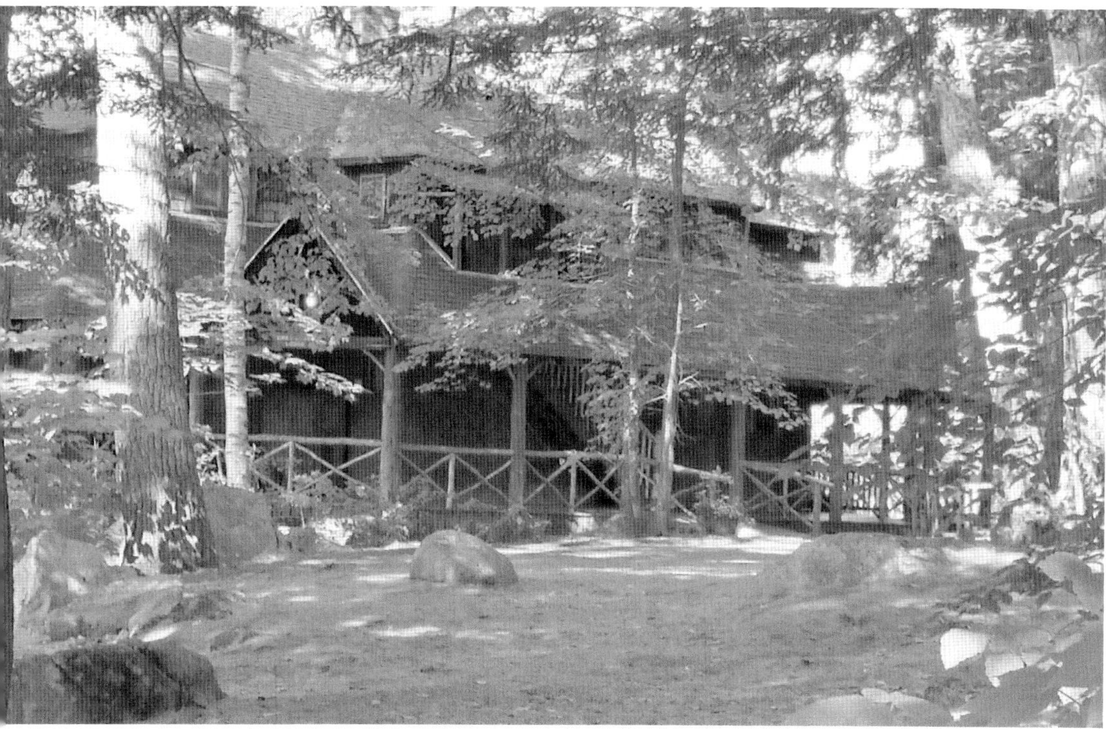

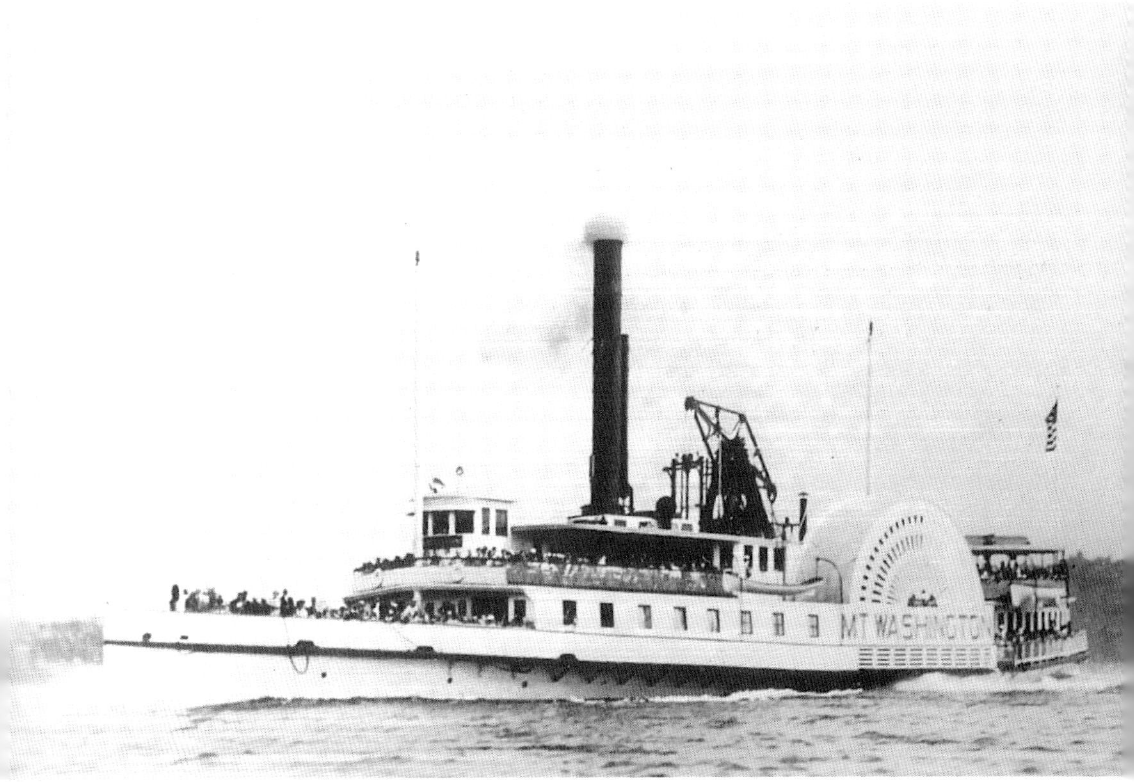

"Here Comes the *Mount*"

The *Mount Washington*, the passenger ship that sails around Lake Winnipesaukee, has been an integral part of Lakes Region life since the first iteration, in 1872. Since that time, there have been innumerable changes—most significantly, the replacement of the original boat with a newer version in the 1940s.

One former captain of the boat deserves special attention. When increases in automobile travel spelled the end of freight use for the original side-wheeler, Capt. Leander Lavallee bought the ship from the Boston & Maine Railroad and turned it into a passenger tourist vessel—a role it still fills ably today. It took time for businesses to reward his confidence, and he was fond of saying, "I'm boat poor and boat crazy."

After a fire destroyed the original *Mount* (above) in 1939, Lavallee worked diligently to find a replacement and fund its refitting and launch. (Courtesy of Lake Winnipesaukee Historical Society.)

Airport on Ice

It is the only FAA-approved ice-covered airfield in the continental United States. But it might not be in Alton Bay if not for Paul La Rochelle, Steve Bell, and Roger Sample.

The three local men were concerned after the winter facility, which had been in operation since the 1980s, closed down after a longtime snowplow man said he could no longer do the job. Community leaders loved the way the airfield drew in pilots from around the East and supported the effort.

Several meetings with state officials meant the airfield could reopen and continue to host its popular winter festival in February if La Rochelle and his cohorts would accept official responsibilities. Now, almost 10 years later, the trio is on the job every winter, updating online airport information for pilots and generally keeping the unusual operation going. La Rochelle is pictured here. (Courtesy of the La Rochelle family.)

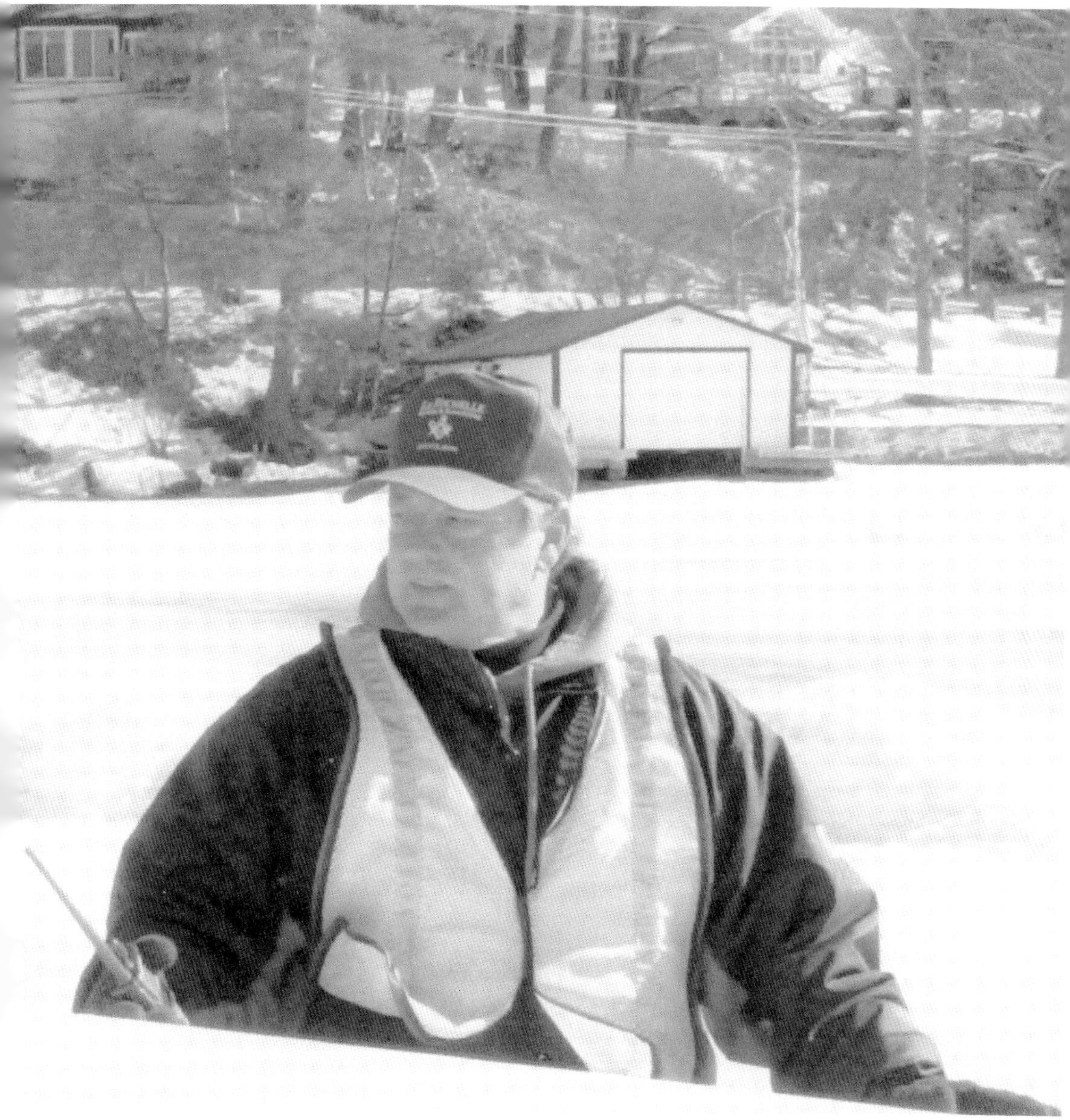

Castle in the Clouds (BELOW AND OPPOSITE PAGE)

In 1859, Thomas Gustave Plant was born in Maine to poor parents of French-Canadian heritage. He left school and started working at the age of 14 as a manual laborer. Around 1880, Plant left Maine and wound up in Lynn, Massachusetts, which was then known as the "shoemaking capital of the world."

Plant worked his way through several skilled shoe manufacturing jobs and eventually purchased a share in a small shoemaking company. He later shared ownership in two different companies before starting the Thomas G. Plant Company in 1891. A few years later, he moved his operations to Boston and developed a state-of-the-art factory. Eventually, his business could claim to be the most successful shoe-manufacturing firm in the country; its Queen Quality and Dorothy Dodd women's shoe lines were sold all over North America.

Plant was a so-called "enlightened capitalist," a supporter of the Progressive Party and Pres. Theodore Roosevelt. His factory instituted numerous manufacturing innovations and unusual recreational and service facilities, as well as an adjacent park for his employees.

But after a very public and bitter corporate battle with the monolithic international United Shoe Machinery Company, Plant sold his factory and his shoe machinery patents and retired a millionaire in 1919, as one of the wealthiest French-Canadians in America.

Several years later, he decided to build a country home on a Moultonborough mountain overlooking Lake Winnipesaukee. The estate, which he and his wife, Olive, named Lucknow, included over 6,500 acres of unspoiled land. The castle, which is still standing, is an excellent example of luxurious country living of the early 20th century. It includes many then-modern conveniences, expensive furnishings throughout, and living quarters for servants. Built in the Arts and Crafts aesthetic, the exterior façade of cut stone, oak timbers, and terra-cotta tile roofing was designed to harmonize with the natural surroundings.

Plant was a better industrialist than an investor, and his net worth soon toppled. By 1924, Lucknow was for sale. Plant could have achieved some financial stability by harvesting its timber, but he refused to mar the area's beauty.

Shortly after the stock market crashed in 1929, Plant declared bankruptcy. His creditors allowed him to live at Lucknow for some time. He died just before it was seized in 1941.

Today, the nonprofit Castle Preservation Society manages the property, offering tours and other amenities to the public. (Opposite, portrait by Alphonse Jongers, courtesy of PlantHome.org; below, courtesy of Castle in the Clouds.)

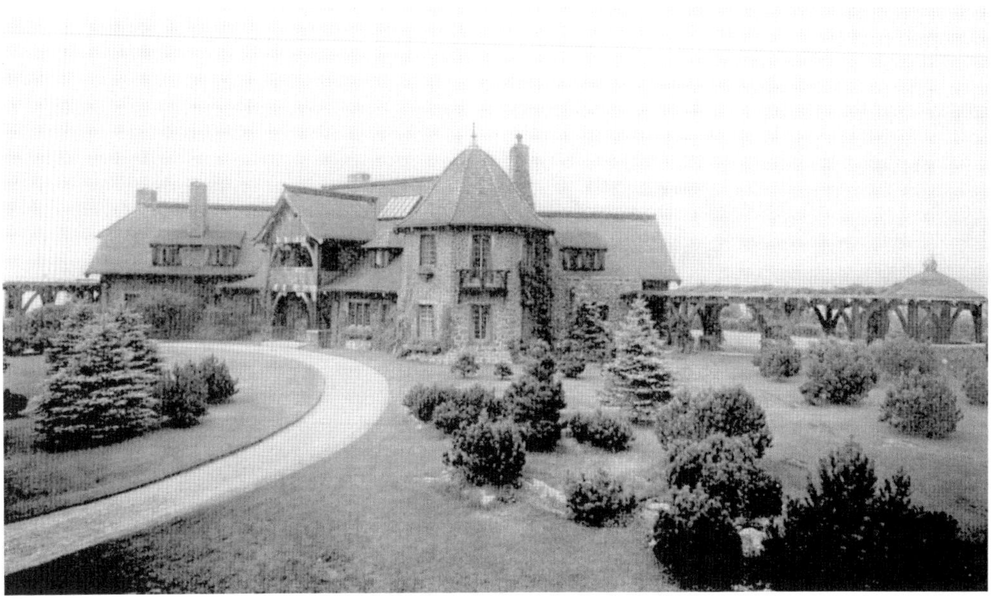

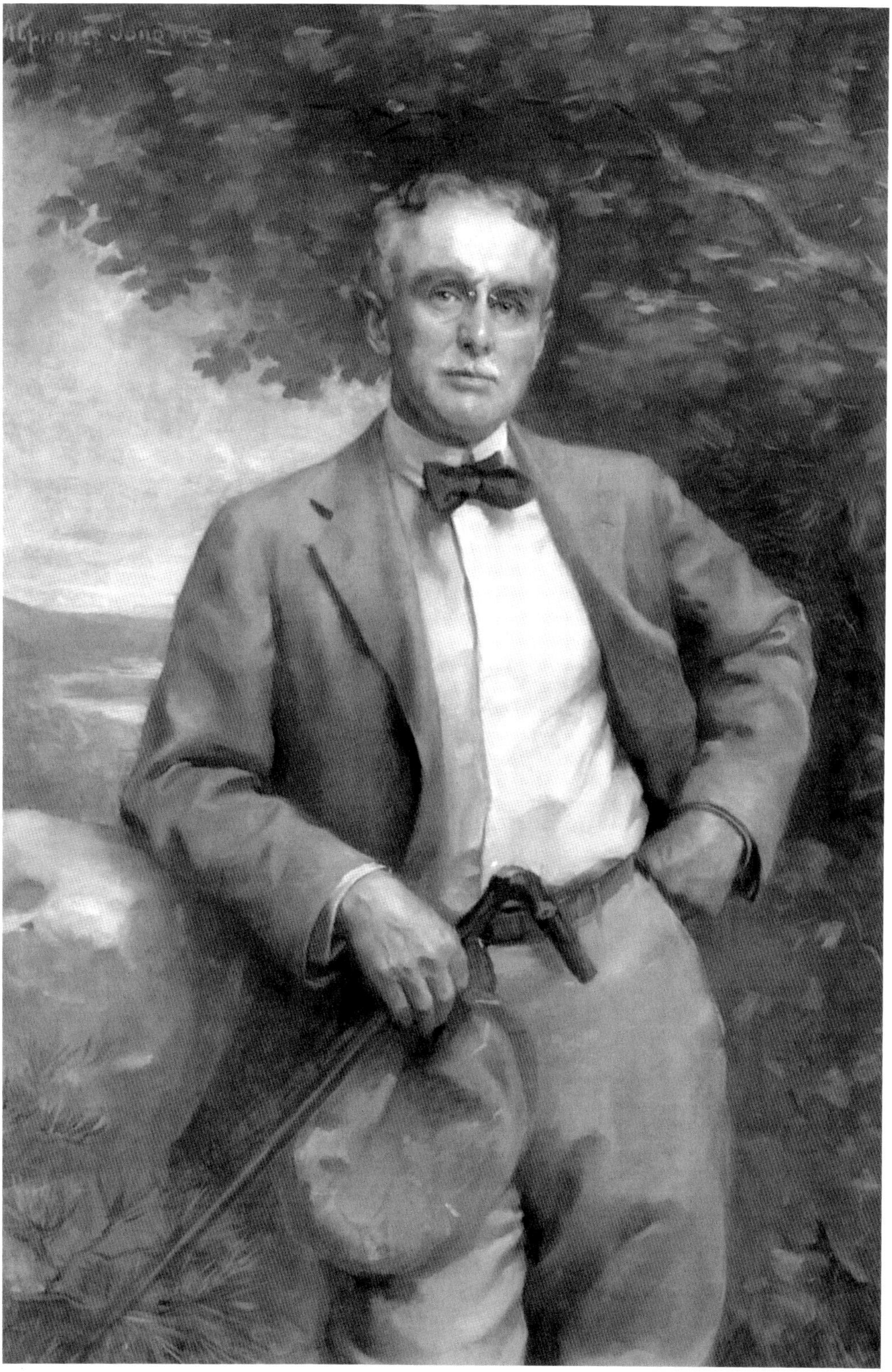

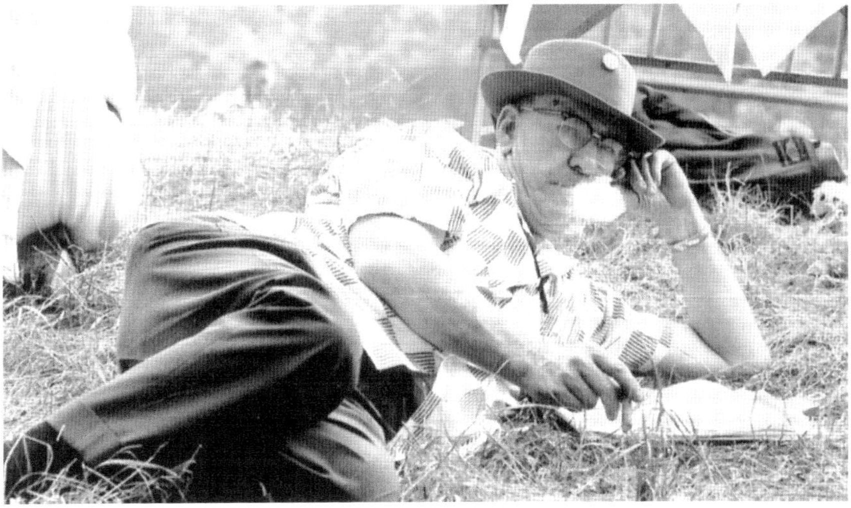

Baer of a Man

Frank "Fritzie" Baer is commonly considered the man who made Laconia Motorcycle Week a significant annual event. Baer was a major figure in modern motorcycling from the 1930s through the 1960s. He was a racer, dealer, club president, announcer, mechanic, sponsor, and employee of the original Indian Motorcycle company.

In 1938, Baer helped draw a popular American motorcycle road race to the Belknap Mountain Recreation Area (now called Gunstock Mountain Resort) in Gilford. With his distinctive red hat and cigar, he was a striking figure overseeing the event. He later became the recreation area's general manager, but remained involved with Motorcycle Week until his death in 1984.

During Fritzie's tenure, an annual motorcycle parade (pictured below) drove down Main Street. (Both, courtesy of Charlie St. Clair.)

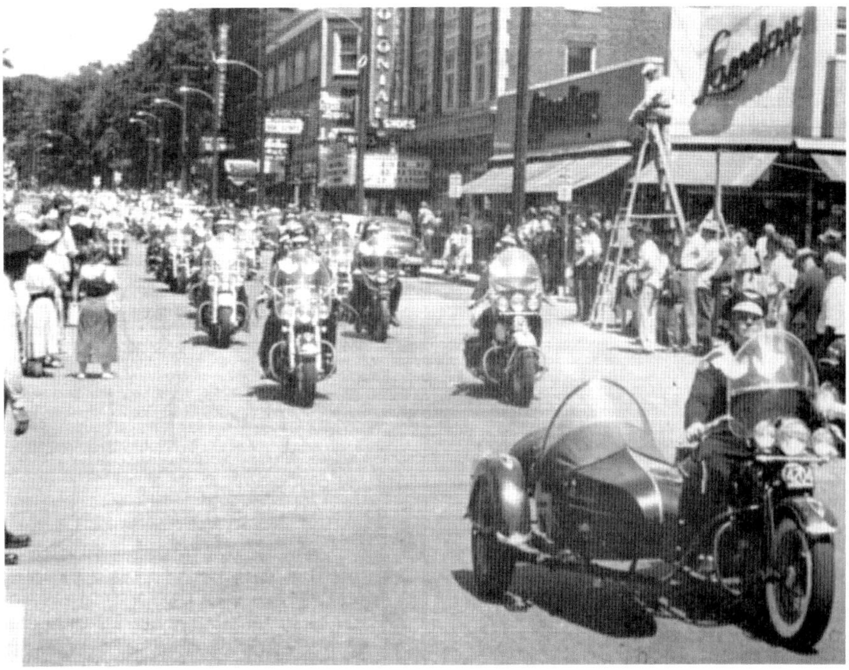

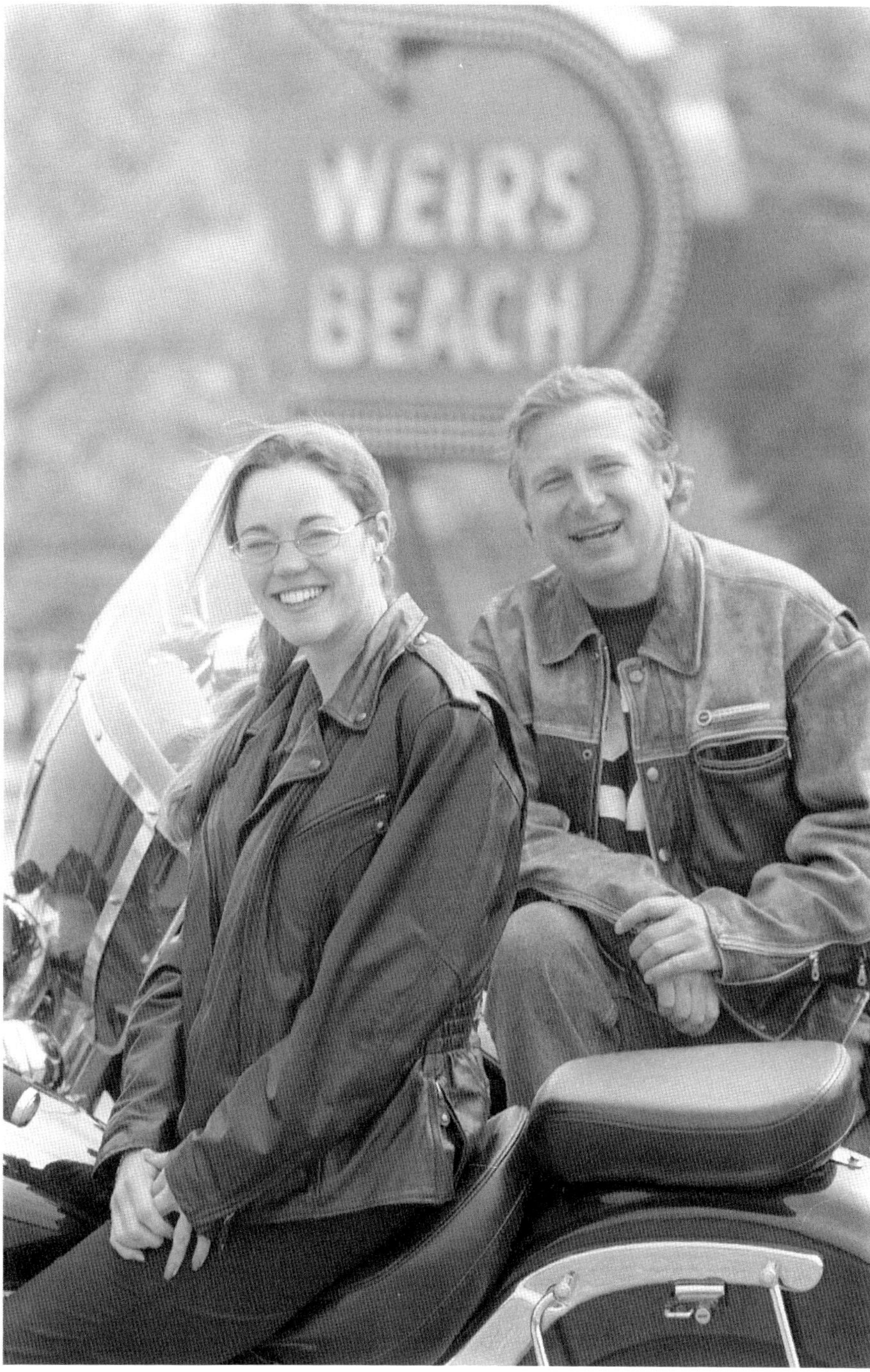

Motorcycle Week Man

Since the revival of Laconia Motorcycle Week in 1991, native Charlie St. Clair has led the charge to get the now nine-day rally recognized and appreciated by local communities, the state, and the nation. He and his colleague Jennifer Anderson now travel around the country promoting the event, which is the oldest rally in America. (Courtesy of Daryl Carlson/Kamara Image Photography.)

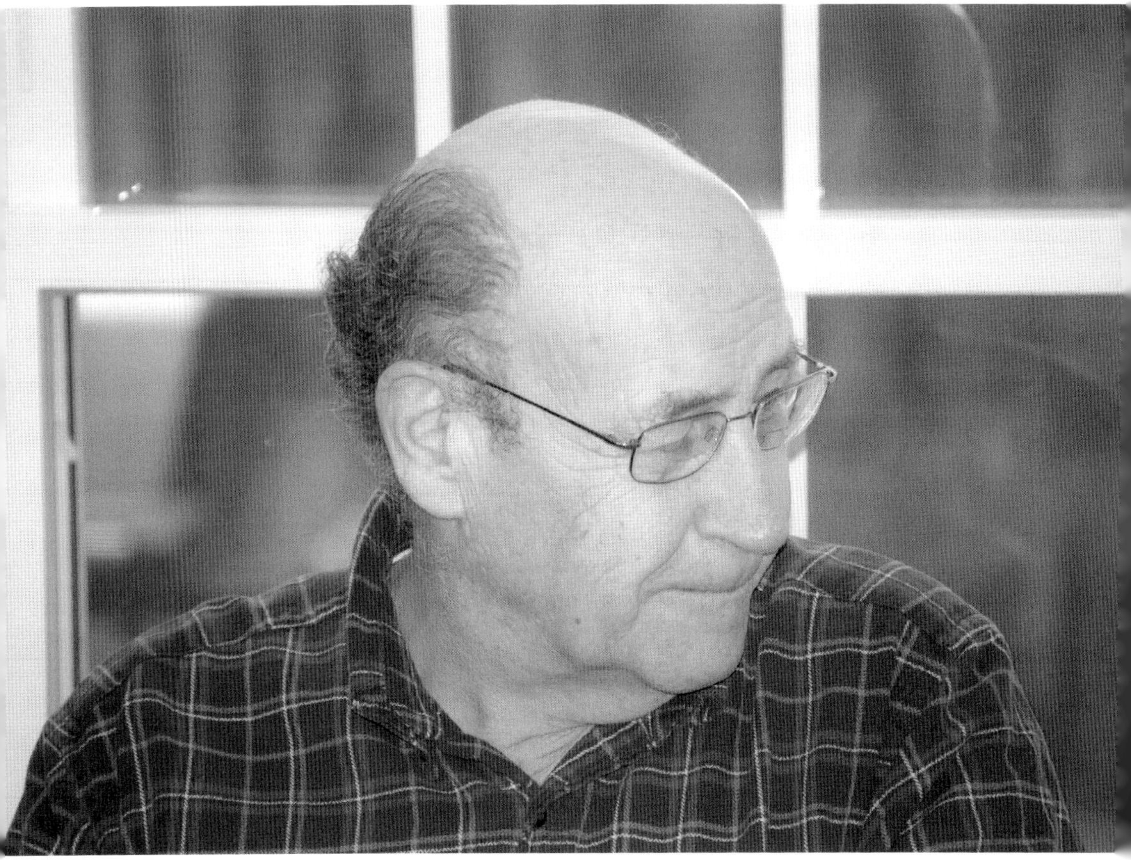

Fish in Water

After his father drowned in Squam Lake, Moultonborough native Rick Davis left school as a youngster to support his family. He bought the Paugus Bay Sporting Goods store in Laconia and ran it successfully for more than 20 years.

In the early 1970s, Davis started the Lakes Region Inland Fishing Association, managing its three-day annual Winni Derby; the event is now the largest landlocked salmon and lake trout tournament in the Northeast and draws thousands of people to the Lakes Region. He also spearheaded a smelt program for the New Hampshire Fish and Game Department and was cofounder of the Winnipesaukee Sportsmen's Club.

Davis was a warm, generous man who loved what he was doing, but, ironically, he did not fish for many years toward the end of his life. A fire destroyed his boat, and he could not bring himself to get back on the water. (Courtesy of the Davis family.)

CHAPTER SIX

In Service

I will always do my duty, no matter what the price.
I've counted up the cost, I know the sacrifice.
Oh, and I don't want to die for you,
But if dying's asked of me,
I'll bear that cross with honor,
'Cause freedom don't come free.

—Toby Keith

The lyrics of this country song are popular because they reflect the deep reverence America has for citizens who take on the roles of service.

In New Hampshire, this respect runs especially deep. And as the people in this chapter indicate, the respect is well placed.

Consider Harrison Thyng of Barnstead, whose exploits as a military pilot in World War II and the Korean War are too numerous to list here. And Carl Johnson, a World War II veteran who became a successful businessman and still served as a community leader for decades. In the Civil War, Maj. Gen. George D. Savage and Charles William Hunt fought bravely in the heroic 12th New Hampshire Volunteer Regiment at the brutal battles of Chancellorsville and Gettysburg.

There are also people included here whose service is closer to home.

Longtime Laconia police chief Mickey Dunleavy left a legacy of community service that is still recalled more than 50 years after he left the police department. Franklin fire chief Edgar Wheeler stands out as a heroic figure who advocated safety codes for buildings decades before they became the rule in many Lakes Region communities.

William Athanas and Tom Clairmont earned their stripes from years of community service. Athanas has been a dedicated educator for almost 50 years, and Clairmont was an innovative medical administrator for more than 40 years.

These are the kinds of people who are the backbone of the Lakes Region.

Without them, no community could stand.

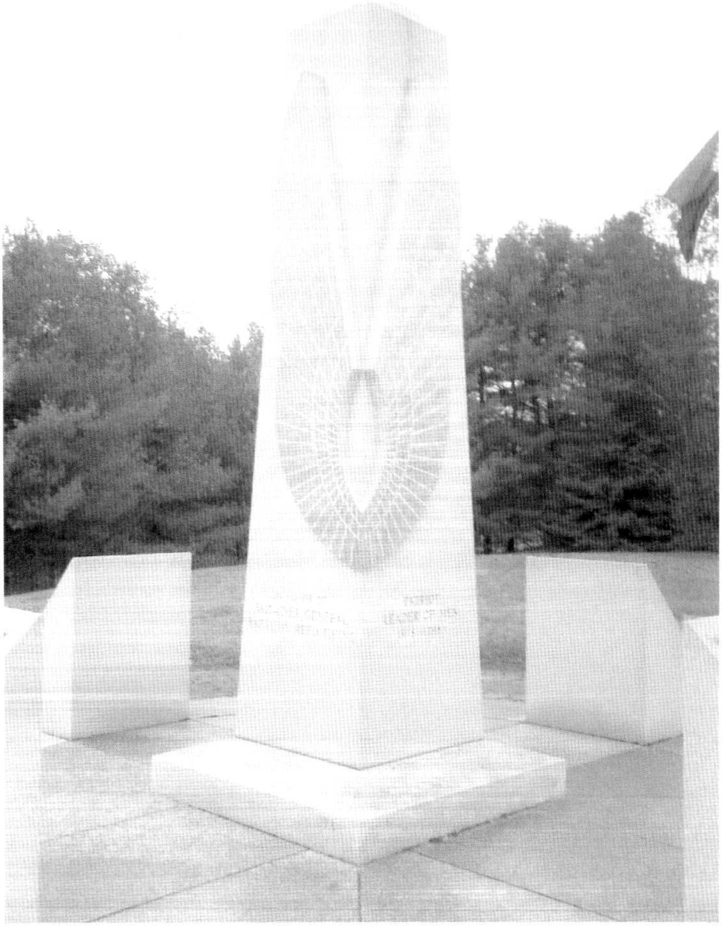

New Hampshire's First Ace

Brig. Gen. Harrison Thyng, born in Laconia and raised in Barnstead, was one of the most celebrated military pilots in American history, an ace in both World War II and Korea.

In 1942, Thyng was among a group of six senior pilots sent to England with their units to learn how to fly the British Spitfires, and he was the first US pilot to engage a German plane in air combat.

That same year, his squadron (along with two others) was secretly transferred to North Africa to fight in the invasion, America's official entry into World War II. He was once shot down by friendly fire and once crashed due to engine failure. Both times, he flew the next day after miraculous escapes.

In 1945, Thyng organized and trained a group that flew the first single-engine fighter planes over the Pacific Ocean. And, he was in the air close enough to see the atomic bomb drop on Nagasaki, Japan.

Thyng was a wing commander again in Korea, leading the 4th Fighter Interceptor Wing. He once took to the air all alone to fight off 48 enemy planes. "I did it to put some guts into the squadron," he said afterwards. While fighting every day, he still took the time to establish an orphanage for Korean children.

Thyng was called "the premier American fighter-wing commander of his era," and his Korean group was known as "the finest unit ever put into the field by any nation's air army."

After he retired to Pittsfield (adjacent to his hometown), Thyng became involved in local politics, serving on town boards and once running for the US Senate. He was also the first president of Daniel Webster College.

This monument, dedicated to Thyng's memory, was erected in nearby Pittsfield in 2004.

Chief among Equals

Edgar Wheeler served with the Franklin Fire Department for more than 37 years, beginning in 1904 as a hose operator and retiring as chief after serving in that role for nearly a decade.

Wheeler was a pioneer, stressing fire protection and championing building codes to insure safety in the 1930s—more than 60 years before his city formally adopted codes.

In 1930, Wheeler built a fire truck on the chassis of an older vehicle. Then in 1933, as chief, he had another truck built on a chassis; it was the first rescue truck in New Hampshire, carrying first-aid equipment for firefighters at a fire scene. His department was also the first in the state with a trained rescue squad. Another innovation Wheeler used was putting lights on a Mack truck to illuminate night incidents, even though his department's own engineers said it could not be done. Wheeler is pictured here at far right with unidentified members of his department.

Wheeler's career ended abruptly after he got into a dispute with a local storeowner about what the chief considered a fire hazard in the store. He resigned in 1941 but later went on to speak in Concord about the need to separate fire departments from "political pressure (that) can be brought to bear on fire department officials." (Courtesy of Franklin Firefighters Museum.)

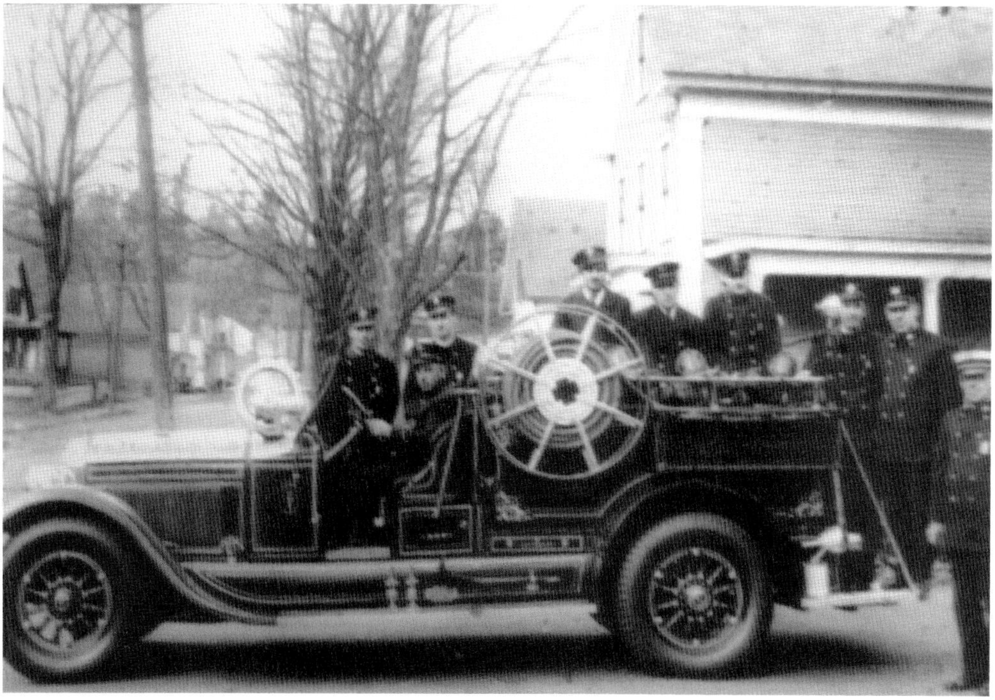

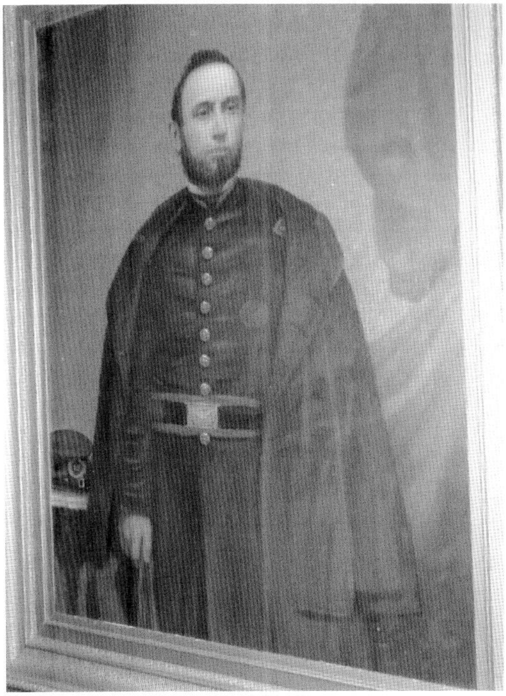

Brave Doctor

Charles William Hunt of Gilford was a member of the 12th New Hampshire Volunteer Regiment (see page 96). Hunt was born in 1832, grew up in town, and practiced medicine in Gilford until the Civil War erupted. He then joined the Union army and was appointed assistant surgeon of the regiment. Military reports assert he was "brave and faithful" during major battles at Chancellorsville and Gettysburg.

At the latter battle, Hunt was taken captive. He died after contracting typhoid fever while treating Southern soldiers in a Confederate hospital. (Courtesy of Thompson-Ames Historical Society.)

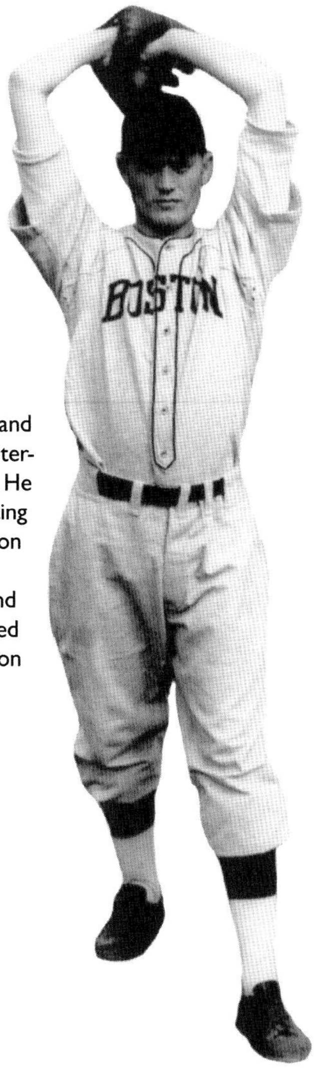

Pitching In

Carl Johnson was the owner of a local distribution company and a committed public servant. He served for decades on the Inter-Lakes School Board and nearly 30 years as a state legislator. He also cared about the natural assets of the Lakes Region, devoting time to the Lakes Region Conservation Trust and the Loon Preservation Society.

Johnson was a Coast Guard veteran of World War II and served in the Pacific for three years. As a young man, he signed a contract to be a professional baseball pitcher with the Boston Braves in 1940. (Courtesy of the Leadbeater family.)

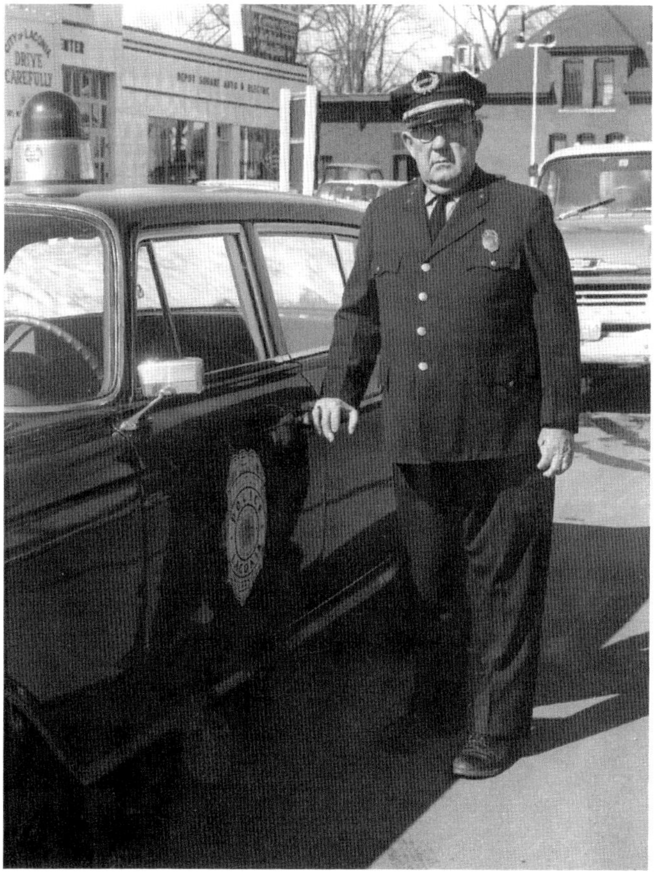

"Common Sense, Good Judgment, and Courage."
Charles Edward "Mickey" Dunleavy was a popular Laconia police chief in the mid-20th century. Born in 1899, the city native was a big Irishman who attended local Catholic schools and served in the artillery during World War I. He joined the police force in 1925, was appointed deputy chief in 1934, and named chief in 1948.

Dunleavy was well known and liked in the city (newspapers commonly referred to him simply as Mickey) for his down-to-earth approach to policing. "Common sense and good judgment, plus courage," are what made a good policeman, he would say.

The chief was particularly committed to the children of the city and frequently participated in special fundraising programs; he attended events like soapbox derbies and Little League games, and his annual Halloween party was famous among local children. His affection spread to both the underprivileged in the city and the developmentally disabled children who lived at the Laconia State School.

Prohibition was still in effect when Dunleavy first joined the force, and as a result, he had his most dramatic experience when he instinctively jumped on to the running board of a bootlegger's car as the driver sped away. Mickey clung on for several miles before finally breaking the back window, crawling through the space, and apprehending the man.

When he retired in 1962, Mickey said he would rather be remembered simply as a policeman than the long-serving chief. He had been honored several times for saving people in dangerous situations while on duty, but he always brushed the compliments aside with the comment that whatever he did was "part of the job."

Dunleavy died unexpectedly in 1966 while picking blueberries at a Gilford farm. (Courtesy of the Dunleavy family.)

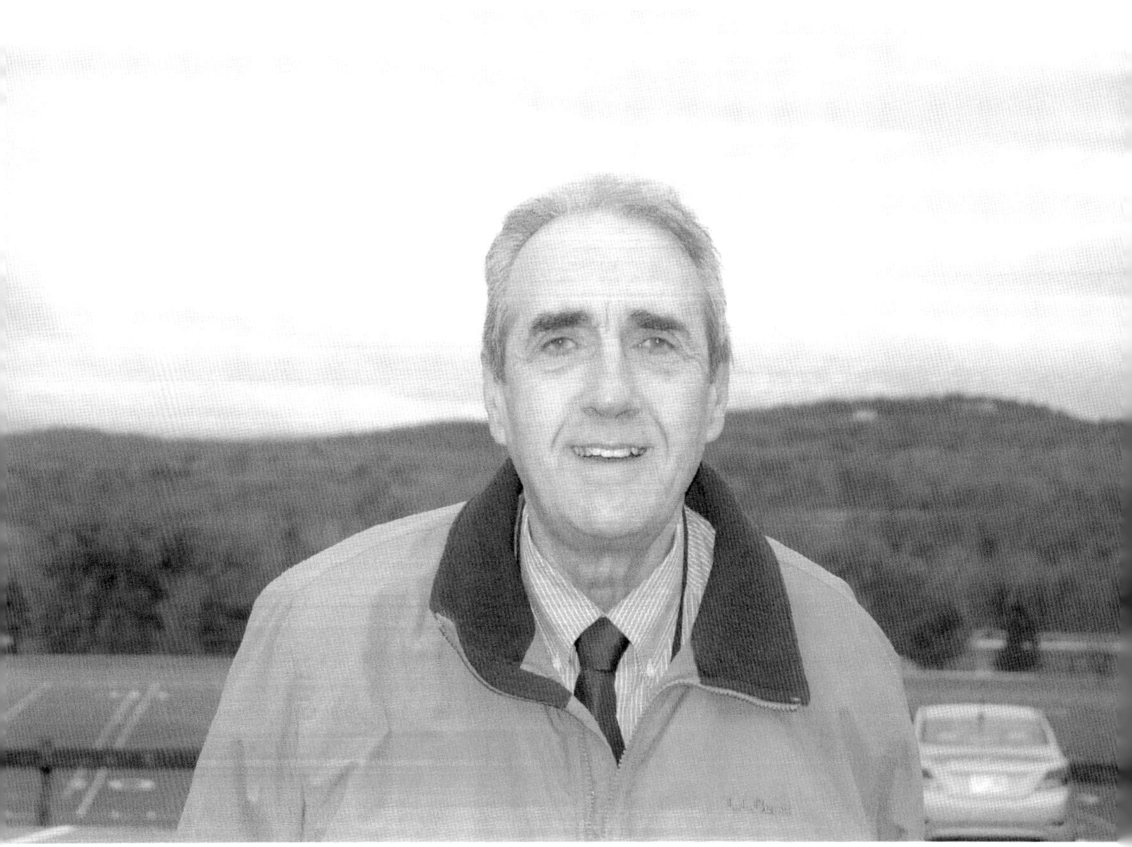

The Legend

"The Legend" is what people call William R. Athanas after his 31 years of service as a teacher and assistant principal at Franklin High School and now in his 18th year as assistant principal at Inter-Lakes High School in Meredith.

"Being around young people keeps me young," he says. Athanas shows care and respect for his students every morning by meeting them as they exit their buses outside in the parking lot—no matter what the weather. He also goes to numerous athletic events and is always available to talk with the youngsters, as well as staff members and parents.

"Someday the principal will call me into his office and say, 'Bill, you can't find your own office anymore," he joked. "Then I'll know it's time to retire." (Courtesy of Inter-Lakes High School.)

From Lakes Region Mayor to Presidential Aide

Bernie Boutin was a Belmont native who owned an insurance company in Laconia and was active in New Hampshire's Democratic Party. After moving to Laconia, he served two terms as mayor, from 1955 to 1959. He also ran as his party's candidate for governor in 1958 and 1960.

Boutin lost both statewide races, but in 1960, he helped engineer an important victory in the state's presidential primary for Massachusetts senator John F. Kennedy. The day after Kennedy was elected president, he called and asked Boutin to "sell the business and come to Washington with me."

Boutin served as administrator of the general services administration under both Kennedy and his successor, Lyndon Johnson. He later was deputy director of the office of economic opportunity and director of the small business administration.

Boutin was particularly fond of Kennedy's wife, Jacqueline. He loved to recall an incident when Jackie Kennedy asked him to revise a plan to redesign the capital's famous Lafayette Square that would have demolished the historic Ford Theatre. When Boutin finally acquired the new plans, the First Lady asked him to come immediately to the White House, and on the floor of the Blue Room, she and Boutin reviewed the designs.

When Boutin left Washington, he continued to serve in various prestigious roles and on numerous regional boards. He was the first layperson chosen to be president of St. Michael's College, a Catholic school in Vermont. Boutin died while living in Meredith in 2011, at the age of 88. (Courtesy of Daryl Carlson/Kamara Image Photography.)

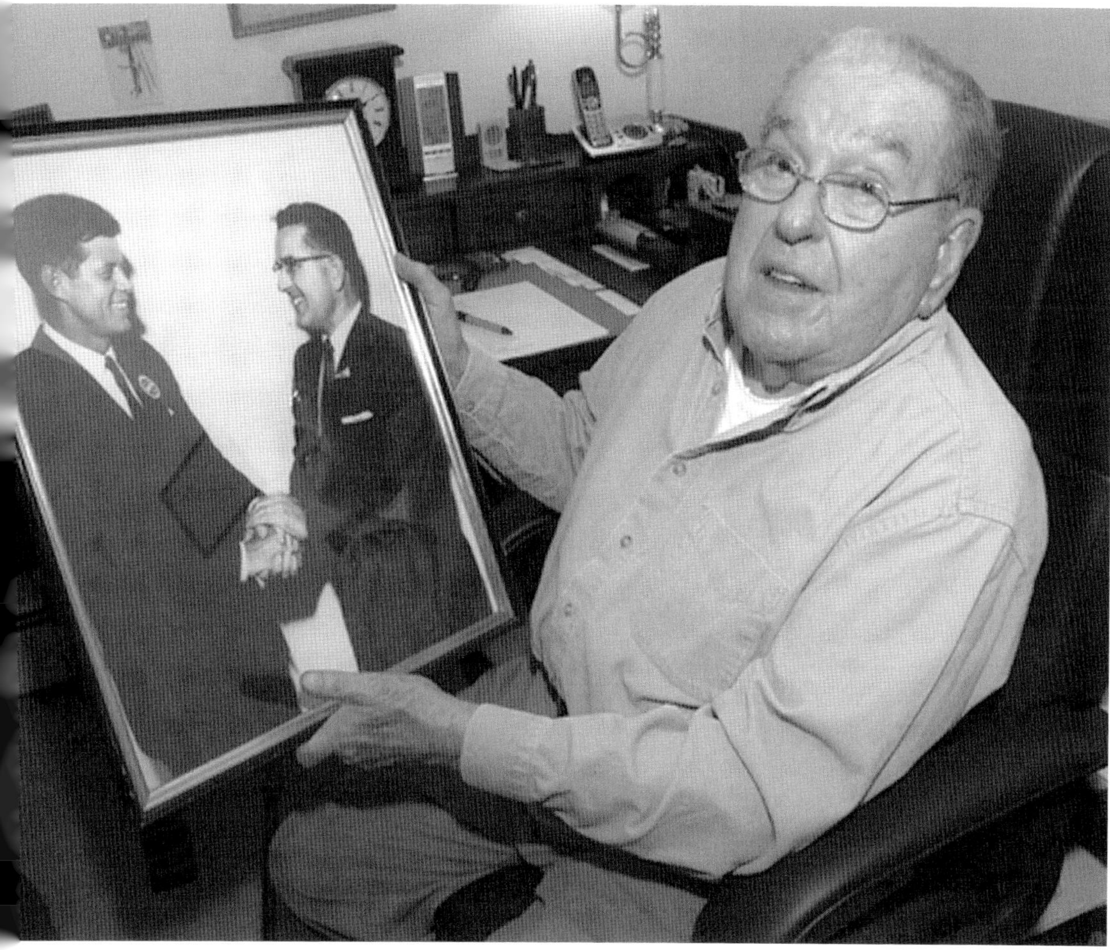

A Horse, a Memorial, a Regiment (BELOW AND OPPOSITE PAGE)

When Maj. Gen. George D. Savage asked to have his horse Old Tom buried in Alton's Old Riverside Cemetery (so it would be at his side, as it was during his military career), town leaders refused. So, the animal was buried outside the fence surrounding the cemetery. But, the cemetery grew as the town did, and eventually Old Tom's plot was incorporated into the grounds.

It is a fitting memorial—not just to the horse but also to Savage and his cohorts in the area's Company A, 12th New Hampshire Volunteer Regiment, which fought for the Union during the Civil War. The group, which trained in what is now Monument Square in front of Alton Town Hall, was in the bloody battle at Chancellorsville in May 1863 and among the units that suffered the greatest casualties. Commanding officers apparently forgot to call them back during a retreat. Savage's brother, Capt. Moses Savage, died in the battle, and Major General Savage was shot through the jaw but managed to survive.

After the war, Savage returned to Alton and operated the Savage Tavern until his death in 1883, regularly giving Civil War veterans and their families special consideration. His building, which was used by veteran groups for decades, still stands in Monument Square.

Another Alton Civil War veteran was Charles Estes, who served in the 3rd New Hampshire Regiment of Volunteers. Estes was wounded twice at the battle for Fort Wagner, South Carolina (the inspiration for the 1989 film *Glory*), and was sent to Washington to recover from his injuries. That is how he happened to be among the military guards who moved Pres. Abraham Lincoln after he was shot at Ford's Theatre to the boardinghouse across the street where the president later died.

After the war, Estes moved to Alton and was good friends with a fellow veteran named Nathan Chesley, who had served with Savage. Estes proudly carried Chesley's raised sword in local patriotic parades for many years. (Below, author's collection; opposite, courtesy of the Alton Historical Society.)

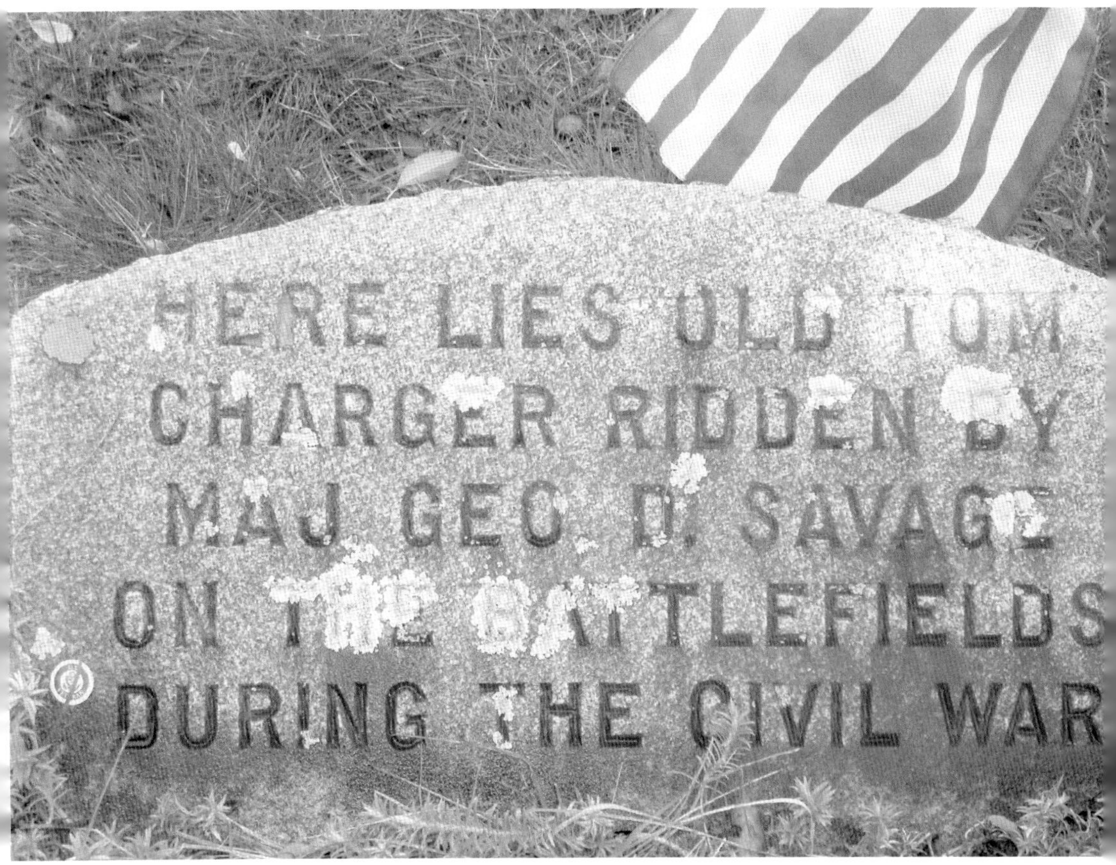

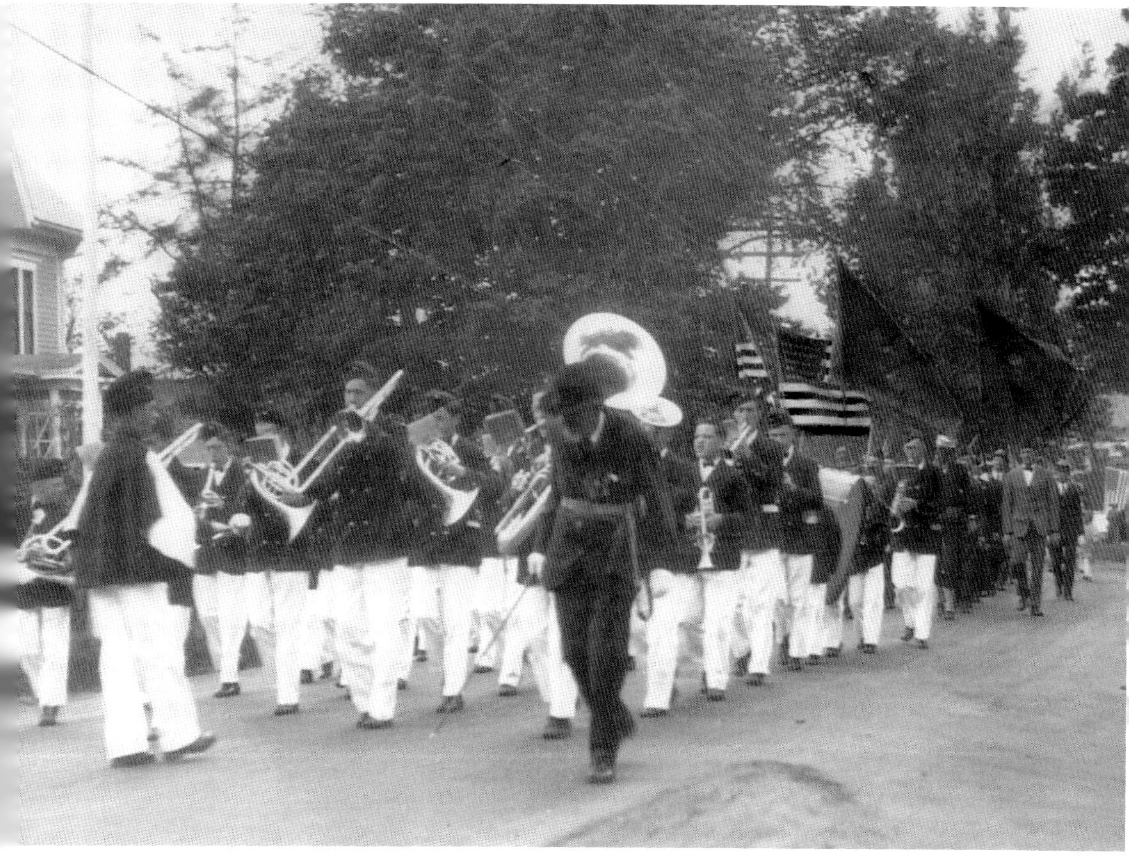

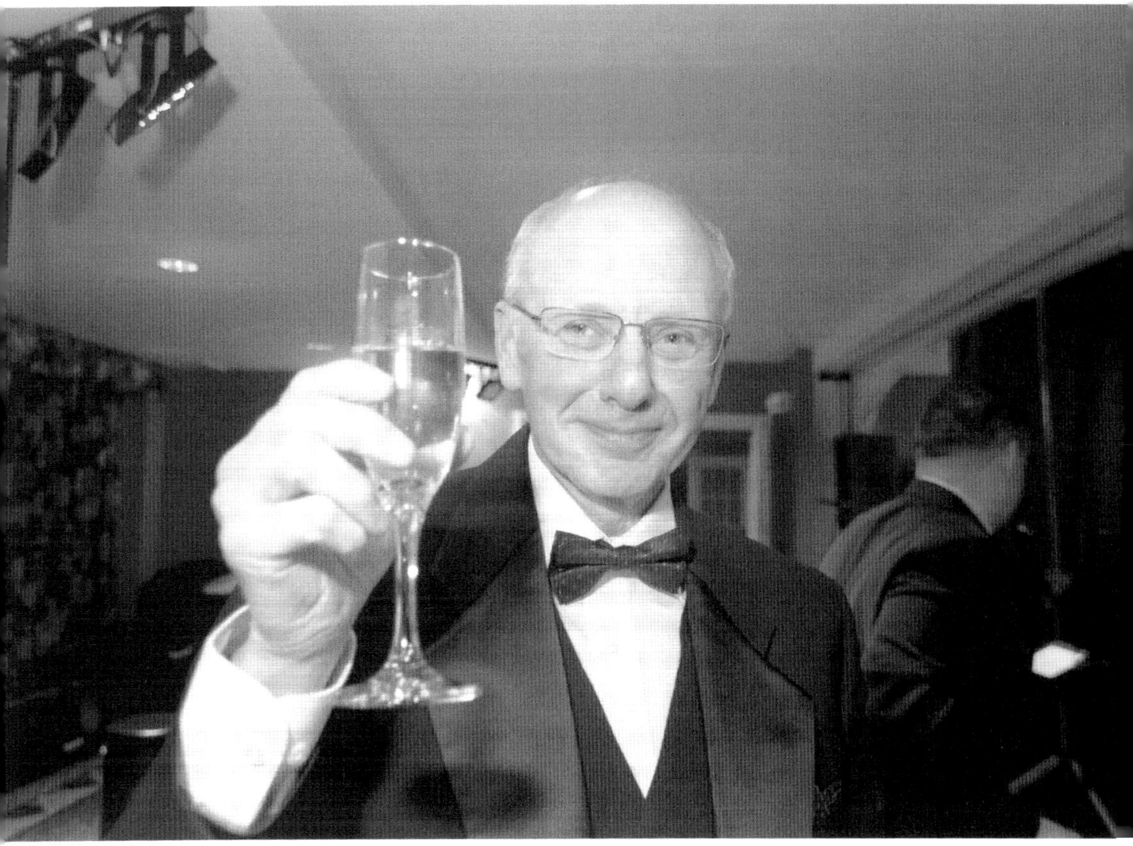

Just a Belmont Pig Farmer

Tom Clairmont liked to describe himself as a "pig farmer from Belmont." He was that—and a supporter of the use of bio solids—but he was also the man who helped turn Lakes Region General Hospital into LRGHealthcare, the largest healthcare provider and employer in the area.

During his 43 years with the organization—the last 25 as its president and chief executive offer—Clairmont repeatedly showed an encompassing interest in the overall health and wellbeing of people in the Lakes Region. Under his leadership, LRGHealthcare agreed with Laconia to share the costs of city ambulance service, built the Inter-Lakes Medical Center in Meredith, put a 97,000-square-foot addition onto LRGH, merged with Franklin Regional Hospital and renovated that facility, developed a local Convenience Care clinic, added a psychiatric department to FRH, and introduced specialties like MAKOplasty knee and hip surgery and the Weight Institute of New Hampshire.

Independently, he also supported the creation of local fitness programs, elderly daycare, a dental service center, and a holistic health center. In addition, Clairmont was a key player in getting the Lakes Region online in the 1990s.

He resigned from his LRGHealthcare position in 2014. (Courtesy of LRGHealthcare.)

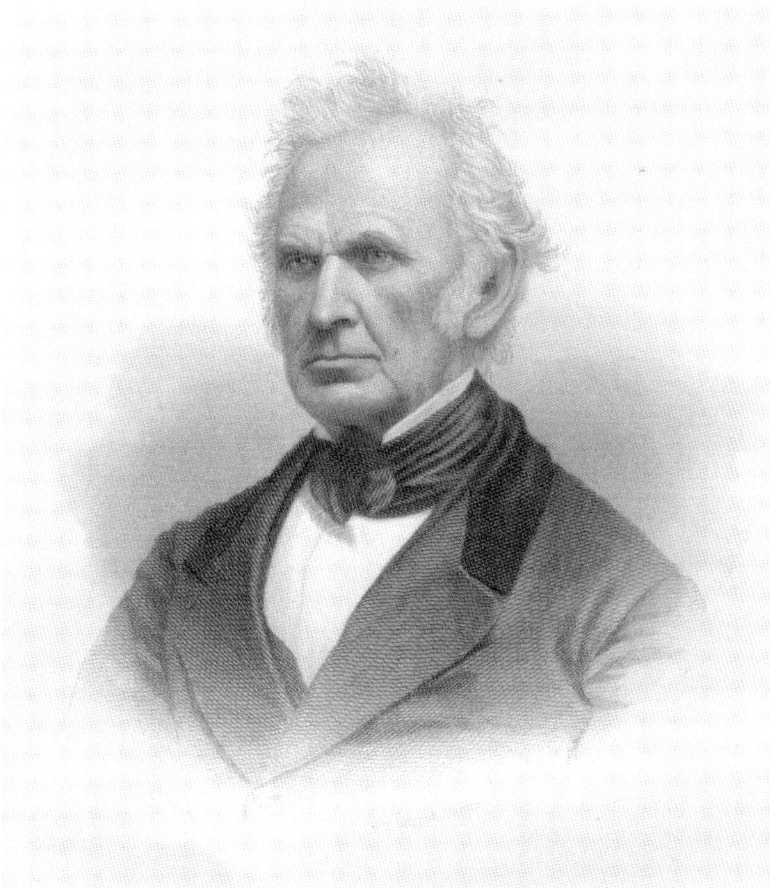

Franklin's Judge and Benefactor

Judge George W. Nesmith was the presiding judge of the New Hampshire Supreme Court in the late 1800s, but he was also well known and loved in his home community. Nesmith was so respected that when a local club of former military men formed, it took the name Nesmith Rifles in his honor. And when the organization disbanded in 1878, Nesmith, who was still alive, was honored to learn that the name was passed on to another veterans' group.

Nesmith was known especially as a strong supporter of the New Hampshire Orphans Home, which was created especially for children left orphaned by the Civil War.

Rev. Daniel Agustus Mack, who was orphaned himself and whose concern for other orphans was stirred further after serving as a chaplain during the war, initiated the project. Mack wanted the facility to be set in a rural community, rather than the city environs that were common for such homes. Mack "made his first public address on its behalf in the Methodist Episcopal Church at Newport," according to *The History of Franklin, New Hampshire* by local historian Albert Garneau. "The Hon. George W. Nesmith was present . . . and was convinced . . . He allied himself with the movement."

The facility was eventually established at Webster Place, the same farmland where Daniel Webster was born and a spot the famous statesman once called, "the most beautiful place on this earth." (see page 18). Judge Nesmith was the first president of the home's board of directors, and continued supporting the operations with his money and time until his death nearly 20 years later, in 1890.

"The grand old man, the venerable judge, the honored citizen . . . was a father to the home, assuming in large part the responsibility for its success . . . One cannot speak too highly of his service, of his love, and what the home owes to him," Garneau wrote. (Courtesy of Franklin Historical Society.)

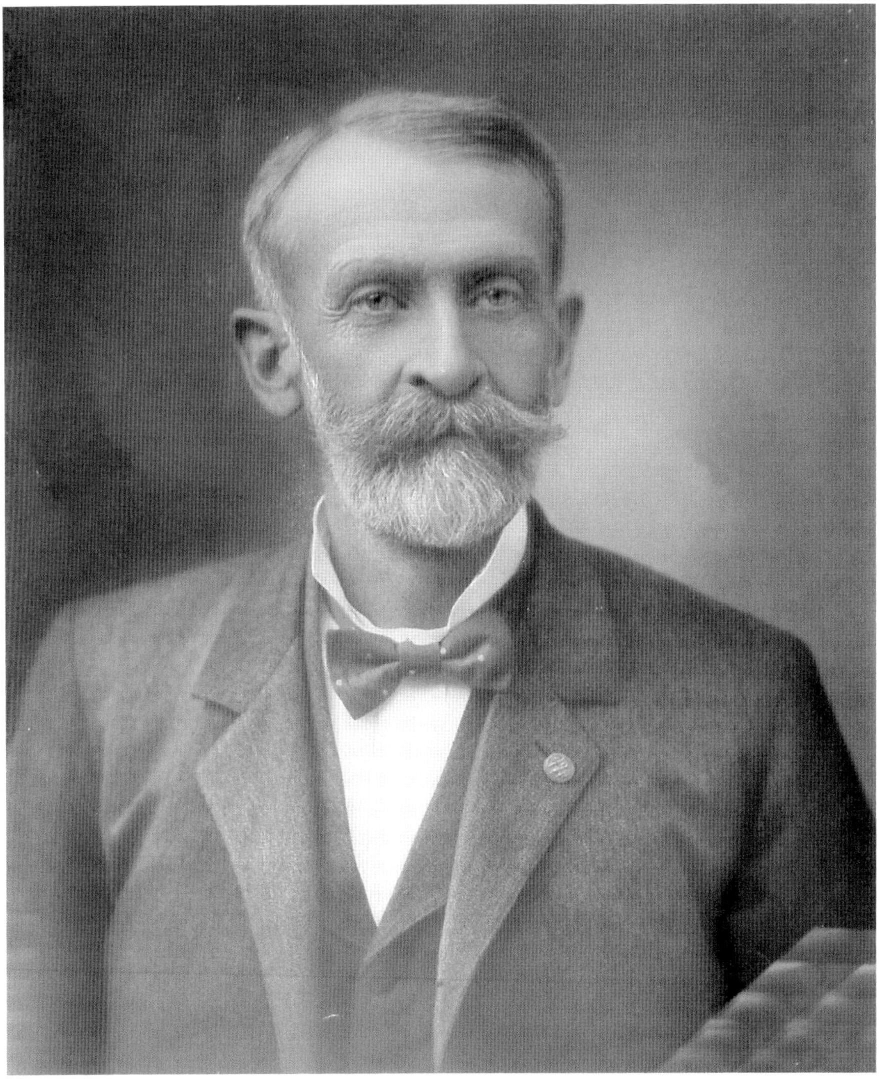

Dedicated to Veterans (ABOVE AND OPPOSITE PAGE)
Like most of New Hampshire, the Lakes Region has always held its military veterans in high esteem. So it is not surprising that about 25 years after the Civil War, the State of New Hampshire constructed the Soldiers' Home in Tilton for war veterans unable to care for themselves due to wounds, old age, or other infirmities. Charles E. Tilton (see page 13), a prominent resident of the town, donated the 30-acre property. The Woman's Relief Corps raised $5,000 to provide furnishings for the "Fortress," which sat on a hill in the Highlands section of town. Commandant Edwin H. Smith, seen above, was the facility's first manager.

In 1899, electric lights and a laundry plant were added. In 1913, an additional farmhouse infirmary was built. By the 1950s, farming operations had ceased, and in 1971, the farmhouse structure was replaced by a 50-bed nursing care addition. Another 50-bed addition was completed in 1978 when the original main building, seen opposite, was demolished. In 1989, a third 50-bed addition was built. More recent additions include areas devoted to helping veterans with dementia, an outdoor pavilion-park area, and the Main Street and town hall section, which provides a venue for larger events.

Today, the facility is called the New Hampshire Veterans Home. (Above, courtesy of New Hampshire Veterans Home; opposite, courtesy of Lake Winnipesaukee Historical Society.)

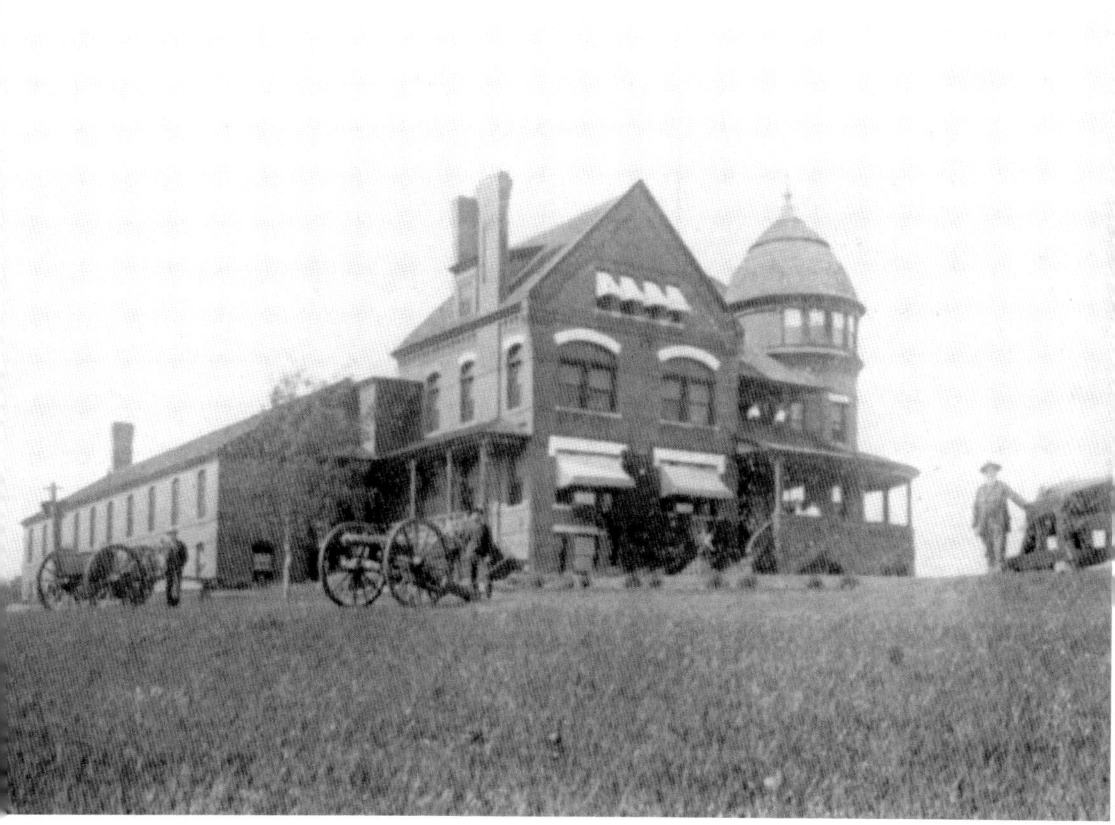

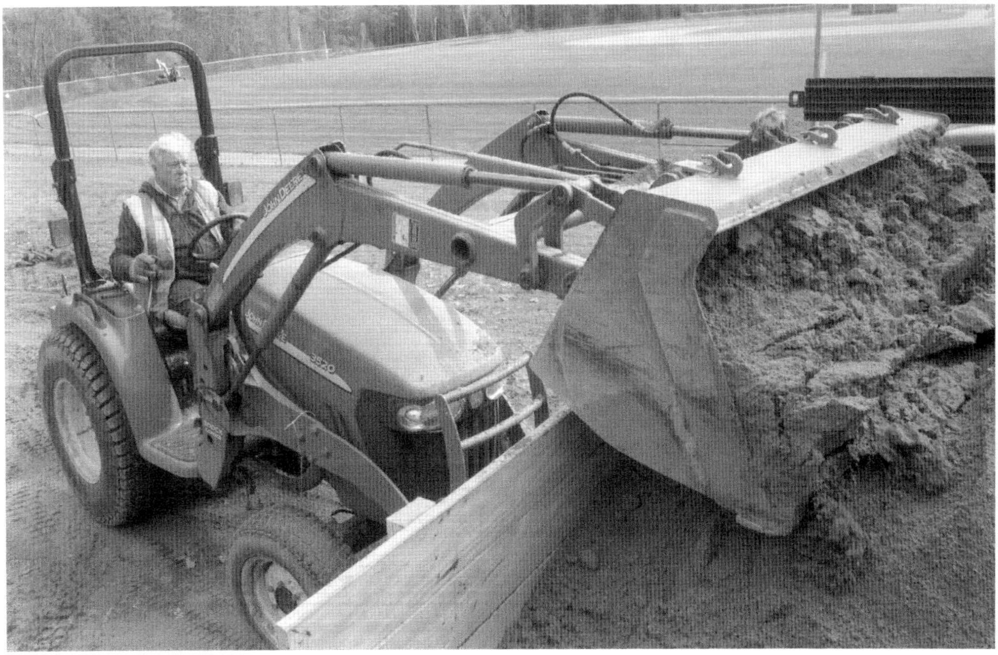

"The Mayor of Belmont."

Ron Mitchell grew up with the words of John F. Kennedy ringing in his ears: "Ask not what your country can do for you; ask what you can do for your country."

Mitchell moved to Belmont in 1971 and started volunteering with the fire department; he eventually served the department for 17 years. He was then a water commissioner for six years and a selectman for seven years. He has now served on the budget committee for the last 15-plus years.

A retired engineer, Mitchell is currently employed as a groundskeeper at Belmont High School. (Courtesy of Daryl Carlson/Kamara Image Photography.)

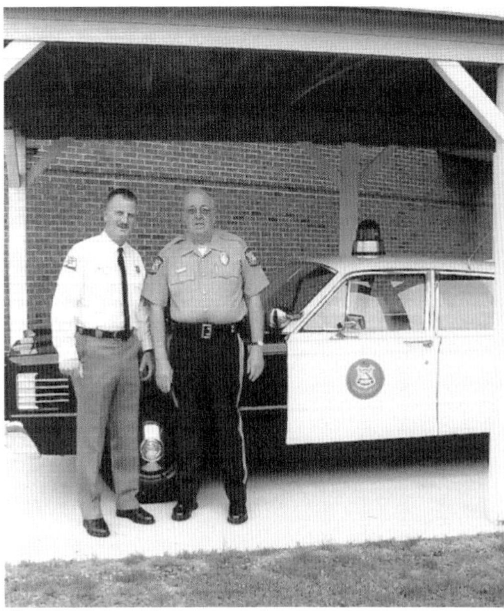

First Officer

Earl Sweeney was only 24 when he was appointed chief of the Belmont Police Department; in 1961, he organized the town's first fulltime department and made it the first New Hampshire department to use blue lights on cruisers and moving radar for traffic. He later joined the New Hampshire Department of Safety, where he initiated the state police's computerized criminal history database. Now assistant director with the DOS, Sweeney also continues his long association with the International Association of Chiefs of Police. Pictured here, Sweeney (right), as a representative of the association, awards a patrol car to an unidentified Arizona state trooper. (Courtesy of the Sweeney family.)

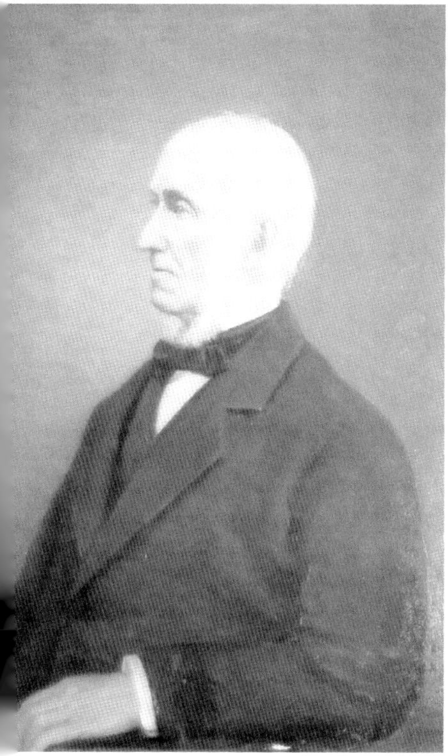

Out of a Kind Heart, a Repository for Knowledge

Napoleon Bonaparte Gale was a well-loved, kind-hearted, and respected banker and community leader in Laconia during the 19th century. "He was a man of unblemished integrity, and conscientious uprightness," according to *The Illustrated Laconian*, published in 1899. "He was a man of great strength of character, kindhearted and generous, public-spirited and enterprising—in short, one of the most honored and respected of Laconia's citizens."

When Gale died, he left much of his fortune to the City of Laconia to fund the building of a public library. Designed by famous Boston architect Charles Brigham, it still stands as a classic example of the Romanesque Revival style that emphasizes weight and mass through rock-faced masonry, heavy arches, and broad slate roofs. The imposing but warm structure has solid oak paneling throughout and several stained-glass windows.

The Gale Memorial Building, which is listed in the National Register of Historic Places, has been called "New Hampshire's most important Romanesque Revival building" and was named "Laconia's Livingroom" by *New Hampshire* magazine. (Left, courtesy of Laconia Public Library; below, author's collection.)

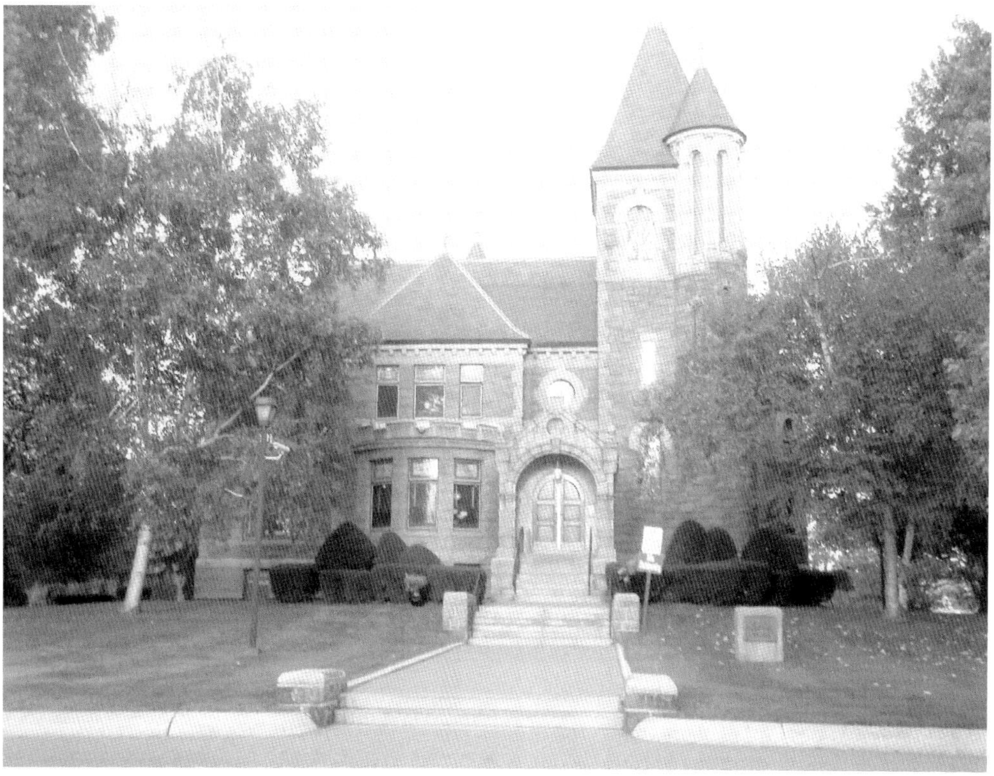

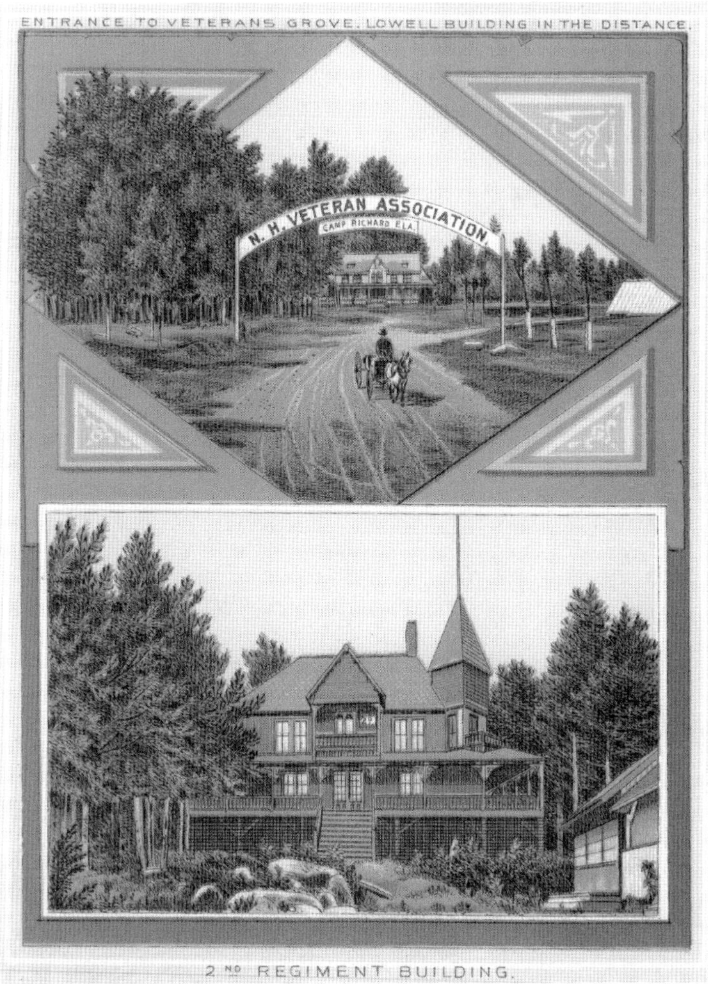

Veterans Stake Out a Beach

In 1878, the New Hampshire Veterans Association (NHVA), made up of men who had served in the Civil War, held their first general reunion and encampment in Manchester. One year later, the group moved the event to Weirs Beach, where it settled in for decades of growth. Four years later, a railroad company made local land available to the association for 43 years.

The NHVA and the annual event, held each August, grew in popularity as veterans from all over the Northeast came to visit the Lakes Region during the summer.

Between 1883 and 1896, a number of large Victorian buildings were built on the property, most of them very ornate and colorful. Many had running water and sewer service long before other summer camps, and most featured large, open areas on the first floors with fireplaces and water closets; upper floors consisted of dormitory-style sleep areas for members of the regiment. These images show the campground's entrance and stately 2nd Regiment building.

In 1924, a large fire destroyed the prominent Weirs Hotel and at least one of the veterans' buildings. A hurricane in 1938 damaged even more structures. Between the 1950s and the 1980s, fires and other structural problems eliminated other barracks, but in the 1990s, preservation efforts were begun on the few remaining buildings in the campgrounds adjacent to Lakeside Avenue. Unfortunately, limited resources have slowed progress on the rehabilitation efforts in recent years. (Courtesy of the Lake Winnipesaukee Historical Society.)

CHAPTER SEVEN

Here and There

Some people do not fit easily into categories. They bring a certain attitude, a certain *je ne sais quoi*, a peculiar character to the community that is hard to explain and almost impossible to duplicate.

Their jobs may not be that unusual. They could be restaurateurs, realtors, pastors, or actors. Sometimes they are athletes, beauty queens, or poets.

And other times—rarely but, unfortunately, they are shysters or even, in one horrible case—America's original serial killer.

But they are a part of the history and the legacy of the Lakes Region.

It is wonderful to see David Wright start the World War II museum in Wolfeboro to honor his father.

It is inspiring to learn that George Brunstad swam across Lake Winnipesaukee at the age of 76.

It is invigorating to read about the varied accomplishments of the late Henry Maxfield of Wolfeboro, the author of the classic *Legacy of a Spy*.

It is remarkable to hear how Hector Bolduc of Gilford worked among the traditional Catholic community in America.

It is fascinating to hear about young Ian Hill of Northfield, the teenage creator of Ian's Wicked Good Donuts.

And it is just puzzling to find out about Sanbornton's Joseph Plummer, the sociable "Hermit of Meredith Hill."

But it is mystifying, to modern minds, to fathom the financial success of doctors Alonzo and Frank Greene. They sold a patent medicine of vegetable extract and liquor that made them wealthy, despite the fact that there is no record that either of them ever actually practiced medicine in the Lakes Region.

And it is simply terrifying to read of the horrible exploits of Herman Webster Mudgett of Gilmanton, later known by his pseudonym Dr. H.H. Holmes of Chicago. In that role, he killed innumerable people, including children. His crimes were not committed here, but in a peculiar way, he remains part of the fabric of the Lakes Region. His childhood home still stands in the village, and his descendants live in the area.

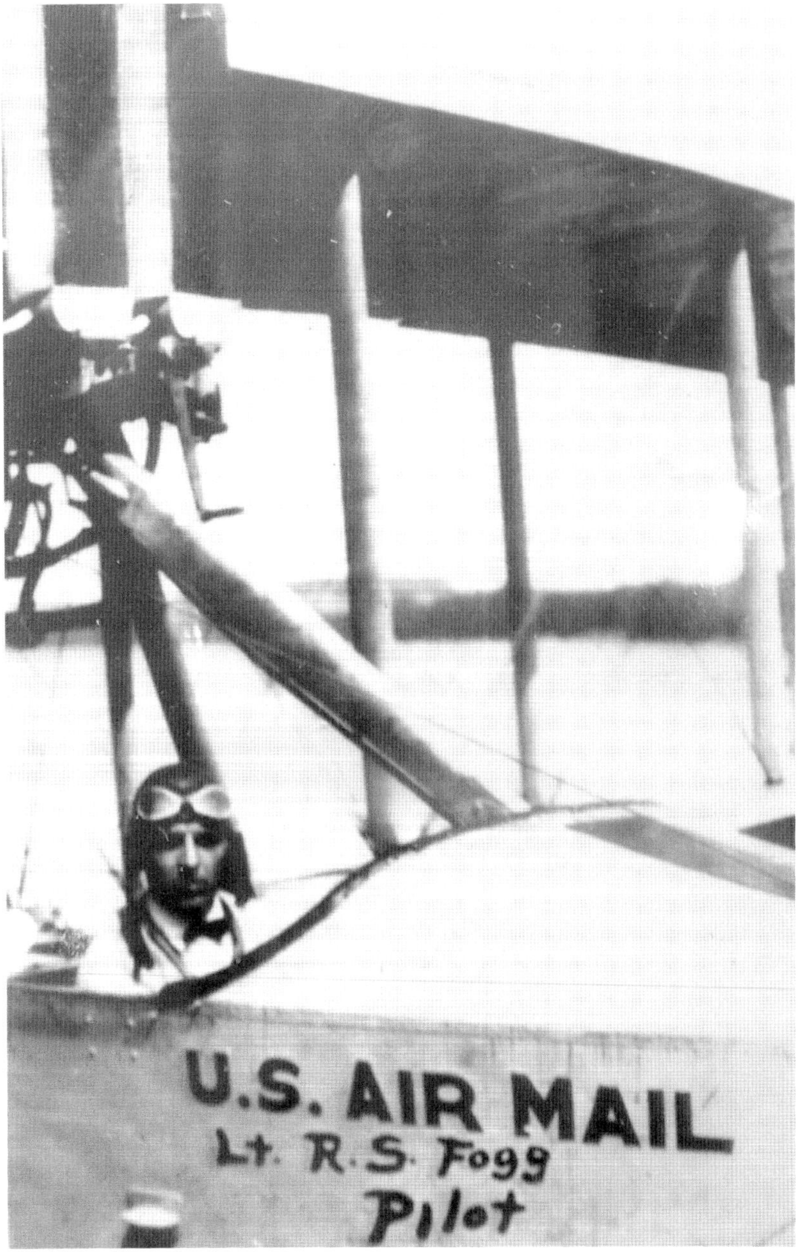

Fly Right

Bob Fogg, one of America's aviation pioneers, operated in the Lake Winnipesaukee area in the 1920s and 1930s. He is shown here in the Curtiss Seagull seaplane that he used for his airmail route in August 1925, which is believed to be the first flight of its kind in the world. Fogg delivered mail to summer residents in Wolfeboro and people who lived along the big lake's shoreline, both on the mainland and on the islands.

Fogg also took some of the earliest aerial photographs of Lake Winnipesaukee and Wolfeboro Bay from his cockpit. Jane Rice of Moultonborough researched the history of Fogg's seaplane base at Weirs Beach, where her grandfather, a World War I aviator, was in business with Fogg in the 1930s. This image is from her recently published book *Bob Fogg and New Hampshire's Golden Age of Aviation*. (Courtesy of Jane Rice.)

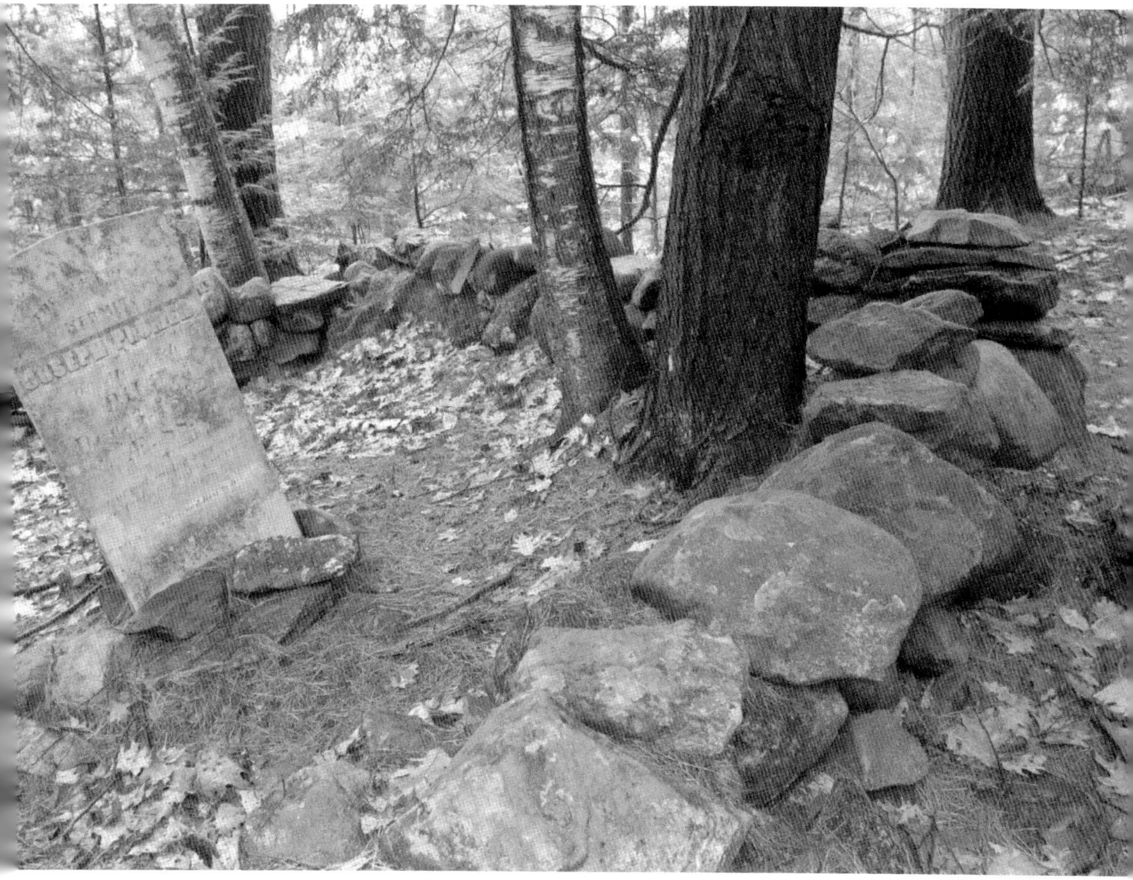

The Social Hermit

If someone is well known in his community, can he still be called a hermit?

If so, Joseph Plummer, the "Hermit of Meredith Hill," pulled it off.

Plummer was born and raised in Sanbornton into a family that looked to all other people as normal. In fact, his siblings grew up to be typical citizens of the 1700s. Joseph, however, spent most of his time alone and did not play with his siblings. When he grew up, he built a one-room house close to the border of Meredith. It had no windows, and its only entrance was four feet off the ground; the chimney was made of sharp stones pointing upward to discourage possible intruders.

Still, children were always treated to cider and apples when they visited Plummer, and folks constantly trekked to his land to meet the hermit. He would appear nervous at their arrival, but he did not chase them away. A student of the Bible, Plummer also met regularly in his cabin with students from the New Hampton Literary Institution.

"It would seem that it was inborn in him a fear of human beings that drove him into solitude," wrote an old friend after he died. "Where this irrepressible fear did not hold sway, he had for the most part, good sense."

Plummer prepared his own grave near his house, and the stone, identifying him as a hermit, is still standing. (Courtesy of Daryl Carlson/Kamara Image Photography.)

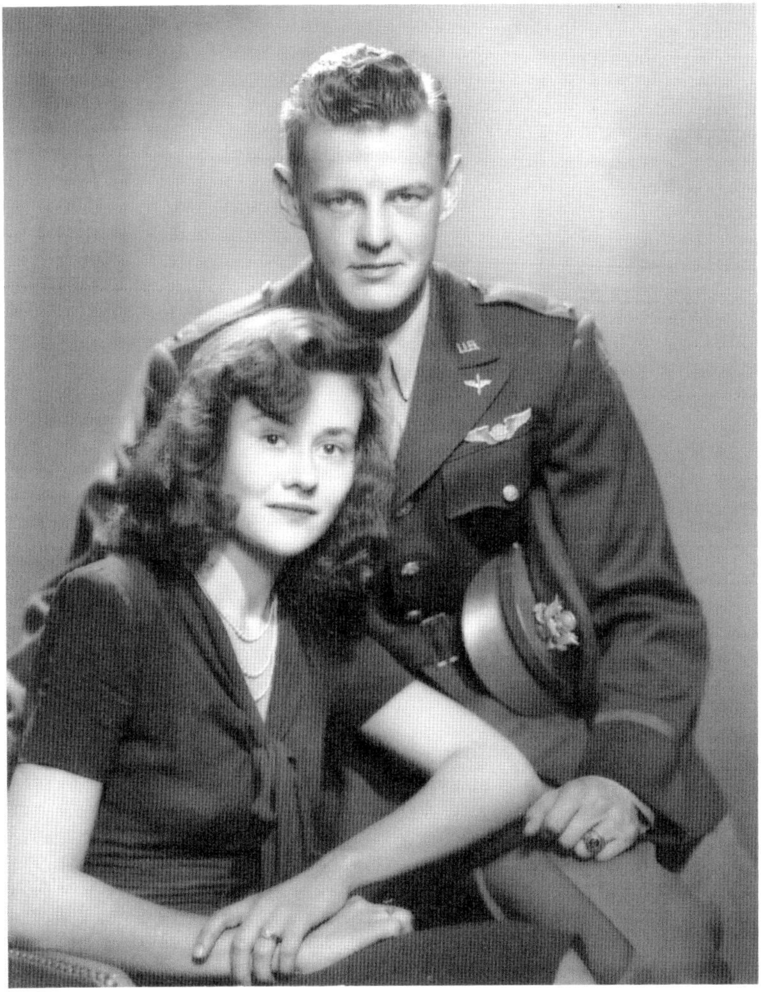

Amazing Life

Henry Maxfield was born in Boston in 1923 and grew up to fight in the Army Air Corps (now the Air Force) in World War II. As a navigator on a B-24 bomber, Maxfield was captured after his plane was shot down over Germany. He served six months in a POW camp before being liberated by Gen. George Patton.

Eventually, Maxfield moved his wife, Elizabeth "Betty," and his young family to Wolfeboro, where he had enjoyed summers at a local camp as a child. He started writing fiction, but to pay the bills he also worked numerous other jobs, including selling shrubbery door-to-door.

In 1951, Maxfield went back to Europe, where he pursued graduate studies and began working for the CIA. He was on the agency's Berlin desk for a while and then moved back to the United States.

Three years later, he left the government agency and returned to Wolfeboro. That is when he had his first significant writing success: his play *Money in the Bank* was produced by television's *Matinee Playhouse*.

In 1958, his first book, *Legacy of a Spy*, was published; still considered a classic of the espionage field, it was made into a movie. His second book, *Another Spring*, was a story of love and passion set in a town much like Wolfeboro. Maxfield believed it would have captured the national attention that *Peyton Place* gained if he had delivered the manuscript to publishers just a few months earlier (see page 57).

Between his writing, the author opened Maxfield Real Estate and became a prominent member of Wolfeboro's business community. He remained interested and active in the town until his death in 2013. (Courtesy of Maxfield Real Estate.)

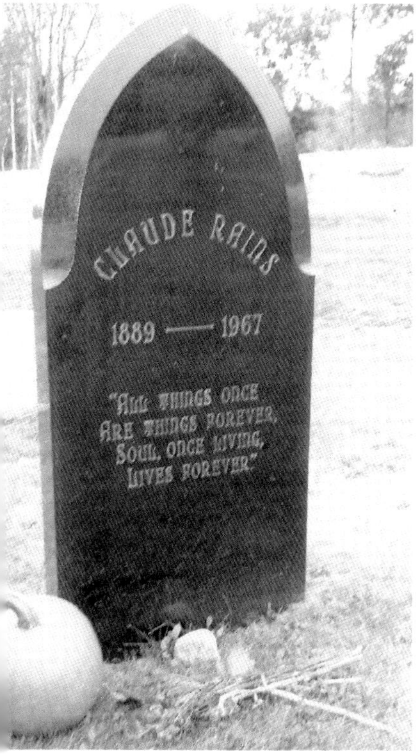

A Beautiful Friendship

Claude Rains was a star of stage and screen long before he visited the Lakes Region in the late 1950s. He played the lead in the 1933 film *The Invisible Man* and followed that with a range of roles that cemented his reputation; he was nominated for an Academy award four times, including his iconic role opposite Humphrey Bogart in *Casablanca.*

Rains first came to Sandwich to see an old friend and fell in love with the town, purchasing an 1800s house in 1963. He respected the historic building and made few alterations; his personal library was lined floor to ceiling with books, and it was said that he read every one.

Rains mourned when his wife, Rosemary, died in the house and spent hours staring out her window. When he tried to resume acting, he fell ill. "I miss Sandwich," he wrote in a letter to a friend at that time, "and I miss my home and garden."

Rains came back, but became ill again and died in 1967 at the age of 77.

Claude and Rosemary Rains are buried in a nearby Moultonborough cemetery. His inscription reads, "All Things Once Are Things Forever. Souls, Once Living, Live Forever."

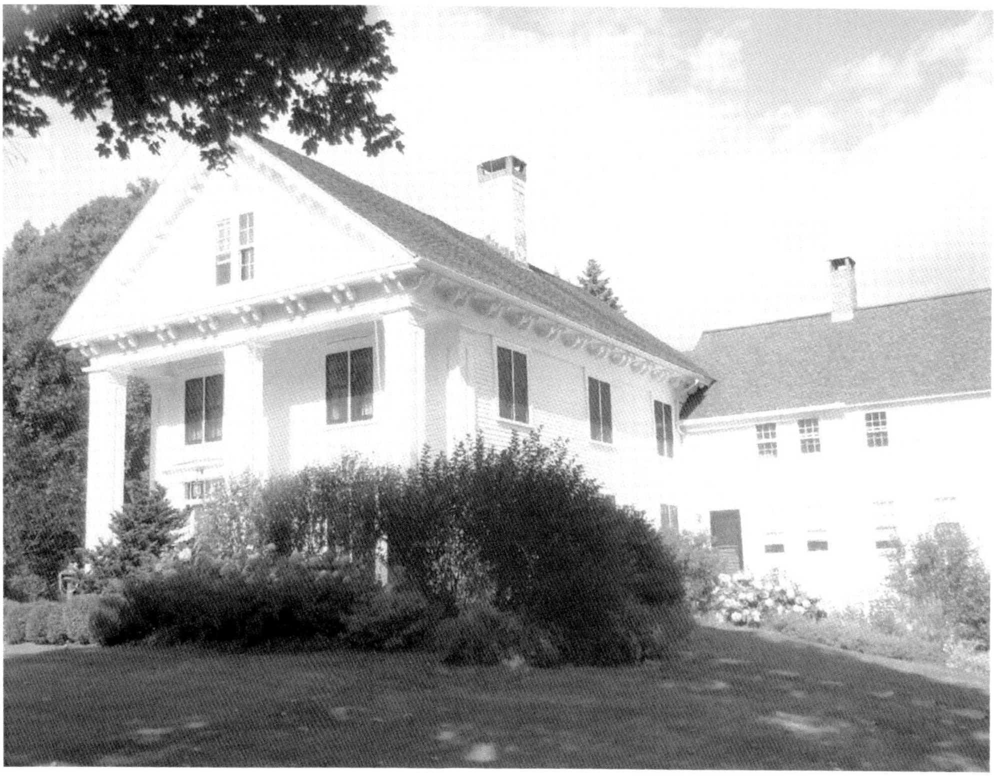

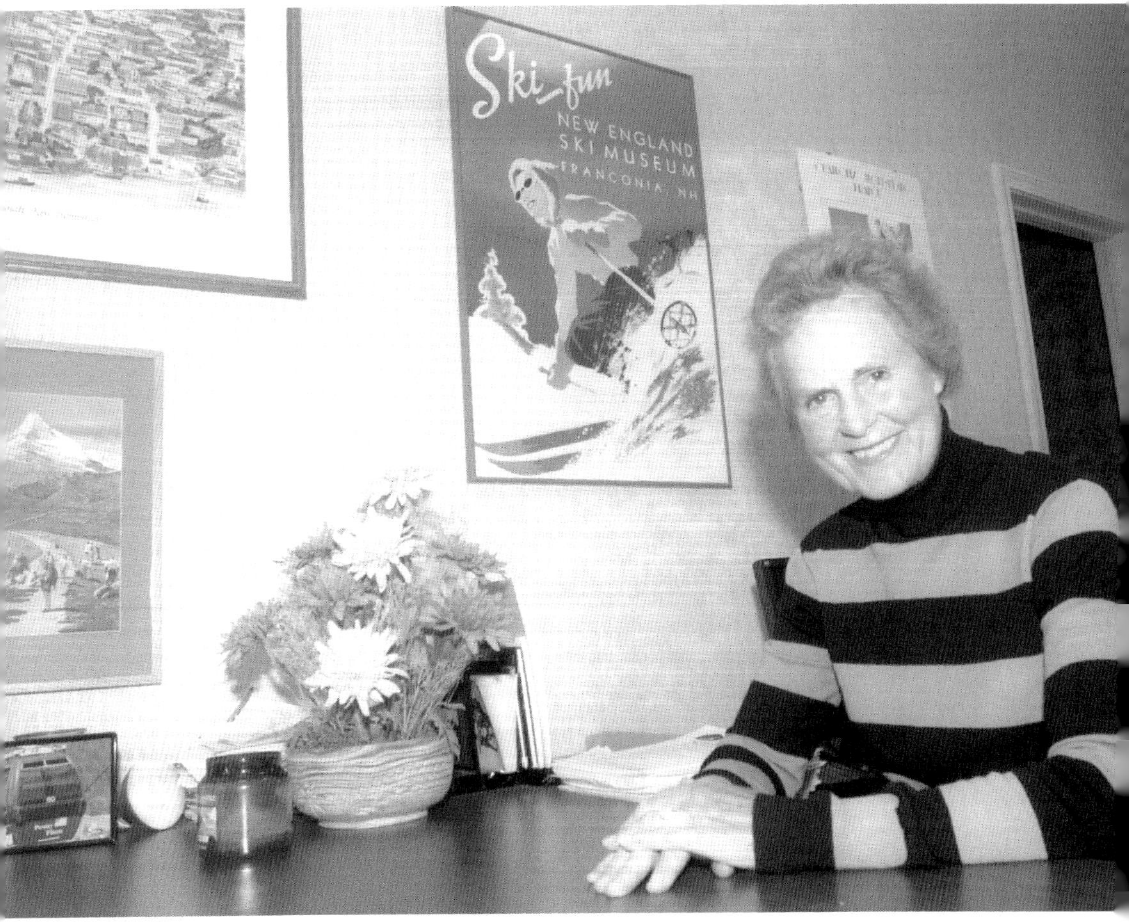

Ski Champ

Penny Pitou was only three years old when her family moved to Center Harbor from New York. She started skiing in her backyard and later joined the Gilford Outing Club, where she sharpened her skills. When Pitou was in high school, she tucked her hair under her helmet to make the all-boys ski team; after officials found out, she was kicked off the squad.

But, Pitou was a talented and determined athlete. She kept improving, frequently skiing at the Gunstock Recreation Center in Gilford, and eventually made the US Olympic teams in 1956 and in 1960. At the latter, she won silver medals in the downhill and giant slalom events, becoming the first American woman to ever medal at an Olympic downhill race.

In 1961, Pitou and her husband, Egon Zimmermann, founded the Penny Pitou Ski School at Gunstock and took over the ski school at the Blue Hills Ski Area in Canton, Massachusetts. Today she owns Penny Pitou Travel in Laconia and leads ski trips to the Alps. (Courtesy of Daryl Carlson/Kamara Image Photography.)

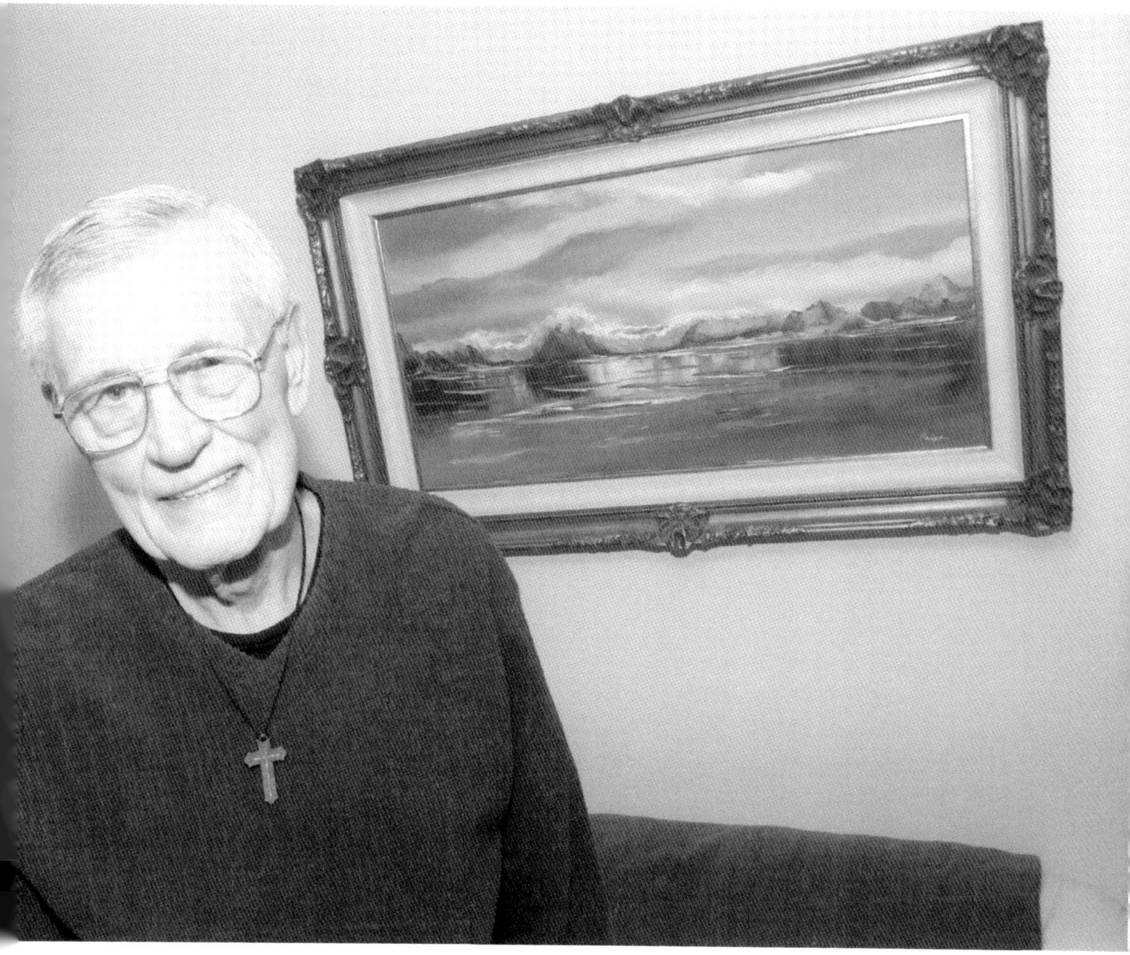

Meredith's Iron Man

George Brunstad swam across the English Channel and across Lake Winnipesaukee from Center Harbor to Alton Bay—when he was more than 70 years old.

Brunstad was interested in long-distance swimming as a young man, and when he retired, he began competing in—and winning—open-water races in the masters category. He took on the daunting challenge of swimming the English Channel in 2004; he completed it in 16 hours and was, at that time, the oldest person to have ever completed the swim. Brunstad was 76 when he decided to swim across Winnipesaukee as a charitable event; he finished in almost 22 hours, a relative crawl due to a paralysis that slowed him down for the last six miles. (Courtesy of Daryl Carlson/Kamara Image Photography.)

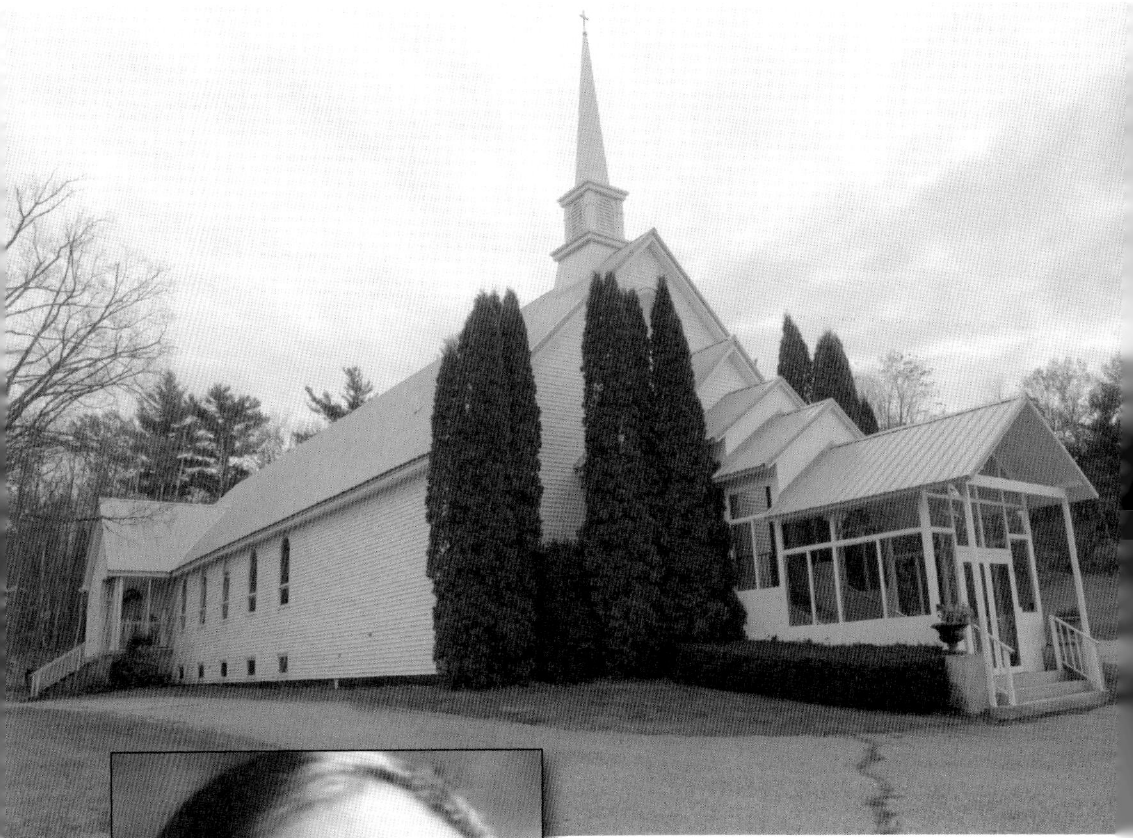

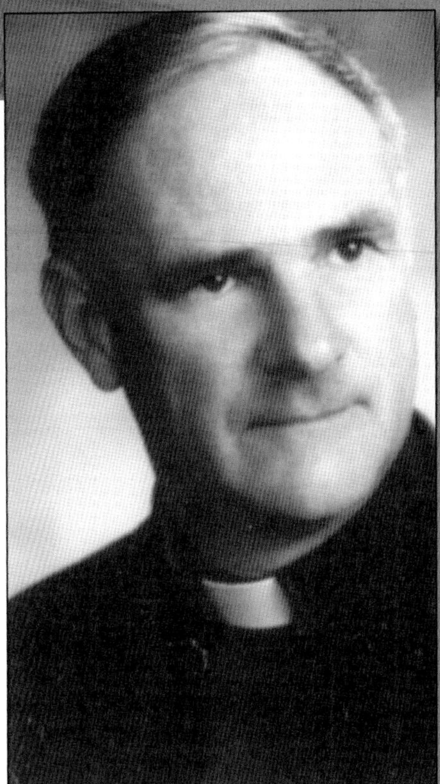

Priest and Pioneer

Fr. Hector Bolduc of Gilford was a world traveler, avid reader, enthusiastic collector, and priest ordained by Archbishop Marcel Lefebvre in 1974.

The last made Bolduc a somewhat controversial figure, as Lefebvre was the leader of the Society of St. Pius X, an international traditional Catholic group that opposes the changes that came to the church in the 1960s. Bolduc was one of the first American supporters of Lefebvre, and he helped establish Immaculate Conception Church in Gilford, which still uses the Latin mass preferred by many traditional Catholics.

Bolduc was a major leader in the traditional Catholic movement in the United States, leading and establishing churches all over the world. (Left, courtesy of the Bolduc family; above, courtesy of Daryl Carlson/ Kamara Image Photography.)

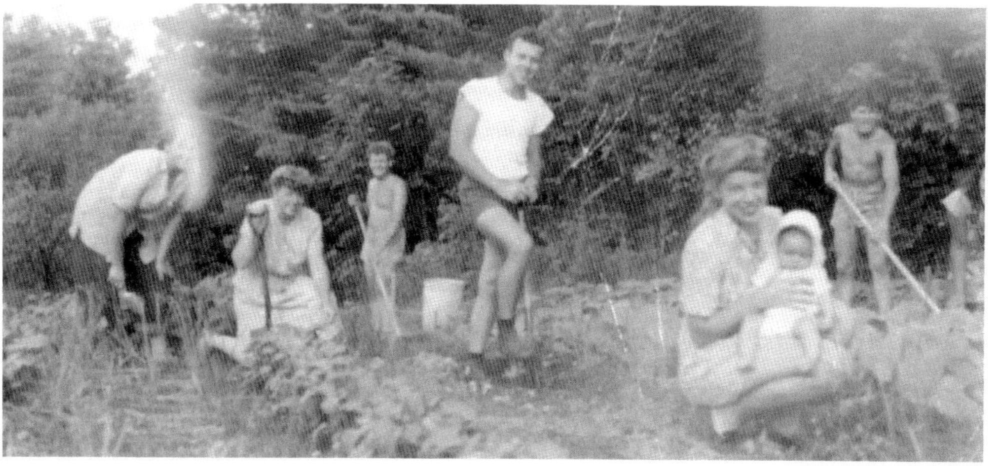

Quality Family

In the late 1940s, brothers Russ and Larry Hart left New Jersey to farm in Meredith. They raised vegetables and apples and sold foodstuffs from the back of a truck. Pictured here are, from left to right, Marilyn Hart, Russ Hart's daughter; Mea Hart, the mother of Russ and Larry Hart; Larry Hart; Bob Hart, brother of Larry and Russ; Hilda "Rusty" Hart, Bob's wife (in her arms is their baby Lee Hart); an unidentified employee; and Russ Hart's wife, Gerda Hart.

In 1953, the brothers decided to focus exclusively on raising turkeys; the next year, they opened a small restaurant specializing in turkey meals. Larry passed away in 1960, and Russ eventually closed the farm to focus on working as chef and restaurateur.

Over 50 years later, Hart's Turkey Farm Restaurant is considered one of the great family restaurants of America. It is managed now by second and third generation Harts including those pictured below, from left to right, (first row, sitting) Russ Hart's daughters Dale and Lynn Hart; (second row, standing) grandson Sim Willey and son Russell Hart. (Above, courtesy of Hart's Turkey Farm Restaurant; below, courtesy of Daryl Carlson/Kamara Image Photography.)

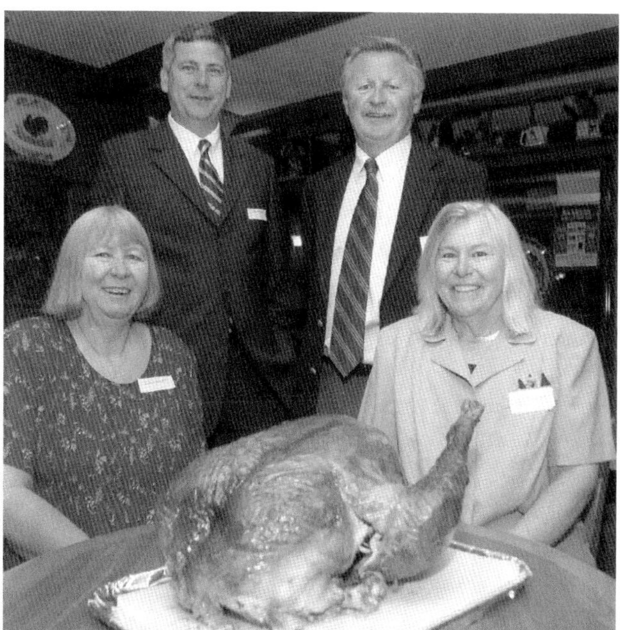

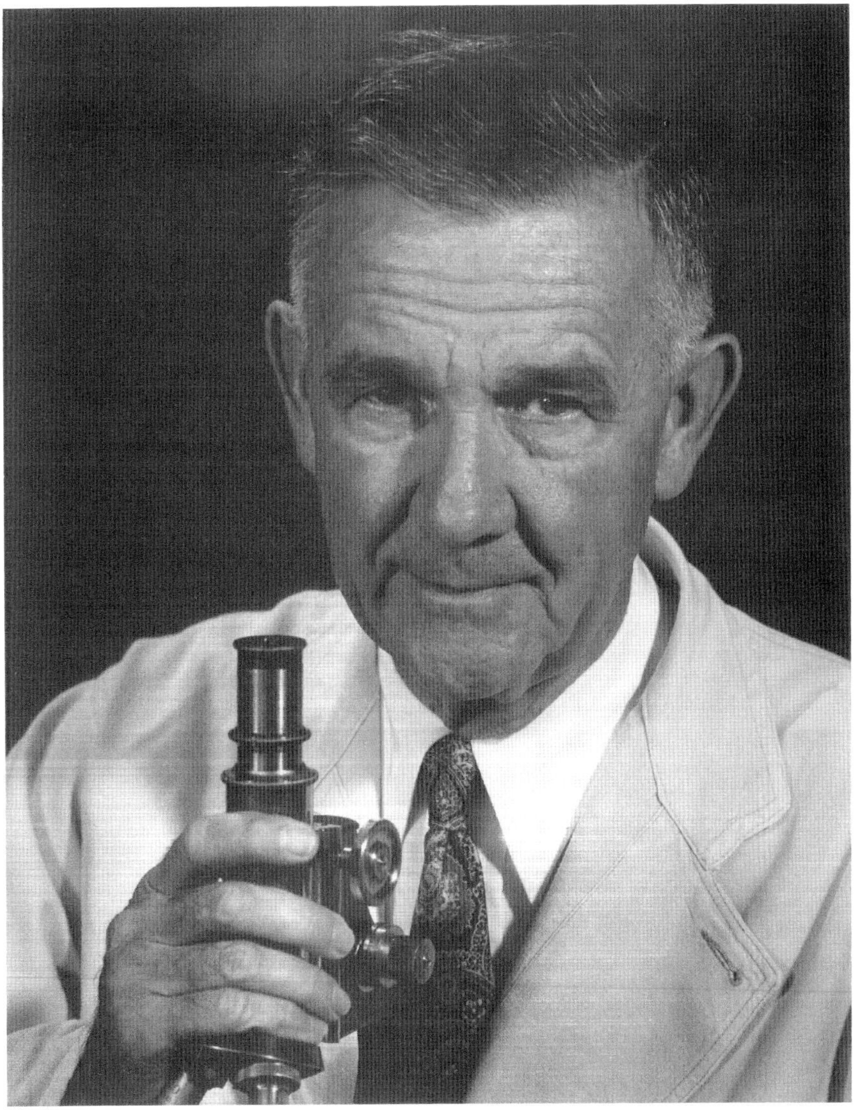

Nobel Doctor

George Hoyt Whipple grew up in Ashland, the son and grandson of physicians. Whipple graduated from Yale University and then received his medical degree from Johns Hopkins University in Maryland. He became involved in research, primarily focused on anemia and the physiology and pathology of the liver.

In 1921, Whipple became the founder and dean of a new medical school at the University of Rochester in New York. He served as dean until 1954 and remained associated with the institution until his death in 1976 at the age of 97.

In 1934, Whipple and two other doctors inspired by his work were awarded the Nobel Prize in Medicine for research that led to care of pernicious anemia, a disease that was killing 5,000 Americans every year in the 1920s.

Although Whipple had left town years before, he maintained fond memories of his home community. In 1970, he bought out the heirs of the family home where he was born and grew up and gave it to the town for a historical museum. The Ashland Historical Society is now housed in the structure. (Courtesy of Ashland Historical Society.)

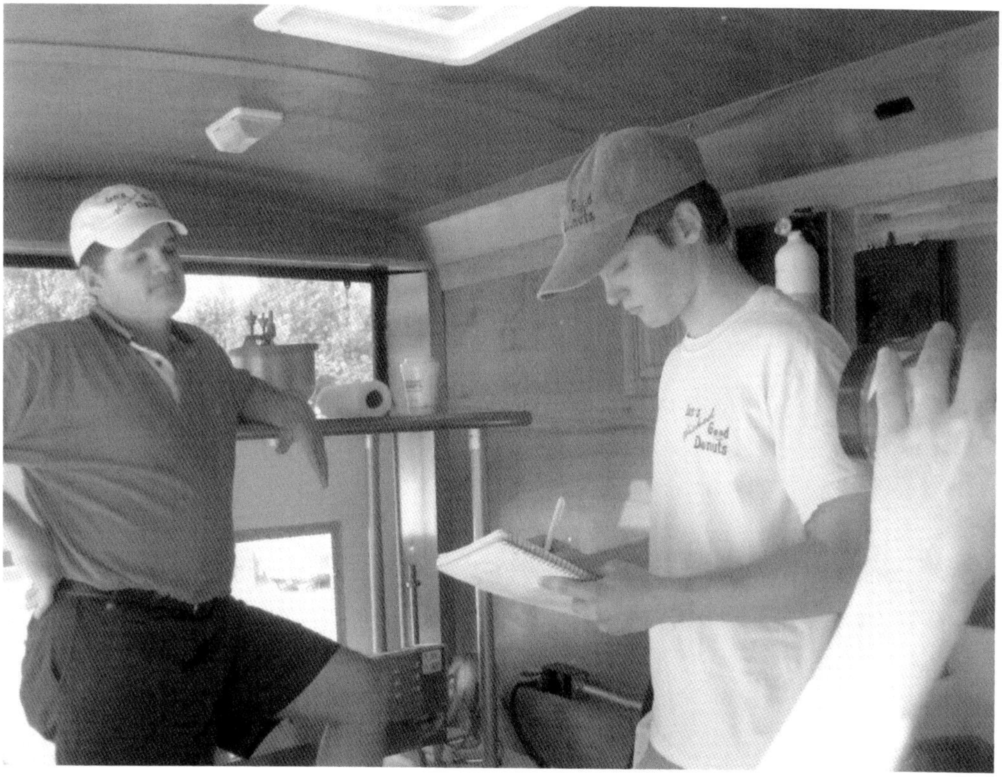

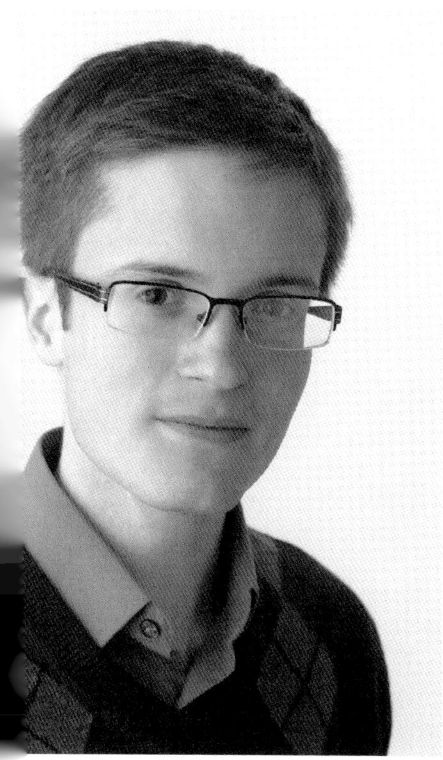

Making Dough

In 2007, the parents of high school student Ian Hill of Northfield were hoping to find something interesting for their young man to do during the summer. They bought a Lil' Orbits Mini Donut Machine, and after some trial and error, Ian started producing some very yummy doughnuts. He sold his first products at the annual Tilton-Northfield Old Home Day that summer.

Now a college student, Ian (with his family's help) has turned Ian's Wicked Good Donuts into an exercise in business and entrepreneurship that is helping to fund his education. His tasty wares are available at Pauli's Restaurant in Tilton and other local outlets, including summertime campgrounds and special events he visits with his mobile bakery. Pictured above are Ian and his father in the mobile bakery. (Both, courtesy of Ian's Wicked Good Donuts.)

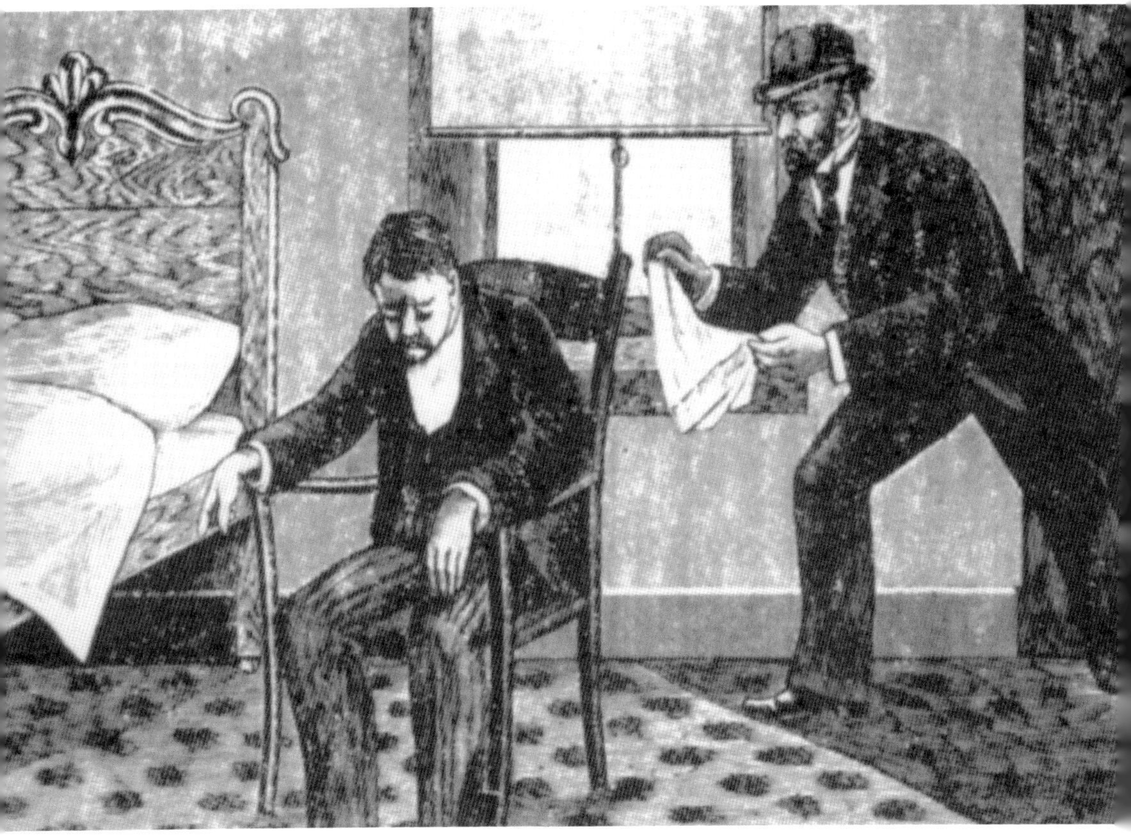

Gilmanton's Shameful Son (ABOVE AND OPPOSITE PAGE)
When Herman Webster Mudgett was growing up in a simple house that's still standing in Gilmanton village, town residents saw no sign of the man he would become. He appeared normal in every way, attending Gilmanton Academy and even studying medicine in Chicago for a while.

But, under the alias Dr. H.H. Holmes, Mudgett became known as one of America's first serial killers. He worked out of a building he had constructed in Chicago around the time of the 1893 World's Fair in Chicago, where he reportedly tortured and killed dozens of people, many transients who came to the city for the event. (The newspaper illustrations pictured here depict two of his crimes: suffocating an unconscious man and gassing two children he locked in a storage trunk.)

Mudgett once said he killed 27 people, but the pathological liar confessed and recanted his testimony numerous times, never revealing a reliable total. Police officials said they could not accurately estimate how many had died at his hands, but some guesses were in the hundreds. "I was born with the Devil in me," he reportedly said. "I could not help the fact that I was a murderer, no more than a poet can help the inspiration to sing."

Mudgett's capture, trial, and execution in Philadelphia were front-page national news in the last years of the 19th century, distressing his Lakes Region family. Local townspeople huddled around the Mudgetts, supporting them during the difficult times.

Several books have been written about Mudgett's horrid exploits, and rumors of a movie based on his life have persisted for years. So far, no one has been able to explain the reason for his unnatural behavior. (Illustrations are from the *Chicago Times-Herald*, *Chicago Daily Tribune*, and *Holmes, the Arch-Fiend or, A Carnival of Crime.*)

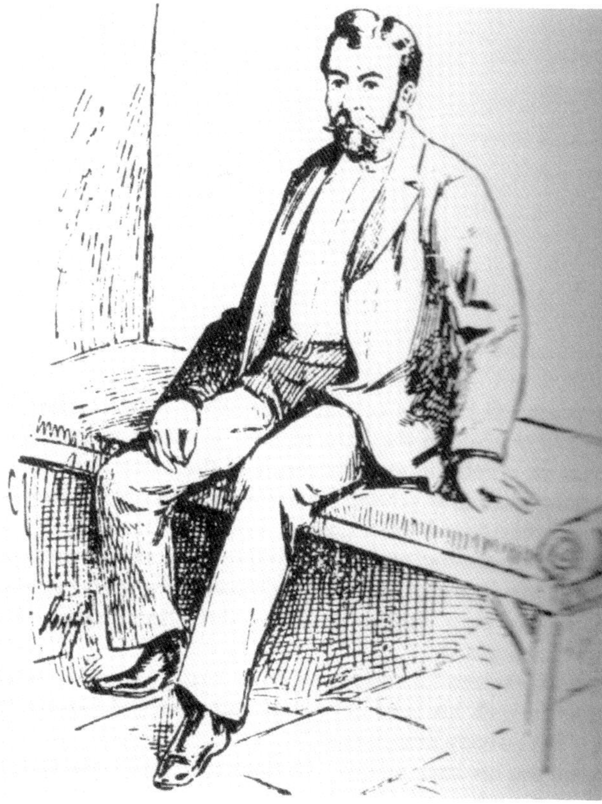

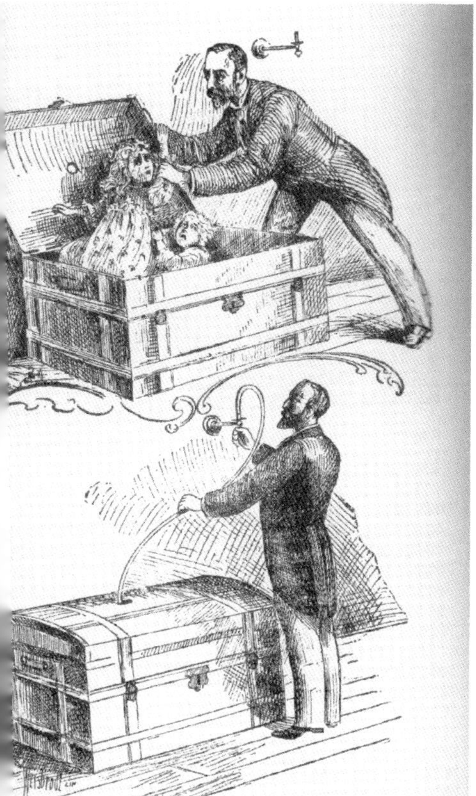

The children now realized their predicament and began to beg piteously for mercy.
Holmes arranged a rubber hose to the gas jet and put the end of the same through the hole into the trunk and turned on the gas.

A Bridge to Nature

Dr. Henry Libby of Wolfeboro was a dentist, inventor, and naturalist. Libby began developing early processes of using gold to fill cavities, and also invented several dental implements. When he was 40, he began studying a wide variety of life forms and collecting samples, which led him to establish his own nature museum in which his various samples—from stuffed animals to locally discovered arrowheads—were displayed. The museum, which opened in 1912, still welcomes visitors during the summer season. (Courtesy of the Libby Museum.)

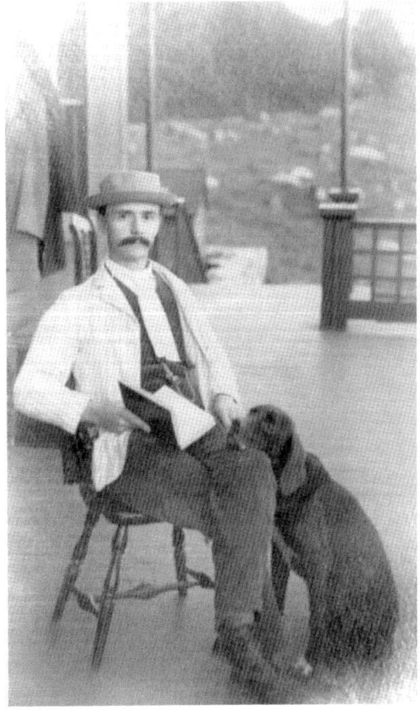

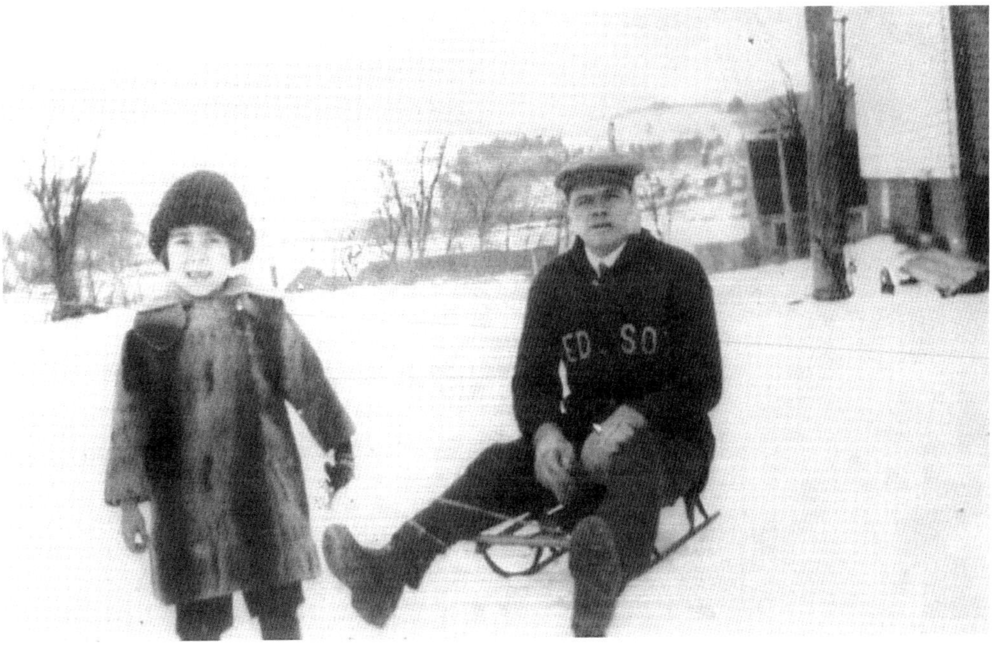

Ruth in the Rough

Some people know that before Babe Ruth became the "Sultan of Swat" for the New York Yankees, he won three World Series rings pitching for the Boston Red Sox in the early 20th century. But not many know that Ruth and his teammates were regularly invited by local businessmen to come up to the Lakes Region during their off-season to enjoy the area's hunting and fishing. As always, Ruth enjoyed spending time with children, and in 1915, he went sledding with Leon M. Hatch of Meredith on Main Street. (Courtesy of L. Michael Hatch.)

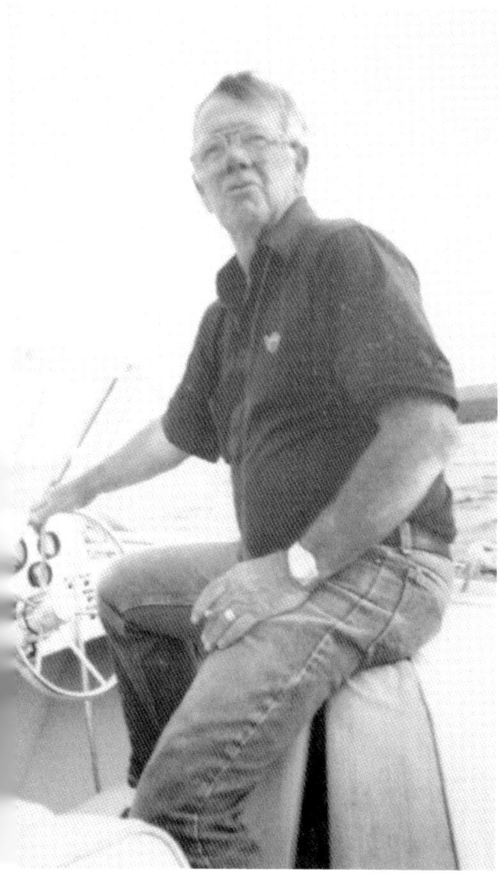

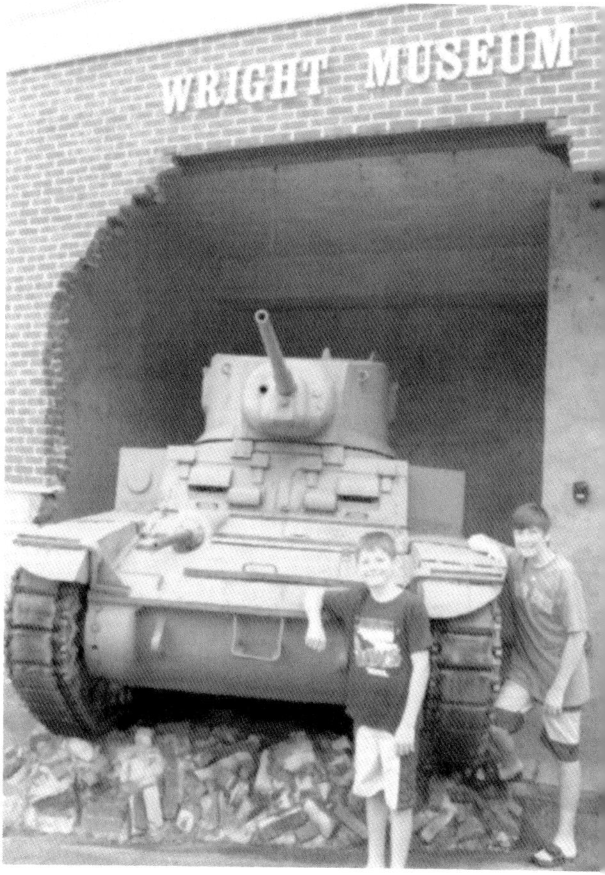

Getting It Wright

Growing up near Worcester, Massachusetts, David Wright was too young to fight in World War II. But, his father was in the military, and Wright was drawn to the worldwide fight between the Allied and the Axis nations. He grew up to become an avid collector of World War II military vehicles, collecting and restoring more than 50. In 1983, he founded the E. Stanley Wright Museum Foundation, named after his father, to allow items from the collection to appear at patriotic events, in parades, and at military functions throughout the Northeast.

But Wright wanted more. He hoped to tell the story of the war on the home front—gas rationing, rubber collections, victory gardens—as many civilians marshaled resources for the war effort.

In 1992, Wright, pictured here on his boat on Lake Winnipesaukee, purchased an eight-acre parcel in Wolfeboro, and two years later, opened the doors of the E. Stanley Wright Museum. The image above right shows the museum's main entrance; the tank appears to crash through the street-side wall of the museum. Since then, 200,000 people have visited the collection. (Both, courtesy of the E. Stanley Wright Museum.)

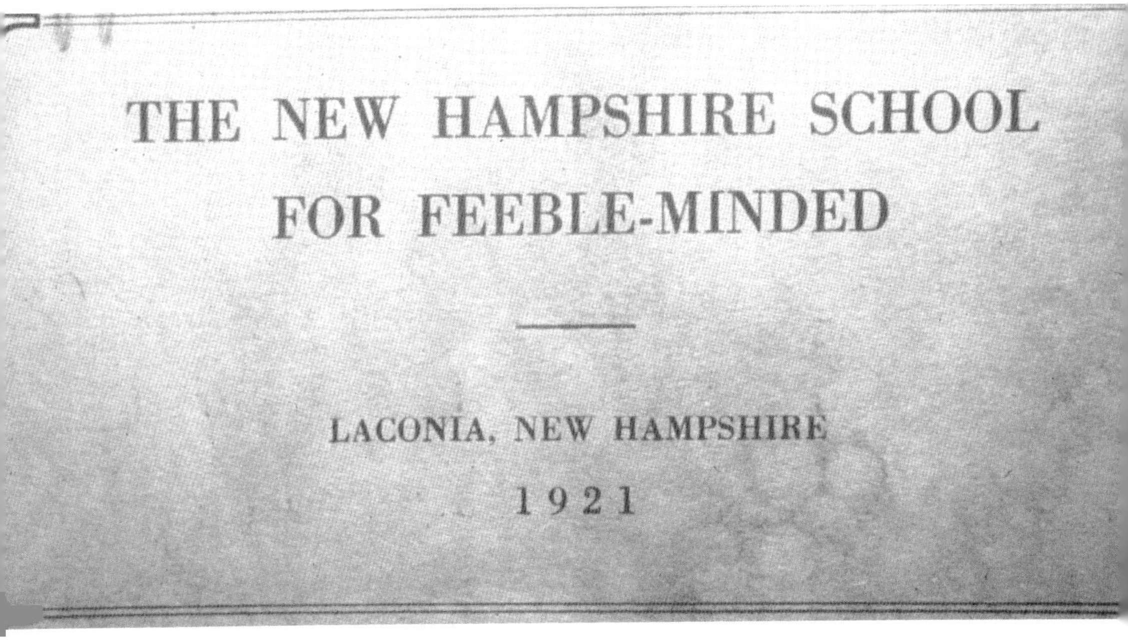

From Treasure to Troubles (ABOVE AND OPPOSITE PAGE)
The Laconia State School opened in 1903 as the New Hampshire School for the Feebleminded. At the time, the large institution was considered a major improvement over the quality of care destitute and marginalized people were receiving in county almshouses, and the citizens of Laconia took pride in the school. But, within a few years, the growing popularity of eugenics—the idea that negative traits could be bred out of humanity by eliminating those who were "defective"—began affecting the conditions of the residents, many of whom had mental or psychological difficulties.

Official neglect led to overcrowding, and the state did not allocate adequate finances to care for the children and adults living on the campus. By the beginning of World War II, over 600 people housed at the facility were living in extremely crowded and poor conditions.

In the 1950s, the tide began to turn when residents' relatives were encouraged to become more involved. In 1956, the LSS Parents Association made a film of the facility that created a furor and provided the impetus for change. Conditions at the institution slowly began to improve, and community resources were developed. In 1975, a new superintendent, Jack Melton, helped to keep things moving forward. But progress was gradual, and in 1978, a federal class action lawsuit filed by a statewide parents' association prompted the eventual closing of Laconia State School in 1991.

Laconia residents had a complicated relationship with the state school. For some years, it was a major local employer, and local people took some pride in the compassionate care they provided there. But, financial resources were never adequate, overcrowding was common, and there were never adequate resources to provide quality care. Pictured above is the institution's original sign. Opposite, top, is a young girl's group, and opposite, bottom, is the Keyes building. (All, courtesy of Bil Rogers and Gordon Dubois.)

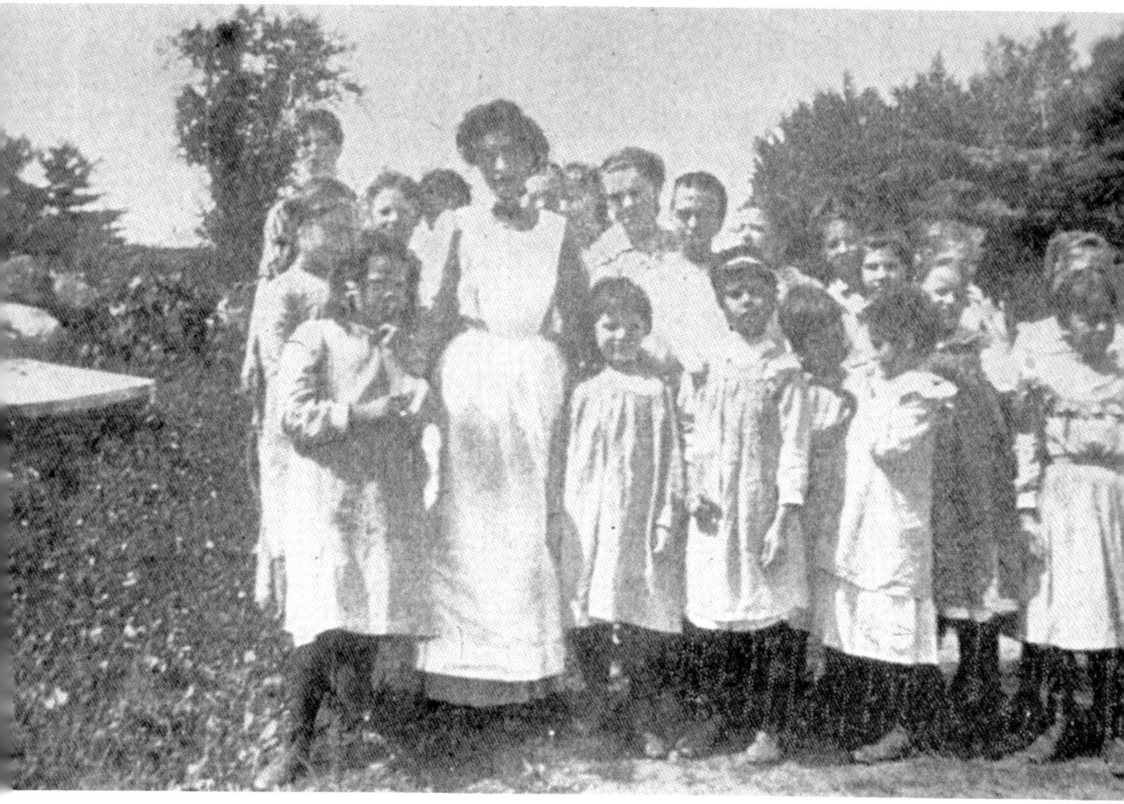

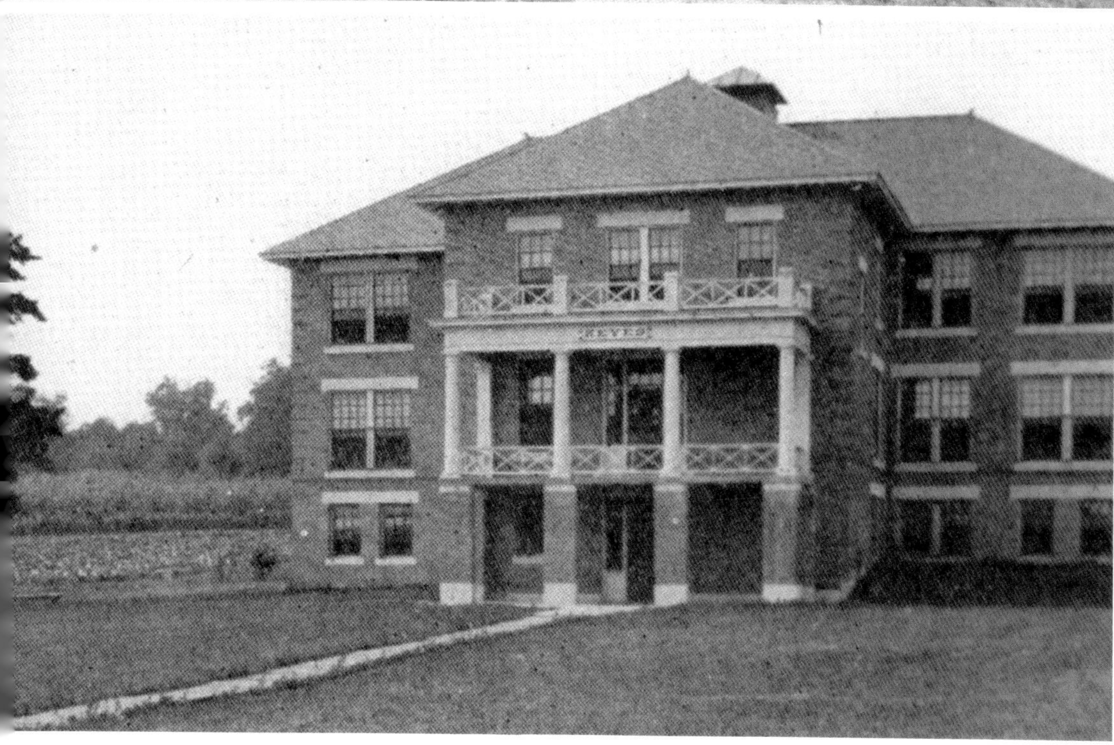

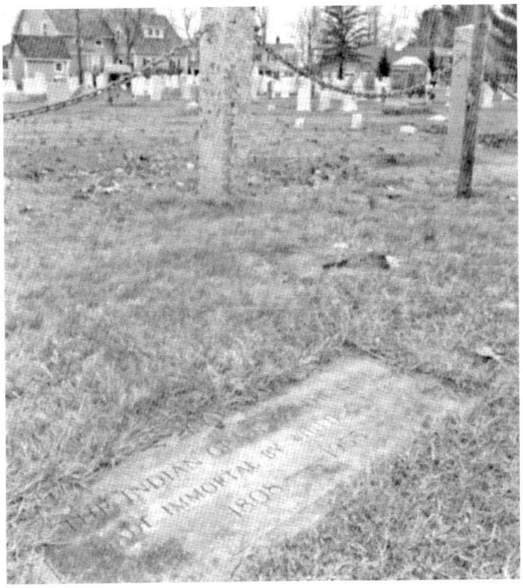

"Deep Below, as High above, Sweeps the Circle of God's Love."
John Greenleaf Whittier was one of America's most famous 19th-century poets. The Quaker abolitionist had strong ties to the Granite State, particularly the Lakes Region, in his later years. *Among the Hills* was a collection of his poems that reflected the bucolic life he had experienced here, including his visits to Ossipee, Holderness, and Sandwich. His stays with the Sturtevant family in Center Harbor were so regular that the family kept a room for his exclusive use. A historical marker near the Melvin Village Community Church in Tuftonboro commemorates Whittier's poem about a Native American's burial place found in Melvin Village, "Indian Grave by the Lake." (Courtesy of Daryl Carlson/Kamara Image Photography.)

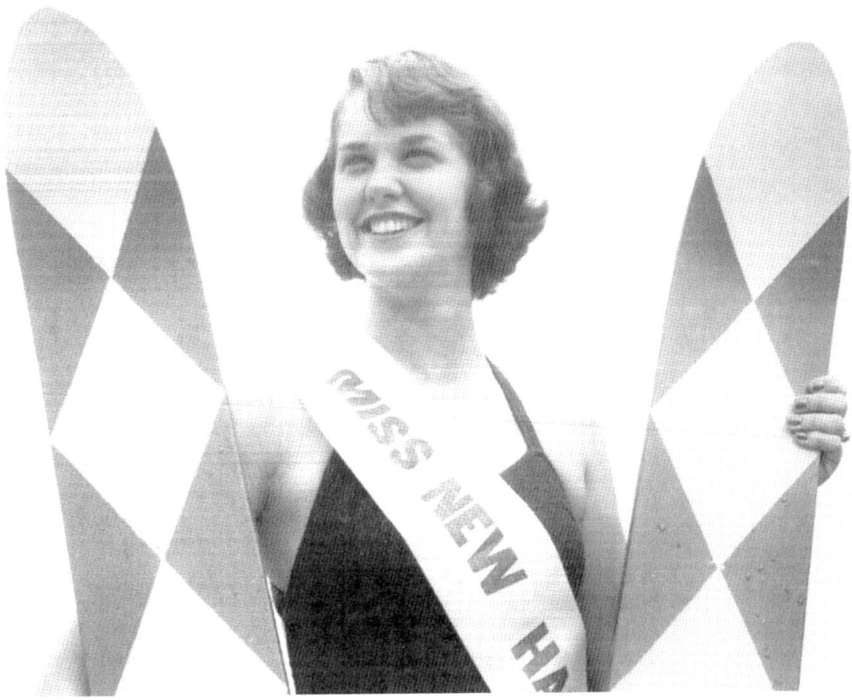

Miss Winnipesaukee Skis
Waterskiing was a popular part of America's recreational life after World War II. In 1947, champion skier Bruce Parker opened a school in downtown Wolfeboro, and in 1949, the Weirs Ski Club was formed. The Weirs group grew to be one of the largest in the country, with as many as 350 members. Members did shows in Alton Bay, Meredith Bay, and Weirs Beach. The National Water Ski Championships were held in the Weirs in 1954 and 1959. One member of the club, Coleen Gallant, was named Miss New Hampshire and entered the Miss America competition, where her talent was waterskiing; it was presented to the judges by means of movies of her performing on Lake Winnipesaukee. (Courtesy of Lake Winnipesaukee Historical Society.)

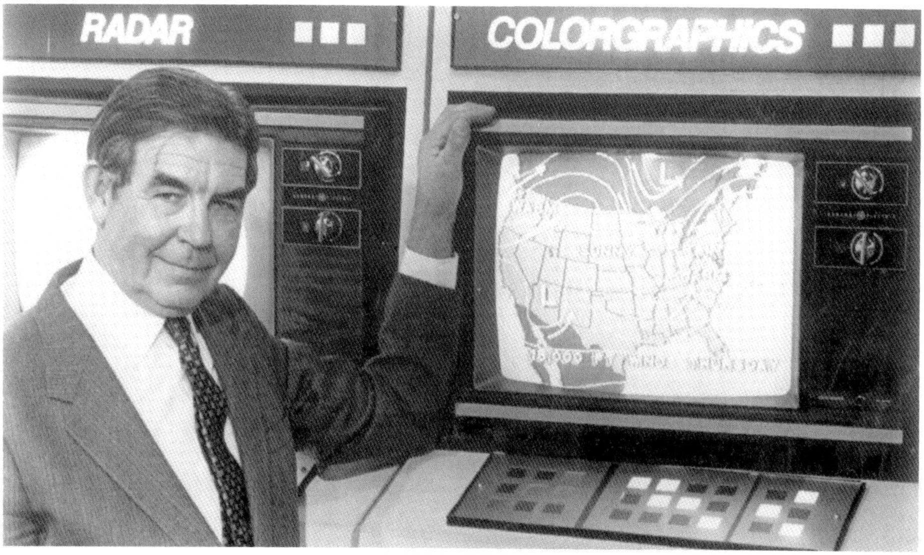

Boston's First Televised Weatherman

Don Kent was the face of weather forecasting in the Boston area for three decades, broadcasting his forecasts and his advice: "You're going to need an umbrella," he would announce to millions of people. Kent was fascinated by the weather and seemed to be able to get more out of looking at the sky than many highly trained meteorologists could get from studying reams of computer reports.

Kent began visiting the Lakes Region because his wife's family came from Sanbornton. He eventually retired to the town and spoke about how much he loved the area. Kent is shown above as a young broadcaster and below as a New Hampshire resident, peering out his window at the changing weather conditions. He died in Franklin in 2010. (Above, courtesy of the *Patriot Ledger*; below, courtesy of Daryl Carlson/Kamara Image Photography.)

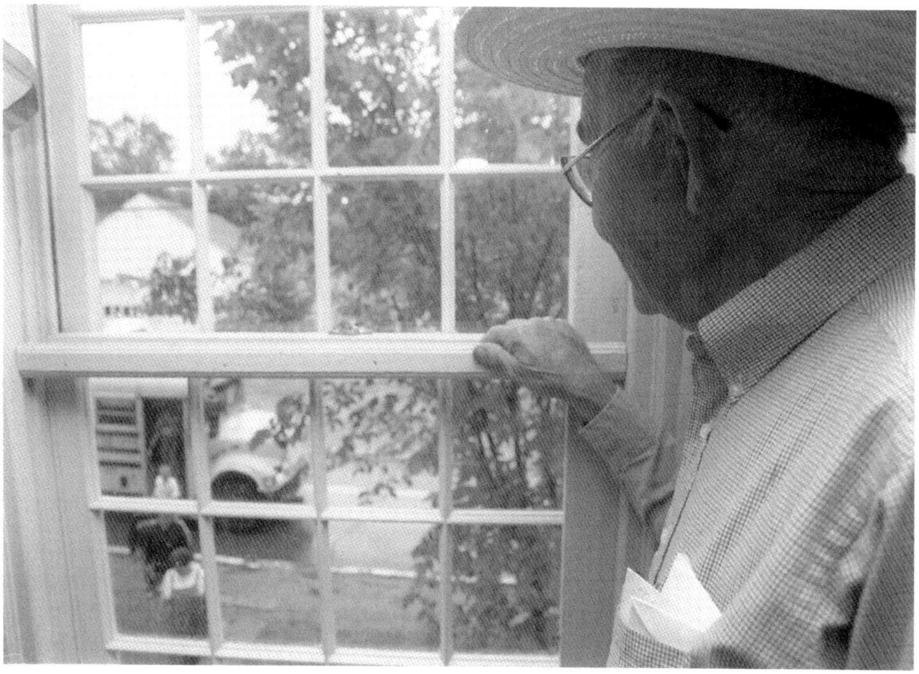

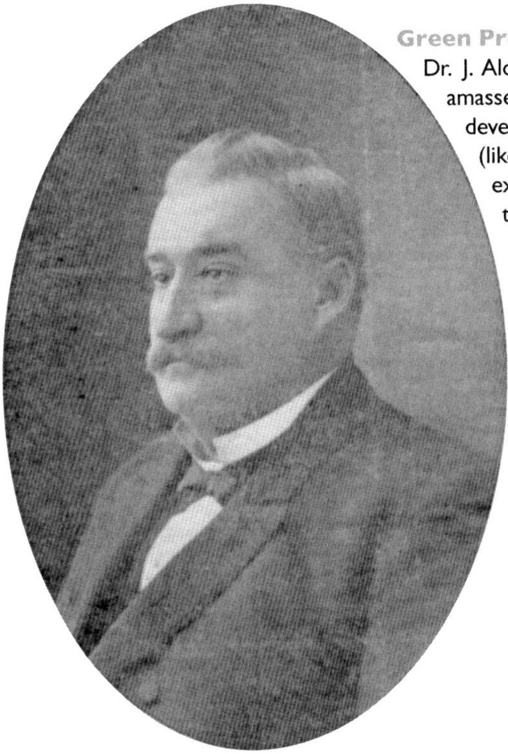

Green Product

Dr. J. Alonzo Greene and his brother Dr. Frank Greene amassed a fortune through the sale of a product they developed called Greene's Nervura. The patent medicine (likely a mixture of vegetable extracts and alcohol) was extremely popular, allowing Alonzo Greene to own the largest poultry farm in New Hampshire, on Moultonborough Neck. Later, he was proprietor of the New Hotel Weirs, which *The Illustrated Laconian* of 1899 called "the most commodious and best hotel in the lake region." A Civil War veteran, he also served a term as Laconia's mayor. (Courtesy of Lake Winnipesaukee Historical Society.)

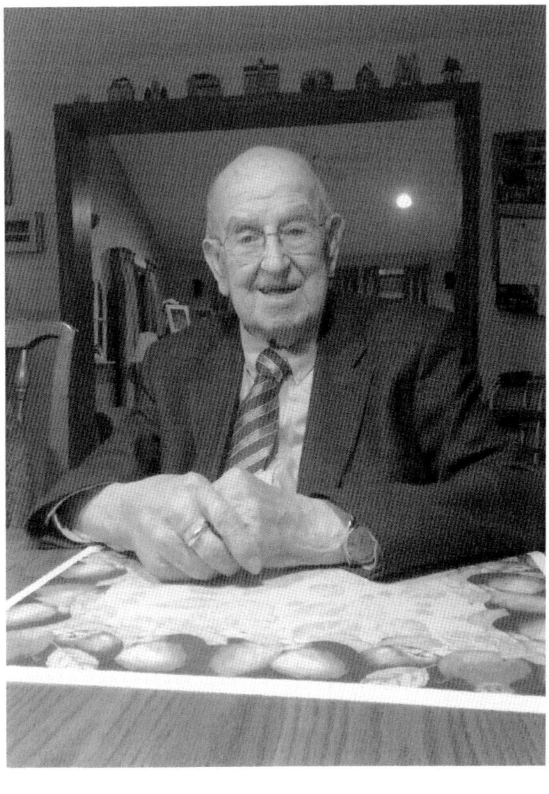

Smokin' Community Fan

In the 1960s, Laconia became part of a federal urban renewal project that called for demolishing numerous older buildings and replacing them with new edifices. City leaders generally supported the idea, but some residents felt the project was insensitive to local history. Peter S. Karagianis, the owner of the Laconia Spa and Happy Jack's Pipe & Tobacco Shop, was particularly concerned about the Belknap Mill property on the Winnipesaukee River (see page 29). He worked with others to form the Save the Mill Society. After a mighty campaign, the structure was left standing. The now-restored mill is listed in the National Register of Historic Places and is recognized as an American treasure. (Courtesy of S. Peter Karagianis.)

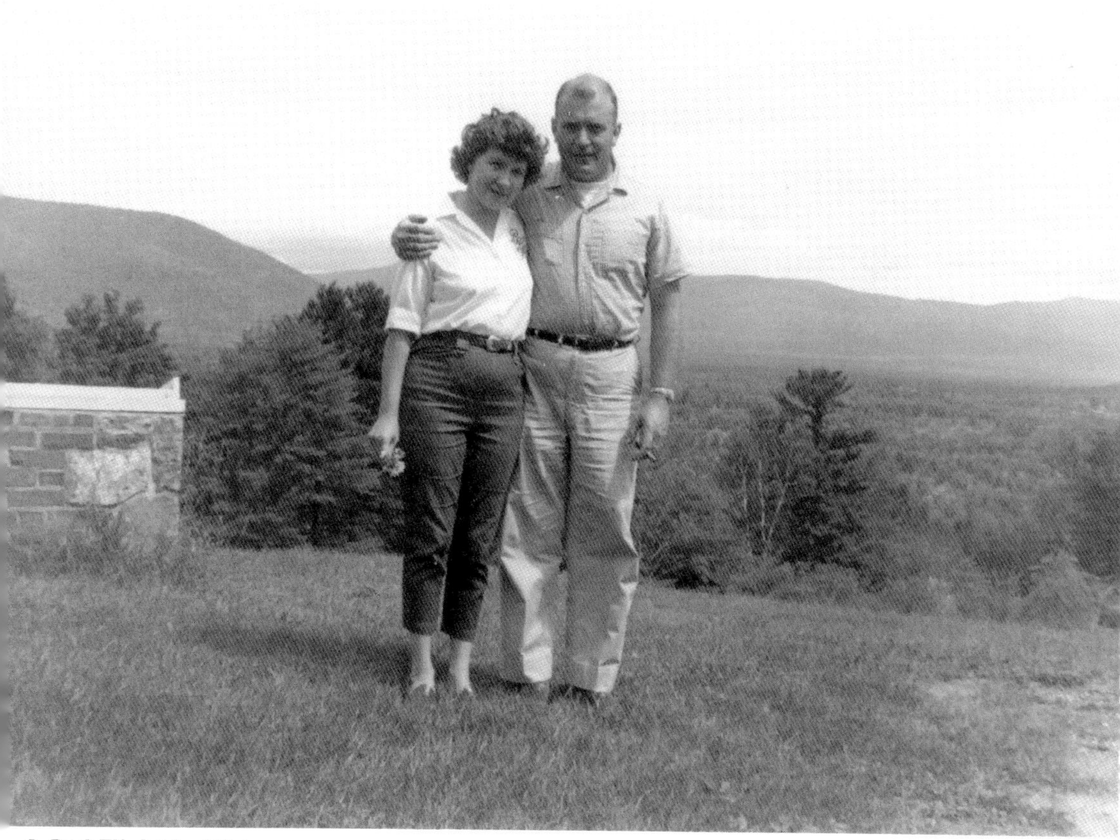

A Sad Flight in History

Col. Lewis Hanson, who was born and raised in Moultonborough, was a longtime military pilot who had a seat on one of the most historic flights in American history.

Hanson was a member of the flight crew for Air Force One, the plane that serves as the president's personal aircraft, when Pres. John F. Kennedy was assassinated in Dallas in 1963. While Kennedy was away from the airfield, Hanson went to see a relative, but she met him at her door in tears, saying he needed to get back to Dallas immediately after hearing reports on the television that the president had been shot. "My mind rejected the idea," Hanson recalled.

Later, he was on the plane when Kennedy's body was brought aboard, and he stood in the cockpit doorway as Lyndon Johnson took the official oath of office.

Hanson eventually retired to Center Harbor, where he served on the Board of Selectmen for 36 years before his death in 2005. He is seen here with his wife, Bess, shortly after buying the property.

Hanson's son Charley, who still lives in Center Harbor, said his father rarely spoke about that fateful day in 1963. "He was a lifelong Republican but he really liked and respected Kennedy." (Courtesy of Charles Hanson.)

INDEX

Adams, Sherman, 21
Against Me!, 69
Ames, Sid, 77, 78
Anderson, Jennifer, 86
Armstrong, Mary Alice Ford, 80
Armstrong, Samuel Chapman, 81
Athanas, William, 89, 94
Bacon, Alice Mabel, 80
Badger, Joseph, 11
Baer, Frank, 86
Ballantine, A. Cooper, 74
Bankhead, Tallulah, 42
Bare, Mary Lamprey, 50
Beach Boys, 73
Bell, Steve, 83
Bennett, Morrison, 16
Benét, Stephen Vincent, 15
Bogart, Humphrey, 109
Boissoneau, Ray, 31
Bolduc, Hector, 105, 112
Boston Pops, 68
Boutin, Bernie, 95
Brigham, Charles, 103
Brunstad, George, 105, 111
Burton, Ray, 42
Carlson, Daryl, 2, 6
Cash, Johnny, 68
Captain Jack, 10
Carver, Raymond, 56
Charles, Ray, 68
Checker, Chubby, 68
Chesley, Nathan, 96
Chiang Kai-Shek, Madame, 7
Clairmont, Thomas, 7, 89, 98
Clinton, Bill, 4, 47
Clough, Russell, 19, 20
Cogswell, Thomas, 7, 9, 11
Coolidge, Mary, 74
Cornwallis, Charles, 11
Cutillo, Ralph, 24
Dale, Greg, 21
Dane, Ernest, 7, 41
Davis, Rick, 77, 88
Demuth, William, 10
Downing family, 16, 17
Dresden Dolls, 69
Dunleavy, Mickey, 89, 93
Dunn, Red, 7
Eisenhower, Dwight, 42
Ellington, Duke, 73
Estes, Charles, 96
Fallon, Jimmy, 8
Fitzgerald, Jim "Coach," 37, 44
Fogg, Bob, 106
Fonda, Henry and Jane, 64
Forrester, Jeanne, 52
Forts, Annie, 4, 46, 47
Fowler, John "Bud" (aka John W. Jackson Jr.,), 39
Frates, Larry 63
Gale, Napoleon Bonaparte, 103
Gallant, Colleen, 122
Garneau, Albert, 99
Gelotte, Bill, 68 (Meadowbrook, 55)
Graton, Milton, 58
Greenberg, Clement, 62
Greene, Alonzo and Frank, 105, 124
Guignol, 69
Hale, Mel, 7
Halperin, Johanna and Bryan, 60
Hampton, Lionel, 73
Hanson, Lewis, 125
Harding, Bob, 68
Hart family, 113
Harvey, Linda, 37, 52
Hatch, Leon M., 118
Heald, Bruce, 7
Hepburn, Katherine, 64
Herrmann, Pepi, 66
Hill, Ian, 105, 115
Hold Steady, 69
Hunt, Charles William, 89, 92
Huse, Warren, 6
Ince, Jonathan, 9, 10
Irwin, Jim, 7, 73
Johnson, Carl, 89, 92
Johnson, George, 37, 43
Johnson, Lyndon, 95
Johnson, Spencer, 8
Karagianis, Peter S., 124
Kennedy, Jacqueline, 95, 125
Kennedy, John F., 95, 102, 124
Kennedy, John F. Jr., 4, 47
Kennedy, Rose, 42
Kent, Don, 123
Kimball, Benjamin Ames, 79
Kingsmen, 73
Laconia State School, 120, 121
Lamprey, Bob and Stuart, 50
Landry, Bolder, 7
Lane, Charles and Sophia, 7, 61
La Rochelle, Paul, 83
Lavallee, Leander, 82
Laubenstein, Norvin, 57
Lawton, Bob, John, and Randy, 19, 25
Leadbeater, Eliza, 34
Leavitt, Dudley, 7, 15
Lefebvre, Marcel, 112
Libby, Henry, 118
Lin Bi, 19, 30
Lincoln, Abraham, 96
Locke, Kent and sons, 35
Lorenz, Jonathan, 55, 72
Lynch, John, 42
Lyon, Hal, 72
MacDougall, Ruth Doan, 4, 63
Mack, Daniel Agustus, 99
Maroon 5, 68
Maxfield, Henry, 105, 108
McBride, Barnard, 4, 54
McKim, Stephanie, 19, 33
McLear, Edward, 26
Meadowbrook, 55
Melton, Jack, 120
Metalious, Grace, 57, 108
Mitchell, Ron, 102
Montana, Bob, 76
Morin, J. Paul, 29
Morin, Joseph, 19, 29
Morris, Ralph, 7, 36
Morrison, Lyndia 16
Morrissey, Bill, 55, 56
Morton, Robert, 10
Mudgett, Herman Webster (H.H. Holmes), 105, 116
Murphy, Lori Gigliotti and Morgan, 64
Nagy, Ivan, 67

Nelson, Willie, 68
Nesmith, George W., 99
New Hampshire Veterans Assoc., 104
New Hampshire Veterans Home, 101
Newman, Paul, 42
Nicolay, Franz, 7, 55, 69
Nureyev, Rudolf, 67
Old Tom, 96
Olitski, Jules, 55, 62
O'Sullivan, Maureen, 64
Oullette family, 21
Page, Henry, 19, 28
Pankhurst, Neil and Lesley, 60
Parker, Bruce, 122
Patten, Cindy and Chris, 54
Patton, George, 108
Percy, Loren, 55, 59
Peters, Esther, 42
Piscopo, Benjamin, 36
Pitou, Penny, 7, 110
Plant, Thomas Gustave, 7, 84
Plummer, Joseph, 105, 107
Poussin, Nicolas, 55
Quimby, Lee, 40
Rains, Claude, 109
Ray, Alex, 49
Rhodes, Wallace, 4, 48
Ritchard, Cyril, 64
Roberts, Alfred, 22
Robie, Charles, 23
Robie, Marion, 45
Romney, Mitt, 8
Roosevelt, Franklin, 48
Roosevelt, Theodore, 84
Rothafel, Arthur, 42
Runnels, Moses, 14
Ruth, Babe, 188
Sample, Roger, 83
Sandwich Home Industries (League of New Hampshire Craftsmen), 74, 75
Savage, George, 7, 89, 96
Savage, Moses, 96
Scheier, Mary, 74
Senter, Moses, 7
Sherman, John, 9, 10
Shumway, Shelli, 19, 33
Smart, Charles and Harry, 4, 21
Smith, Edwin H., 101
Southwick, Bert, 51
Springsteen, Bruce, 69
St. Clair, Charlie, 86
Stearns, Seth, 4, 38
Steinbeck, John, 56
Sturtevant family, 122
Swain family, 32
Sweeney, Earl, 102
Taylor, Adele, 37, 53
Taylor, James, 68
Thompson, Ernest, 55, 64, 65
Thorndike, Annalee and Chuck, 59, 71
Thyng, Harrison, 7, 89, 90
Tilton, Charles, 9, 13, 100
Toth, Edra, 67
Villella, Edward, 67
Washington, George, 7, 9, 11
Webster, Daniel, 17, 99
Weirs Ski Club, 122
Wentworth, John, 7, 12, 77
Wentworth, Rueben, 4, 27
Wheeler, Edgar, 7, 89, 91
Whipple, George Hoyt, 114
Whitten, Rueben, 7, 22
Whittier, John Greenleaf, 122
Wilkes, Alton, 7
Winnipesaukee Playhouse, 55
World/Inferno Friendship Society, 69
Wright, David, 2, 105, 119
Zimmermann, Egon, 110